Fame to Infamy

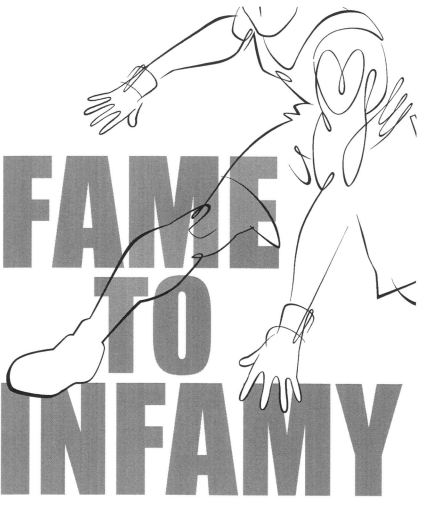

FAME TO INFAMY

Race, Sport, and the Fall from Grace

Edited by David C. Ogden and Joel Nathan Rosen

University Press of Mississippi / Jackson

www.upress.state.ms.us

The University Press of Mississippi is a member
of the Association of American University Presses.

First printing 2010

∞

Library of Congress Cataloging-in-Publication Data

Fame to infamy : race, sport, and the fall from grace /
edited by David C. Ogden and Joel Nathan Rosen.
    p. cm.
  Includes index.
  ISBN 978-1-60473-751-6 (cloth : alk. paper) —
ISBN 978-1-60473-752-3 (ebook) 1. Sports—United
States. 2. Athletes—United States—Public opinion.
3. Sports—Social aspects 4. Sports—Moral and ethi-
cal aspects. 5. Racism in sports I. Ogden, David C. II.
Rosen, Joel Nathan, 1961–
  GV583.F35 2010
  796.089—dc22   2010017510

British Library Cataloging-in-Publication Data available

Contents

vii Acknowledgments

ix Foreword: The Power of Nine
—ROY F. FOX

3 Introduction: Thoughts on Fame and Infamy
—DAVID C. OGDEN AND JOEL NATHAN ROSEN

8 Barry Bonds: Of Passion and Hostility
—LISA DORIS ALEXANDER

30 Kirby Puckett: A Middle American Tragedy
—SHERRIE L. WILSON

45 Don't Believe the Hype: The Racial Representation
    of Mike Tyson in Three Acts
—THABITI LEWIS

61 Lost in Translation: Voice, Masculinity, Race, and the
    1998 Home Run Chase
—SHELLEY LUCAS

76 Branch Rickey: Moral Capitalist
—ROBERT F. LEWIS II

102 Inextricably Linked: Joe Louis and Max Schmeling Revisited
—C. OREN RENICK AND JOEL NATHAN ROSEN

122 Mortgaging Michael Jordan's Reputation
—JEFFREY LANE

146 A Precarious Perch: Wilt Chamberlain, Basketball Stardom,
     and Racial Politics
—GREGORY J. KALISS

170   Jim Brown: The Rise and Fall (and Rise) of a Cultural Icon
      —ROBERTA J. NEWMAN

191   Afterword: Sports and the Iron Fist of Myth
      —JACK LULE

199   Contributors

203   Index

Acknowledgments

The editors would like to extend our appreciation to everyone who has helped to make this venture possible. Our contributors have graciously given of their time and talent, exceeding all our expectations and putting to rest the long-held myth that enormously talented people cannot and should not be expected to pay heed to deadlines and other such minutiae. More important, your ideas and the words with which you have expressed them have taught us that we are anything but alone in our broader vision for this project. We are grateful.

Craig Gill and the entire staff of the University Press of Mississippi offered persistence, encouragement, indulgence, and a wide berth. Their reputation as a university press that encourages creativity and the breaking of intellectual boundaries is both accurate and well deserved.

The contributions of Malisa Konkolics at Moravian College have been invaluable and most appreciated.

Finally, we thank our friends and families, who have watched this project go from idea to fruition. Their patience, their enthusiasm, and most of all their encouragement are much appreciated. Extended writing and editing can lead to some awfully lonely times, but their support—material and otherwise—has proven invaluable, and we would be remiss if we did not put those sentiments to words.

Foreword: The Power of Nine

—ROY F. FOX

In the summer of 1958, in Kansas City, Missouri, my grandfather, Pop, hooked me on listening to radio broadcasts of the Kansas City Athletics' baseball games. The small brown plastic radio on the counter of his break-fast room held us there, standing, expecting at any moment to hear the roar of the crowd as the announcer's voice quickened before bursting out of his throat: *There's a high drive to left-center. . . . Tuttle goes back . . . back, way, way, deep. . . . He leaps. . . . HE MAKES THE CATCH! Wow! Bill Tuttle takes away Mantle's home run!*

Of course, the A's seldom won any games against the Yankees. Pop referred to Yankees manager, Casey Stengel, as "Stinky," and during those hot summer days, when segregation was still common, Pop somehow communicated to me that pitcher Satchel Paige was an aging, brilliant, funny rascal in a league all his own. In deep, shapeless ways, I was changed by "Ol' Satchel." A year later, I could not understand why my favorite As announcer, George Bryson, committed suicide. How could such a warm voice, someone who could elon-gate a home run with such passion, end? Not that it makes much sense now. In many baseball-ish ways, I am still nine years old.

During this time, I began collecting baseball cards, each one a piece of evidence proving that all the drama and heroes of this game were real, were valuable, despite the profound lack of interest in baseball held by my family, except for Pop. I kept my cards (five cents per pack) in a metal box. I studied them, trading only a few, in my long attempt to secure As left fielder Bob Cerv, my hero. Cerv's teammate, Roger Maris, had not yet hit his stride. My interest in Maris greatly increased in 1959, when his sixteen home runs led the team. That total was modest even at that time, but for the eternally cellar-dwelling As, it bordered on a miracle. Immediately following that summer, the As, in true farm team fashion, traded him to the Yankees, where he hit thirty-nine homers in 1960 and sixty-one in 1961. This I will never forget. I remain nine years old.

In addition to the wrinkled, worn Cerv card, which I finally obtained in a trade with Donnie Hales, I had other seemingly golden cards, includ-ing a joint Mickey Mantle/Yogi Berra and another that featured "Words of

Wisdom" from a fatherly looking Stengel apparently schooling World Series hero Don Larsen on the art of throwing the knuckleball.

Such pairings seemed natural to me. I was well aware that certain players had long been closely associated with each other. I seldom heard or read of one player without the other. In essence, they became one word: Tinker-Evers-Chance; Ruth-and-Gehrig; Mantle-and-Berra; Fox-and-Aparicio; and for one year in Kansas City, Cerv-and-Maris. Too, these players were often photographed together, in similar poses. The names on the Larsen-Stengel card are hyphenated and encircled in red, bringing the two men closer together.

In magazines and books, I pored over the iconic photos of Ruth's and Gehrig's farewell ceremonies at Yankee Stadium, sensing that the similar poses, body language, and formation of players constituted the most sacred recognition humanly possible, reserved for these two gods on Mount Olympus. Of course, such close associations in deed, word, and image communicate teamwork, collegiality, friendship, all of which I took for granted at the time.

Fast-forward to the 1990s and the present. A typical image from Barry Bonds's Web site shows his follow-through on one of his trademark massive swings. Bonds's name appears twice in all caps as part of the site's logo; his number 25 appears twice; and his image appears four times. All Barry and nothing else. No one else. Here and elsewhere, the other players are missing. In the same way, I continue to wonder why today's victorious baseball team members shake hands with each other and not their opponents. I miss the collegiality and collaboration with other players (or at least the appearance thereof), a natural phenomenon, I guess, when you're still nine years old.

Several years ago, armed with tape recorders, I researched how rural high school students made sense of in-school, mandatory television commercials broadcast over Channel 1 television. Students are required to watch the news and ad messages, and neither students nor teachers can alter the volume or turn off the monitor. A few times every day for months, the program ran a commercial promoting Michael Jordan's Nike athletic shoes with a catchy jingle, "Be Like Mike." Students sang it in the hallways, on the bus, in the locker room, and in the cafeteria, turning the school into an echo chamber of commercial ploys.

In one small group of students, I began to draw out Ken, noticeably shorter than his classmates, a quiet ninth-grader more shabbily dressed, more outcast, than his chatty peers. He slowly told me how he had saved his money for months to buy a pair of Air Jordan basketball sneakers, and how his grandmother helped him out with the purchase. When I asked why he was so interested in this brand, he drawled, "Saw 'em on a cum-er-shel."[1]

About this same time, I discovered an ad from a magazine published in the United Kingdom for the Nike Shop of J. D. Sports. This ad portrays three athletes depicted in a stained glass window of yellows, reds, blues, greens, and purples. The left panel shows a soccer player on bended knee, left hand on heart; the center panel, the largest, shows a basketball player (Jordan, most viewers would assume), with hands folded in prayer; the right panel shows a tennis player in the same pose as the soccer player. Each sports god wears the appropriate ball as a halo. Across the top of this three-paned window, formal, holy lettering, states, "The Temple of Nike." Below this phrase, a more utilitarian font announces, "Hours of Worship Mon–Sat 10–7 pm Thurs 10–8 pm Sun 11–6 pm."[2]

In today's global consumer society, everything—professional athletes, mouthwash, political power, popularity, sex appeal, nature—can be bought and sold. The common and varied forms of narrative—the stories, movies, yarns, jokes, songs, news items, novels, sports pages, soap operas, and so forth—teach us how to construct meaning from the chaos of everyday life. The tellers of these stories used to be grandparents, parents, aunts and uncles, trusted friends, clergy, teachers, and others who had nothing to gain from their storytelling.

However, as George Gerbner reminds us, the storytellers of old have been replaced by story *sellers*—those who have something to gain from the stories they tell.[3] When my grandfather told me stories about Satchel Paige, he had nothing to gain from it except the cultivation of his relationship with me and the imparting of knowledge for its own sake. America's main storytellers are now electronic media, especially Internet and television advertising. Many readers of the Temple of Nike ad may find it clever, funny, or cute. Some readers may interpret it as a legitimate (if edgy) tribute to the supreme athletic/fashion shoe. Some readers may believe that this ad promotes materialistic attitudes. Others may be offended by the ad's mocking of religious values.

I do not strongly disagree with any of these interpretations. The logic of this ad, though, seems clear: sports are holy; Nike is sports; therefore, Nike must be holy. And holier than sports and even holier than Nike is spending money. The ad also suggests that no entity outside of ourselves is bigger than Michael Jordan, that those who adopt the stance of prayer—the most private and vulnerable of acts—are fair game for exploitation.

Maybe the most important issue here is that religion no longer serves as any kind of guiding narrative or set of rules or mythology to which we can adhere during our time on this wild earth. We no longer have a single language or body of literature to fill this void. Most of us no longer live within any kind of community where everyone believes the same thing. Religion and myth no longer serve as stable forces of social cohesion and psychic unity. And what fills this yawning gap? We buy stuff. We worship technology.

These are just a few of the reasons why *Fame to Infamy* is a needed, important, and ambitious project. This collection of essays is about far more than the upswings and downturns of sports stars' reputations. The essays collected here concern countless issues that reach down into race, gender, class, language, nationalism, dreams, history, religion, materialism, culture, mass media, psychology, personality, violence, learning and teaching, economics, symbols, nostalgia, genetics, values, environment, attitudes, cognition, beliefs, emotion, identity, and more. These entanglements are greater in number and intensity for these athletes—a by-product of fame and infamy—than for most of us. Reading many of these accounts results in the feeling that these men's lives off the playing field qualify them as heroes just as much as their points per game or RBIs. The athletes explored in this book *are*, after all, mere mortals—people who have intensely engaged with this fluid, wired, weird world; who have chosen their own directions, up or down or sideways; who have been buffeted into confusion and desperation by the ricocheting, random forces of history and contemporary life.

One of the forces teased out in these chapters is racial bias, both as it previously existed and as we can see it now, from a distance. Some of these players have elicited and continue to elicit racial bias from both fans and writers. Some players "receive" bias with calm dignity. Others try to ignore the whole issue. None of them, though, can really escape it. Maybe, more important, this book illustrates how today's racial issues can breed indefinitely on the sidelines and in the shadows, seemingly invisible and culturally harmless, until a flare-up reveals a lurking pattern. These chapters demonstrate that Ralph Ellison's "Invisible Man" has new meaning in postmodern America: prejudice can arise from neutral, even pristine intentions and then mutate in the maze of print and media symbols that saturate our information-gone-berserk landscape.

Maybe the most important reason for this book is that in the rise and fall of sports heroes' reputations, we may find some stability within a culture not prone to stability. We may find a framework, a set of rules, a pattern, an ordered mythology—yes, a game—where we can observe and evaluate those stones and shafts of light randomly thrown at us by the gods. Maybe, in small ways, sport serves as one of our few remaining religions or mythologies. The first function of a living mythology, as Joseph Campbell states, is to help us "reconcile consciousness to the preconditions of its own existence."[4] He continues, "A mythological order is a system of images that gives consciousness a sense of meaning in existence, which, my dear friend, has no meaning—it simply is. But the mind goes asking for meanings; it can't play unless it knows (or makes up) some system of rules."[5]

This book explores those times when the ordered universe of each athlete's game did not or could not apply to his life. These players' lives off the field had different rules, or rules that the men could not or did not learn, or rules too incomprehensible for them, or no rules at all.

None of this, however, should diminish another truth: for most of us, most of the time, the rules of any sport set us free. They enable us to see—even beyond the playing field—what's great, what's evil, what's sad, what's needed. Participating through the radio in Pop's kitchen in pathetic losses to the Yankees, impossible catches up against the wall in center field, and endless Sunday afternoon pitching changes has helped me to remain nine years old. Most of the time, that's not such a bad thing.

NOTES

1. Roy F. Fox, *Harvesting Minds: How TV Commercials Control Kids* (Westport, CT: Praeger, 2000), 47.

2. "The Temple of Nike" (advertisement), reprinted in Roy F. Fox, *MediaSpeak: Three American Voices* (Westport, CT: Praeger, 2001), 121.

3. George Gerbner, "Telling Stories; or, How Do We Know What We Know?" in *Against the Mainstream: Selected Works of George Gerbner*, ed. M. Morgan (New York: Lang, 2002), 116–31.

4. Joseph Campbell, *Pathways to Bliss: Mythology and Personal Transformation* (Novato, CA: New World, 2004), 3.

5. Ibid., 6.

Fame to Infamy

INTRODUCTION
Thoughts on Fame and Infamy
—DAVID C. OGDEN AND JOEL NATHAN ROSEN

INTRODUCTION

Promising beginnings are one thing most notable athletes share. Such athletes often burst on the scene, raising the specter of a new era for their team or sport. As such, these athletes bring with them hopes and aspirations that fans quickly adopt. And as such, athletes become part of the fabric of everyday existence for individuals, families, neighborhoods, and cities.

In our first collaboration, *Reconstructing Fame*,[1] we examined athletes who were branded as "outliers" who found community acceptance difficult, if not impossible, early in their careers, though they were afforded such acclaim later in their postcareer lives. Those athletes, like the ones profiled here, found that it is not enough to serve as a conduit through which the community vicariously experiences thrills and triumphs. The athlete is expected to reflect community mores and set a standard for civil behavior. Athletes are expected to be dedicated stewards of the trust and faith fans place in them. So it is little wonder that when an athlete's promising beginning turns sour, fans and the community take these changes quite seriously and quite personally.

The process by which an athlete's reputation erodes over time is of little interest when compared to the aftermath of that erosion. That aftermath, as portrayed by press and media, usually encompasses the athlete's betrayal of the public trust and the fans' emotional investments. Press and media not only convey public disapproval and disappointment but also in some cases exacerbate public frustration with the athlete. Such disappointments are often framed within the athlete's promising beginnings.

Tracing the downward spiral from the pinnacle of the athlete's career can make the fall from grace, as we have deemed it, seem that much farther, which indeed is the case for the collection of athletes featured in this volume. Kirby Puckett's domestic violence problems and allegations of sexual assault, for example, turned the once-adored outfielder into a virtual pariah. Wilt Chamberlain's self-proclaimed sexual prowess clouded his historic career on the court and turned him into a laughingstock and a symbol of recklessness in a world seemingly preoccupied with sexual expression and the threat of transmitted disease as well as lingering questions posed by black male sexuality.

In some cases, however, the sports figure changed less than the social and cultural forces around him. Branch Rickey's groundbreaking approaches to building and managing a baseball team became outmoded and ineffective as society and the game changed. Some African Americans publicly chastised Michael Jordan for failing to take advantage of his position and fame to champion civil rights. In the context of the cultural and social zeitgeist, Jordan's indifference was considered betrayal. Yet neither Jordan nor Chamberlain nor Puckett nor even the venerable Rickey represent anything completely unexpected in this mounting age of celebrity. In fact, there are times when it becomes (prohibitively) easier to simply assume that one way or another the figurative second shoe is going to drop. The promise of all-encompassing glory quickly morphs into something much less glorious, a tumble in popular perception best exemplified in the very public fall of the once universally adored O. J. Simpson.

THE JUICE CAME LOOSE

If there is one American sports figure who exemplifies the idea of the public crash, it is indeed Orenthal James Simpson, who once held remarkable sway within public discourse. His fall from grace has been so thoroughly dissected and publicly retold that we decided that a chapter devoted to him would offer nothing new. But much as an aging Muhammad Ali embodied the subjects in our first collection, Simpson serves the same purpose in this second go-round. Simpson's acclaimed career saw him make the precipitous leap from college and professional football to popular culture through countless ad campaigns alongside television and feature film appearances. Simpson had seemingly broken the iron barrier that reminded earlier generations that a black man could never move farther forward than the milieu that brought him his initial acclaim would allow. Yet Simpson, with his radiant smile and engaging demeanor, had indeed moved beyond that boundary, gaining an unprecedented degree of celebrity at a time in his career when the majority of once-famous men of color were still expected to make a slow decline into obscurity. Simpson, however, seemed to be made of spun gold, a man with a Heisman Trophy and an astonishing record of accomplishments between the lines that would catapult him headlong into the American culture. With the backing of the more traditional machinery, he reinvented himself by running through airports in countless Hertz car rental ads and serving in such high-profile supporting roles as the agonizingly ill-fated Nordberg character in

The Naked Gun trilogy.[2] Still, just as it looked as if he would be one of those palpably transcendent figures, everything came crashing down on him. The allegations against him and subsequent murder trial replaced the image of the lovable all-American goofball with that very haunting and notably darker image as seen in his doctored but no-less-significant mug shot made public in newsstands across the landscape.[3]

Like the swift change of direction in public perception in the case of Muhammad Ali, Simpson's fall was rapid yet telling. Once adored, he was summarily and universally shunned. Once a symbol of raceless acceptance (some might say acquiescence), he was quickly reconnected to his past gang affiliations, his youthful indiscretions in his native San Francisco, and the mass of secrets strategically hidden from view regarding his first marriage and his subsequent marriage to the woman he allegedly nearly decapitated in a fit of rage. In a word, this wholly American icon was reracialized in such a way as to suggest that the darkening of O. J. Simpson was not the tale of a wayward celebrity sucked into the vagaries of fame but rather the logical outcome of a man who crossed a barrier for which he (and perhaps even we) were never fully prepared to cross. The thud that marked Simpson's fall, then, represented a most predictable end to a tragic experiment gone awry.

WRESTLING WITH TROUBLING REPUTATIONS

Simpson is by every measure indicative of the sort of man who might be chronicled in this volume. Although star athletes are lauded for their constructed roles in American life, they are hardly taken at face value, a situation that at the very least lends itself to some comparatively unusual if not troubling juxtapositions. As many of our contributors underscore, the distance between fan favorite and villainy is microscopic, while the change in direction is as easily tendered by virtue of an unfortunate turn of phrase (Chamberlain), a supposition (McGwire, Sosa, and Bonds), or a transgression that garners the public's eye while taking over its imagination (Puckett, Brown). Ideally, our heroes never suffer such setbacks, but as most observers will admit, sport neither constitutes an ideal situation nor can be divorced from its social or cultural context. Indeed, sports (at least in its American translation, though we suspect that this holds true wherever sport and culture seem to galvanize a populace) are products of the forces that govern the behaviors—collectively and/or individually—of those who participate. Thus, the factors that one takes into account relative to any sort of transgressive moment cannot simply be deducted from society writ large but are thrust against its backdrop. In this regard, the thread that binds the individuals whose stories grace this volume is indelibly linked to the very temporal and spatial circumstances with which their once-celebrated reputations were formed. In other words (to paraphrase the Bard himself), such falls can be seen less in these stars per se and more in how the trajectory of their narratives either fails to transcend expectation or (especially in the case of Mike Tyson) captures precisely what we as members of a general public have come to expect. And this is where the intersection of two very real and formidable variables in the social sciences collide: nature and the socially constructed meaning of race. This pairing has long relied on the inherently spurious notion that behavioral expectations and the capacity to adapt are somehow encoded collectively in our DNA. The athletes depicted in this volume may not have succeeded in negotiating the shifts in public opinion or conquering the heights of public expectation, but their public profiles racialized through centuries of misapplied logic rather than any perceived genetic shortcomings ultimately exposed them to the subsequent buffeting by disenchanted fans and disgruntled media. Accordingly, the authors of the essays in this volume not only strive to find deeper social and cultural reasons for the downfall of the athletes featured here but also remind us how quickly fortunes can change (even for the most beloved celebrity) and how circumstances can relegate celebrated careers to the dustbins of history.

BOOK NOTES

This work, which encompasses a range of subjects and approaches (in no small part because of the consciously interdisciplinary approach we have brought to this venture as a whole), contrasts directly with *Reconstructing Fame*. In that volume, we explored the question of how once-tainted reputations—specifically, those initially sullied through the presence of the sport-race conundrum so omnipresent in American culture—could be rehabilitated through the march of time and by the changing nature of race and racialized thought. Central to the narratives in that volume were the means by which nostalgia and collective memory can help redraft if not deliberately reinvent the past. In this regard, *Reconstructing Fame* was about the past and its effect on men of color forced to endure an admittedly overt and unforgiving racial landscape. However, that book was also about the present and how the contemporary rehabilitation of these once virile and gifted warriors, once kept at arm's length by the racial mores of the time but subsequently whitewashed in the public consciousness, played out in discussions of their newfound standing and that of their more modern counterparts. As a consequence, the plotline that underscored those particular narratives held that embedded within these rehabilitative shifts was perhaps a more subtle but no less problematic notion that the modern male athlete was hopelessly unable to match on or off the field the sort of competitive spirit and the community footing evidenced by Jackie Robinson, Roberto Clemente, Bill Russell, and others.

In sharp contrast, this collection explores what we have long considered the mirror image of that initial trajectory. This volume takes up the notion of shifting reputations not only from the perspective of the sport-race conundrum but also from the paths of men who began their careers as lauded figures but who subsequently plunged into public disrepute, with the question of color in the American consciousness at the base of this journey. Unlike Robinson, Clemente, Russell, and Jim Thorpe, the men whose stories grace this effort were once considered racially insignificant; at the very least, their racial makeup and its consequent expectations and/or latitude allowed for a certain degree of popular acceptance that in effect was shown to have an endpoint, if not a breaking point. Moreover, this lapse into disregard, dishonor, buffoonery, or the like shows that the consequences of such shifts—intended or not—can be felt beyond each man's individual tale of woe. Thus, if the rehabilitation of the once-tainted can lead to questions regarding the comportment and value of the young athlete less encumbered by a previous century's racial norms, the discrediting of those once even marginally accepted by the public can only lead to a further cluttering of a racial climate that continues to falter amid ominous and unrelenting expectations that pose race as both a material obstacle to progress and a genuine marker of human efficacy.

Many people continue to resist the idea that so much can come from critiques of sport, but these matters remain a persistent marker of American life, and this discussion remains very much in need of a little rehabilitation in its own right. Thus, it is with an admixture of pride and apprehension that we once again toss our collective hats into the ongoing discussions of race against the backdrop of masculinity through the following collection of essays and their resulting analyses.

NOTES

1. David C. Ogden and Joel Nathan Rosen, *Reconstructing Fame: Race, Sport, and Evolving Reputations: The Redemption of Yesterday's Villains and What It Means for Today's Athletes* (Jackson: University Press of Mississippi, 2008).

2. See *The Naked Gun: From the Files of Police Squad!* (Paramount Pictures, 1988); *The Naked Gun 2½: The Smell of Fear* (Paramount Pictures, 1991); *Naked Gun 33⅓: The Final Insult* (Paramount Pictures, 1994).

3. The most notorious of these covers was that proffered by *Time* magazine with the caption "An American Tragedy" (June 27, 1994).

BARRY BONDS
Of Passion and Hostility
—LISA DORIS ALEXANDER

INTRODUCTION

There are athletes whose reputations become more favorable as time goes on, and there are those athletes who are framed as less likeable over time. And then there is Barry Bonds, whose reputation has evolved from bad to worse over his twenty-one-year career in Major League Baseball. Merely mentioning the slugger's name engenders the type of passion and hostility usually reserved for crooked politicians or terrorists. It seems that ever since Bonds landed in Pittsburgh and throughout his embattled years in San Francisco, sportswriters and fans have focused more on his actions off the field than his achievements on the field.

Wisdom would dictate that in a sport that is obsessed with statistics, a player who holds the records for career home runs, single-season home runs, career walks, single-season walks, single-season on-base percentage, and single-season slugging percentage—plus seven Most Valuable Player Awards and eight Gold Gloves—would be praised in every ballpark in the nation. Instead, Bonds is framed and, by extension, viewed as a pariah. When Bonds won his first MVP Award in 1990, the *Sporting News*'s Bob Hertzel claimed, "Bonds is smog. . . . Bonds is a sneer."[1] After Bonds broke the single-season home run record in 2001, Dave Kindred remarked in the same publication, "Bonds is a natural loner with a sneer for those he considers his inferiors—which, to judge by the frequency of his surly behavior, seems to be most of us. Somehow this husband, father and professional athlete has reached 37 years old without learning to play with others."[2] When Bonds broke the career home run record, thought to be the greatest achievement in sports, Jim Reeves, a sportswriter for the *Fort Worth Star-Telegram*, wrote, "It is now officially a national day of mourning. Black bunting should hang from every ballpark in America. A riderless black horse, its saddle empty, its stirrups filled by a pair of Hank Aaron's cleats turned backward, should be led around every warning track tonight. The greatest record in sports has fallen to a liar and a cheat."[3]

How did Bonds go from a tolerable presence to baseball's nemesis? One could argue that Bonds is a miserable and unpleasant human being. One might also conclude that sportswriters reserve special contempt for Bonds because he does not make their jobs easy. At the same time, from 2001 to 2007, Bonds served as baseball's poster child for performance-enhancing drugs despite the fact that he has never failed a drug test. Finally, the fact that Bonds is a black man comes into play as well. Bonds biographer Steven Travers argues that "the reality is that most whites love to like blacks. It makes them feel good. It helps convince them that racism is not what it used to be. What is not on the surface, however, is that most whites love to like *certain kinds* of blacks. Barry Bonds has not always been the kind of black athlete that they love to like."[4] This chapter tracks Bonds's fall from grace as a result of a combination of personality, the specter of performance-enhancing drugs, and the omnipotence of race.

A FAMILY THING

Before we can track the course of Bonds's reputation, it would be helpful to ponder who might be orchestrating this downfall. According to the 2006 Associated Press Sports Report Card compiled by the Institute for Diversity and Ethics in Sport, the racial makeup of sports columnists, assistant sports editors, and sports editors at newspapers across the United States is not as diverse as many would think. The study found that 88.9 percent of sports columnists, 86.9 percent of assistant sports editors, and 90 percent of sports editors are white.[5] Only 7.7 percent of columnists, 5.3 percent of assistant sports editors, and 1.6 percent of editors are African American.[6] In addition, in 2007, 80 percent of radio/television broadcasters were white, while African Americans made up only 3 percent of that group.[7] These are the men (and a few women) who are framing Bonds's image. Even if sportswriters' dramatically homogeneous background is set aside for a moment, race would still play a role in what they choose to write about and how they choose to write about it. Unless sportswriters and editors were born and raised on *Star Trek*'s fictional planet, Vulcan, they are "imprisoned by the history of racial subordination in America" and exist in a society where "racism is an integral, permanent, and indestructible component."[8] This is not to say that all sportswriters are racists; however, one school of thought suggests that everyone who is exposed to this "history of racial subordination" is informed by such racism. For the purpose of this discussion, it is helpful to differentiate between *racist* behavior and policies, which are designed to have a "differential or harmful effect on minority groups," and *racial* behavior and policies, which are "neutral in intent but ... have a differential or harmful effect on minority groups."[9] Since intent is nearly impossible to prove, this chapter suggests that there is a racial component to the ways in which athletes in general and Bonds more specifically are framed.

Bonds's stature as one of the best if not *the* best baseball player ever is not an accident, nor did his relationship with the media begin when he played his first game in Pittsburgh. Bonds is baseball royalty. His father, Bobby Bonds, played fourteen seasons in the Majors and had a lifetime .268 batting average, won three Gold Gloves, and made three All-Star appearances.[10] Sportswriters touted him as the next Willie Mays—Barry's godfather—but when the elder Bonds failed to live up to that label, they framed him as an underachiever despite the fact that he hit thirty home runs and had thirty stolen bases in five seasons, a feat Mays accomplished only twice.[11] Bobby Bonds was frustrated by how sportswriters discussed his career, and he was not afraid to tell reporters exactly how he felt, noting later in his life, "I probably had more success than anyone they ever put that [underachiever] label on. You show me another guy who's going to do 30-30 five times. But all the writers kept talking about was potential. You haven't reached your potential yet, they say. Well, unless you win a Pulitzer Prize, you're not living up to your potential either, are you?"[12] The point that the elder Bonds had a productive baseball career has been raised more frequently since his death in 2003. As *Sports Illustrated* writer Ron Fimrite argued, "As the son continues to topple records, researchers have discovered that the old man was himself a superior player and that his reputation as an underachiever was unfair."[13] Only two players in baseball history have hit more than three hundred home runs and stolen more than four hundred bases, and both are named Bonds.[14]

Another factor in the younger Bonds's popular construction is his relationship to Mays. Considered by many to be one of the best players ever, Mays won the Rookie of the Year Award in 1951 and later won two MVP Awards.[15] Mays accumulated twelve Gold Gloves, played in twenty All-Star Games, and played in five World Series.[16]

In addition to witnessing Mays's exceptional on-field heroics, both Bondses learned from Mays "that to be a superstar, one must carry himself like a superstar. That meant being occasionally difficult with the press[,] blowing off the media, blowing off teammates; [making] sarcastic comments that stung like snakebite. Mays knew he was royalty, just as he knew those frumpy-looking [sportswriters] with inkstains on their sweaters weren't of his ilk."[17] Barry Bonds evoked comparisons to Mays in terms of both talent and personality. As one sportswriter remarked, "Both [are] great players, of course, but both [are] mercurial characters. Both men can be a royal pain in the rear."[18] The men who taught Barry Bonds how to play baseball also may well have taught him that sportswriters were not to be trusted.

RISING EXPECTATIONS

Between his baseball lineage and his status as a first-round draft pick, Barry Bonds faced a mountain of expectations when he arrived in Pittsburgh in 1985. The Pirates were in a rebuilding period. The team had lost 104 games the previous year and was caught up in a very public drug scandal. Everyone looked to the new superstar and the new manager, Jim Leyland, to turn the franchise around. To be fair, when Bonds arrived in Pittsburgh, he did not bring a warm and fuzzy personality with him. He rarely acknowledged his teammates and was very aware and vocal about his talents.[19] As a rookie, Bonds was described as "confident, just this side of cocky,"[20] and his relationships devolved from there. In 1986, Bruce Keidan of the *Pittsburgh Post-Gazette* wrote,

> Reading his own press clippings seems to have an intoxicating effect on 21-year-old Barry Bonds. After a wretched outing during the Pirates' last home stand, Bonds refused to talk to the news media. The following day, he deigned to talk to newspaper reporters but kissed off a request to appear on the Philadelphia Phillies radio network's star-of-the-game show. And a day or so after that, he instructed reporters to hold all questions until after he had finished his post-game snack. All this from a young man less than two months removed from the minor leagues. Makes you wonder what sort of boor he will become when and if he grows into his enormous potential and becomes a superstar.[21]

It did not help that it took a while for Bonds's production to match expectations. Given some sportswriters' tendency "accidentally" to call him "Bobby" and the frequent comparisons and allusions to his father, it should not have been a surprise that Barry Bonds grew frustrated with media representatives.[22] Resentment quickly grew on both sides. In 1990, the *Sporting News*'s Tom Barnidge maintained that Bonds "occasionally has been branded as moody and uncooperative. And just as frequently, he has resented the label. When a note pad nears Bonds's locker, the pages sometimes stand on end."[23] Hank Hersch of *Sports Illustrated* made a similar point, noting that "the Pittsburgh press branded Bonds 'a bad guy to have in the clubhouse' and 'the Pirates' MDP—Most Despised Player.'"[24] To make matters more interesting,

Bonds referred to one of his teammates, Andy Van Slyke, as "Mr. Pittsburgh" and the "great white hope."[25] The racial gauntlet was thrown down after the Pirates signed Van Slyke to a three-year deal worth $12.5 million at the same time that two white pitchers, John Smiley and Doug Drabek, won their arbitration cases.[26] It was simply a coincidence that Bonds and Bobby Bonilla, black men in their fifth year of service, lost their arbitration cases that same year. Ulish Carter from the *New Pittsburgh Courier* agreed with Bonds that the financial winners and losers that season were not cases of luck: "The fans, local media and Pirates treated [Bonds] as if he was some kind of villain because he wanted to be paid close to what the market would bear. . . . The treatment of Bonds was no exception; it was the rule for Pirate fans toward Black superstars, starting with Roberto Clemente and continuing with Dave Parker, Al Oliver, and even Willie Stargell."[27] Given the situation, it came as no surprise that when Bonds became a free agent, the Pirates did not offer him a contract.

Bonds signed a contract with the San Francisco Giants worth $43.75 million over six years.[28] The contract was the largest in baseball history to date, meaning that Bonds again faced some very high expectations. During his first year with the Giants, sportswriters generally focused more on Bonds's talent than his personality. Scott Ostler of the *San Francisco Chronicle* wrote, "Bonds came to San Francisco and turned the franchise around like the cable-car operators turn their cars around at Market and Powell. Bonds had become an absolutely riveting character. . . . But what about Barry the Guy? Most attempts to analyze and characterize and psychoanalyze him have fallen flat, and one school of thinking is: He's a great player. Who cares what he's like off the field? Just appreciate him as an athlete."[29] Mark Purdy provided a similar combination of praise and criticism when he wrote, "Bonds is not merely dominating baseball, he is making it sit up, beg, and roll over. . . . He can be both charming and loutish, sometimes in the same sentence. But charm has been more prevalent with his fresh start in San Francisco."[30] Writer Bruce Jenkins compared Bonds to previous Giants' superstars: "He's perfect for the Giants. It's really kind of amusing, how they've assembled Bobby Bonds (as a coach), Hall of Famers Willie Mays and Willie McCovey, all-world talent Will Clark and Barry Bonds in camp. It's a wonderful statement about the Giants' image, both past and present, suggesting a band of dangerous sluggers about to administer a 15–3 thrashing. But nobody should mistake this scene as a warm, public-relations gesture, because there isn't a goodwill ambassador in the bunch."[31] Bonds apparently had left his churlish image in Pittsburgh, and San Francisco was willing to focus more on his play on the field than his personality off the field. But for how long?

According to the cliché, familiarity breeds discontent, and such seems to have been the case in Bonds's relationship with sportswriters. In the years following his San Francisco debut, especially after the disastrous 1994–95 MLB strike, which produced its fair share of hard feelings, discussions about Bonds's behavior began to overshadow his MVP-caliber play. Bob Nightengale of the *Sporting News* began one article by writing that Bonds and Albert Belle "are considered the bad boys of baseball. Their reputations have been sullied. They frighten management, are vilified by the media, and disliked by many of their teammates."[32] In that same vein, Jeff Pearlman of *Sports Illustrated* wrote in 2000, "For 13-plus years Bonds had an unmatched record of standing up reporters, of blowing off autograph seekers, of dogging teammates, of taking every opportunity to remind everyone that there is only one Barry Bonds—and you're not him."[33] What changed? San Francisco sportswriters may simply have needed some time to discover Bonds's more interesting personality quirks. In addition, the cancellation of the 1994 World Series as a consequence of the work stoppage left many sportswriters and fans bitter and ready to lash out at any and all baseball players. Bonds's reputation made him an easy target. Finally, the subtle shift in focus also has racial implications. Bonds himself brought up race in a 1994 interview: "It's only because I'm a black man. . . . When black ballplayers have a lot of money, it's a big issue. Why are people saying 'Is Barry Bonds going to live up to his contract?' You don't hear one word about Cal Ripken and Ryne Sandberg. It's always 'Can Barry live up to 40-some million dollars?'"[34] Bonds saw a difference between the way he was treated and the way white players were treated, and he spoke out about it.

The racial component of Bonds's treatment was not mentioned again by the mainstream press for some time, and the slugger simply continued to live up to his contractual expectations. The *Sporting News* named Bonds its Player of the Decade for the 1990s because he ranked in the top three for walks, home runs, slugging percentage, and RBI; racked up three MVP Awards and eight Gold Gloves; and became the first player to hit four hundred home runs and steal four hundred bases.[35] Any goodwill that Bonds generated, however, wore off in 2001, when the slugger dared to break Mark McGwire's single-season home-run record.

DOUBLE STANDARD

In 1998, McGwire became the nation's savior, the epitome of the new baseball slugger: a white working- or middle-class American male who was slightly uncomfortable with the spotlight; spoke proper English; was abrasive at times; had a personality flaw or two, which only made him more appealing; and had a happy-go-lucky ethnic sidekick, Sammy Sosa, waiting in the wings. Baseball still had not fully recovered from the 1994–95 strike, and a home run race brought fans back to the ballpark. During that season, when it seemed, as one reporter put it, that McGwire would "rather get hit in the head with a Randy Johnson fastball than answer one more question from the media,"[36] sportswriters continued to follow his every move and frame him as shy as opposed to surly. Though Bonds seemed to conform to the same curmudgeonly image as McGwire, that image worked for McGwire because he is white but not for Bonds arguably because he is black.

McGwire was not alone in his quest for baseball immortality. When McGwire began his march toward the single-season home run record, Sammy Sosa was unknown to most people outside Chicago, although it is the third-largest U.S. media market. But once baseballs started flying out of Wrigley Field, writers started paying attention. Throughout the home run chase, Sosa played the role of the black athlete society wanted: a sidekick for McGwire who was "friendly and deferential; he was loyal both to dominant societal values ... as well as to individuals who seemingly upheld them; he projected a safe, nonthreatening black identity."[37] At one point, Sosa was quoted in newspapers and magazines across the country as saying, "Baseball has been berry, berry good to me."[38] While Sosa has a noticeable Spanish accent, it is difficult to believe that sportswriters could not differentiate between *very* and *berry*. It is also possible that sportswriters and maybe even Sosa himself were referencing a classic *Saturday Night Live* skit in which Garrett Morris portrayed a Latin ballplayer, Chico Escuela, who had difficulties with English. At the same time, this is not the first time that sportswriters have misquoted Latin baseball players: when Hall of Famer Roberto Clemente said that he "hit" the ball, journalists would quote him as saying he "heet" the ball. Journalists sometimes changed Latin players' names: Clemente became Bob Clemente, and Orestes Miñoso became Minnie Minoso. Framing Sosa as a deferential sidekick further separated him from McGwire and made it easier for journalists to tout equality, since Sosa was being embraced by sportswriters specifically and America more generally, while reifying racial hierarchies with white players on top and black and Latin players vying for second place. At the same time, McGwire was still *the man*, while Sosa was *the sidekick*, which cultural critic bell hooks defines as the "happy darkies who are all singing, dancing ... and having a merry old time even in the midst of sad times and tragic moments."[39] While Sosa could/would play the role of the black athlete white audiences adore and would reap the accolades that go along with that image, Bonds would not play that role and consequently was framed as a malcontent.

In 2001, when Bonds began his quest for the single-season home run record, most of the surrounding commentary fell into two camps: those who begrudgingly asked fans to overlook the slugger's attitude and focus on his achievements, ironically calling even more attention to his attitude, and those who focused solely on his attitude. Pitcher and *Sporting News* guest columnist Todd Jones relayed an impassioned plea: "Please don't lose sight of what he has done just because you don't like him. Nobody likes him."[40] *Sports Illustrated*'s Rick Reilly began one article on Bonds, "Someday they'll be able to hold Bonds' funeral in a fitting room."[41] These sportswriters may well have emphasized Bonds's surliness as a means of lessening his professional achievements. This is not to say that a player's personality or off-field exploits should be completely discounted; however, Bonds's personality cannot be detached from his racialized body and those of sportswriters. Though Bonds's season warranted some national attention, the level of attention was more restrained than it had been for McGwire three years earlier. In fact, about 350 journalists were covering Bonds, about half as many as McGwire had attracted.[42]

Given fans' and sportswriters' fascination with home run chases, why did Bonds generate such a different reception from McGwire? Journalist Dave Zirin agrees that Bonds has not always been the kind of black athlete who white fans and sportswriters love to like, noting, "The media have been crushing Bonds without evidence because he has never played their game. If Michael Jordan was the Tom Hanks of the pro sports world, Bonds is Sean Penn, beating down the paparazzi and challenging their self-importance."[43]

Though Bonds could not be described as radical in a political sense, his relationship with the media could symbolize a power shift as he forces sportswriters to meet him on his own terms. Regardless of whether sportswriters like Bonds, his continued dominance forced those writers to deal with him. Conversely, by framing Bonds as a malcontent, sportswriters are attempting to put the slugger "in his place," sending a message to other black athletes: Be the type of black athlete white America wants you to be, or your image will be ruined. Cultural scholar Michael Eric Dyson points out that framing black athletes in general and Bonds specifically as angry black men/athletes can be described as an attempt "to demonize black people, to label them as somehow peculiarly possessed of an unwarranted ungratefulness for what our country offers. These athletes are angry about racism, they're angry about the unfair treatment they are receiving."[44]

By demonizing Bonds for his surly attitude, sportswriters highlight George Lipsitz's notions that "whiteness is the most subsidized identity in our society" and that "the most powerful identity politics are those that protect the value of whiteness."[45] Baseball already had a home run champion in McGwire, and nothing Bonds did on the field could erase that fact from the American consciousness. If Bonds had behaved more like Sosa, whose persona in 1998 was more of a happy-go-lucky sidekick, the commentary would be different.

Even when it may have been in the media's best interest to focus on Bonds's on-field achievements instead of his reputation, sportswriters continued to vilify him. The McGwire/Sosa chase provided the nation with a welcome diversion from then President Bill Clinton's sex scandal with White House intern Monica Lewinsky. In contrast, Bonds's quest for McGwire's record came in the wake of September 11. Though play was suspended for one week after the terrorist attacks on the Pentagon and World Trade Center, it would be misleading to argue that the ambivalence toward Bonds's season resulted entirely from the terrorist attacks. On the contrary, when New York hosted its first home games after the attacks, Mayor Rudolph Giuliani stated that one of the few things that got his mind off the terrorist attacks was baseball; to that end, although he is an avid Yankees fan, Giuliani attended a Mets game.[46]

Instead of framing Bonds's chase as a unifying force around which the nation could rally, sportswriters and fans again focused on the slugger's personality and seemed to resent the fact that he was trying to break McGwire's record. The *Sporting News*'s Ken Rosenthal argued, "If fans seem ambivalent about Bonds's quest, it's because McGwire broke the record only three years ago. It's because Bonds has failed to endear himself to the public."[47] In the wake of national tragedy and on the cusp of his historic achievement, Bonds's personality seemed to soften. As Bruce Jenkins of the *San Francisco Chronicle* observed, Bonds "readily accepted the media's need for interviews, revealed more of his gentle side than anyone thought possible and showed a rare glimpse of emotion, crying at the podium, during the postgame ceremony of his record home run. His reward: 'Yeah, whatever.'"[48] It was clear that nothing Bonds did was going to be enough to repair his reputation and shift the focus to his work instead of his personality.

According to Dyson, the controlling image of the angry black man/athlete "is in some ways a species of un-Americanness. The subtext is that such angry people are not accepting of the American way."[49] In other words, an angry black man was not the white, patriotic, image of America media representatives wished to forward. Instead of playing up Bonds's quest for the record and the fact that he pledged ten thousand dollars to the United Way for every home run he hit for the rest of the season, the focus shifted to the New York Yankees, a team headed, as usual, for postseason play. While some sportswriters maintained a "Been there, done that" attitude toward Bonds's home run chase, the same ambivalence was not levied toward the Yankees, who were making their fourth straight World Series appearance. Recalled Yankee first baseman Scott Brosius, "For the rest of that year anyway, we weren't the hated New York Yankees."[50] While McGwire and Sosa could provide a diversion from a presidential scandal, and the spirit surrounding 9/11 was enough to reform the image of the entire New York Yankees roster, it was not enough to reform Bonds's image. Sportswriters had framed Bonds in such a way that no amount of good deeds or need for national unity could alter that image. A few months after the 2001 season ended, the public learned that Bonds had received death threats similar to the ones Hank Aaron received in 1974. Bonds did not disclose whether the threats were racially motivated or whether he believed they were racially motivated, and sportswriters failed to give the issue much attention. No evidence suggests that McGwire or Sosa received death threats three years earlier. By framing Bonds as a malcontent somehow unworthy of breaking McGwire's record, sportswriters themselves are partially responsible for creating an atmosphere in which death threats are understandable and acceptable.

AN UNENVIABLE REPUTATION

Bonds's dismissive attitude toward members of the press was not the only factor that jeopardized if not outright damaged his reputation. Bonds's involvement with the Bay Area Laboratory Cooperative (BALCO) and the ever-growing steroid scandal helped to further destroy an already tarnished persona. Public discussions surrounding the use of performance-enhancing drugs in professional baseball did not start with Bonds. Rather, they started with McGwire. Before he broke the home run record, and well before planning for the celebrations began, Associated Press reporter Steve Wilstein spotted a bottle of androstenedione (andro) in McGwire's locker. At the time, andro was not banned by Major League Baseball, though the National Football League (NFL), the National Collegiate Athletic Association (NCAA), and the International Olympic Committee had banned it altogether. Instead of focusing on whether McGwire's pursuit of the home run record was somehow tainted by performance-enhancing drugs, the furor focused on media access and an athlete's privacy, and Cardinals manager Tony LaRussa tried to have the Associated Press banned from the team's clubhouse.[51]

Instead of framing McGwire as a cheat, his potentially unethical use of andro was viewed as a slight personality flaw. As the *Sporting News*'s Steve Marantz and Michael Knisley wrote, "Not that [McGwire's] perfect. His use of the over-the-counter supplement, androstenedione, makes us wonder about his judgment. . . . We question that blind spot, yet perversely, find him more appealing because of it, in the way Cindy Crawford's mole accents her beauty."[52] Sportswriters lined up to defend McGwire, and no one even hinted at adding an asterisk next to McGwire's record. As Jack McCallum and Richard O'Brien of *Sports Illustrated* argued, "Get this straight: McGwire's use of androstenedione, which he may not have advertised but didn't try to hide, should not taint his achievement if he breaks Roger Maris's single-season home run record. . . . It's not as if McGwire's home run prowess is purely a product of androstenedione."[53] Despite the information surrounding McGwire's andro usage, MLB did not institute any drug testing or prohibit the use of performance-enhancing drugs until 2003; even then, Bonds's alleged steroid use was not viewed as an appealing character flaw.

Stories alleging that Bonds took illegal steroids were widely published despite the continued assertions made by a lawyer for his trainer, Greg Anderson, that Bonds "never took anything illegal."[54] Since Bonds had arguably been the most dominant player in the game, it is only fair that his relationship with BALCO would raise a few eyebrows. However, other players who were linked to BALCO—specifically, New York Yankees first baseman Jason Giambi—seem to have earned a free pass on the performance-enhancing drugs spectacle. The free pass was issued in that year when Giambi arrived at spring training visibly thinner and proceeded to miss half of the season for unspecified health reasons, which were later revealed to be an intestinal parasite and a benign pituitary tumor, a known side effect of steroid use.[55] Some observers quietly speculated that Giambi's physical changes had resulted from steroid use. Bonds, whose physical appearance and professional aptitude had not changed since 2001, nevertheless remained a poster child for suspected steroid use.

Both McGwire and Giambi benefited from the differential treatment afforded by white privilege. In her influential article, "Unpacking the Invisible Knapsack," Peggy McIntosh defines white privilege as "an invisible package of unearned assets which I can count on cashing in each day, but about which I was 'meant' to remain oblivious."[56] McIntosh cites privileges that range from the mundane (i.e., finding flesh-colored bandages and blemish cover) to the more substantive (i.e., not having race work against her should she need medical or legal assistance).

To be sure, like Bonds, when Giambi's grand jury testimony was leaked, he was viewed as a pariah, particularly by the New York media. But Giambi's white privilege came into play when he was later afforded the opportunity to reform his image. The Yankees explored the possibility of voiding the remainder of Giambi's contract in the wake of the steroid allegations, but approximately one year later, the player previously depicted a liar and a cheater was named the *Sporting News*'s Comeback Player of the Year for 2005, and he was subsequently cheered in Yankee Stadium.

Since Bonds cannot benefit from white privilege, the steroid scandal continues to hound him. After being unceremoniously dismissed by the Giants following the 2007 season, no team in baseball was willing to sign the all-time home run leader to a contract in spite of his still remarkable statistical productivity. But the entire discussion of performance enhancement and records conveniently sidesteps the biggest beneficiaries of white privilege in baseball. As antiracist writer and educator Tim Wise points out, "How can white Americans call for Bonds to have his records marred by an asterisk while continuing to revere the records and performances of their white baseball heroes of eras past—folks with names like DiMaggio, Williams, Ruth and Cobb—who benefited from a much greater 'performance enhancement' than that which steroids can provide: namely, the racist exclusion of black athletes from the major leagues?"[57] No one is suggesting that Babe Ruth, Ty Cobb, or Joe DiMaggio cheated or that their numbers are tainted because of segregation; however, there is little doubt that white baseball players benefited from racism, and sportswriters remain unwilling to discuss this fact.

Despite very public denials and the fact that Bonds has never failed a steroids test, sportswriters and federal prosecutors have placed a bull's-eye on the slugger's back. In 2004, Lance Williams and Mark Fainaru-Wada printed excerpts from Bonds's sealed grand jury testimony in what would become a celebrated article for the *San Francisco Chronicle*. They claim that Bonds admitted to using a cream and a clear substance that Anderson, his trainer and a childhood friend, said were flaxseed oil and a rubbing balm for arthritis, though federal prosecutors believe the substances were designer steroids.[58] Williams and Fainaru-Wada's article and subsequent book, *Game of Shadows*,[59] were taken as gospel, and little or no discussion took place about how the authors obtained the information: there is no legal way to access sealed grand jury testimony. During the 2004 season, Bonds announced that he was being randomly tested for steroids and that the test would clear his name. On ESPN's *Pardon the Interruption*, analyst Tony Kornheiser responded, "I think a lot of people think that Barry Bonds *used* steroids. Fewer people think he *uses* steroids."[60] As Kornheiser implies, even negative tests cannot prove that Bonds did not take performance-enhancing drugs before MLB began steroid testing. Despite his continued on-field excellence, Bonds remains haunted by the media's guilty-until-proven-innocent thread of inquiry.

APPROACHING THE KINGS

As Bonds's grand jury testimony was being illegally leaked, he was poised to pass Babe Ruth on the all-time home run list. During his career (1914–35), Ruth became a baseball immortal, setting seven Major League records. Despite the fact that Ruth's dominance took place when MLB effectively barred U.S.-born black and dark-skinned Latin players, sportswriters never questioned whether he would have hit 60 home runs during a single season or 714 career homers if he had regularly faced Satchel Paige, Willie Foster, or other Negro League stars. The issue of race and records did not formally enter into the mainstream discussion until a February 22, 2005, press conference in which Bonds "played the race card," stating, "Babe Ruth ain't black. . . . I'm black. . . . [W]e go through a little bit more."[61] Though the majority of sportswriters framed Bonds's comment as simply deflecting attention away from steroids, ESPN's *Outside the Lines* discussed the matter with White Sox general manager Ken Williams and writer Howard Bryant. Bryant pointed out that Bonds

> is the third-generation descendant of the forefathers of integrated base-ball. I mean, the stories that you and I had learned in the history books, he learned at his dinner table from his father, from Willie Mays, Jackie Robinson, and Hank Aaron, and I think that when you watch him play, he's playing to erase a lot of slights. He's playing to erase the slights that his father went through, he's playing to erase the double standards that Willie Mays and these great, great superstars had to endure, and let's face it when I—one of the things that I took from listening to him at that press conference was when he was talking about asterisks and steroids and cheating and all these other things, I heard him say, "Now wait a second. Babe Ruth and the rest of these stars had to play 60 years not playing against black competition or Latinos." So, I mean, why wouldn't you put an asterisk on that? I mean, how unfair is that? I saw a guy who was very, very driven by what he considers to be a historical inaccuracy.[62]

Such was the extent of the mainstream media's racial discussion until the 2007 season, when the Associated Press conducted a poll and discovered that 40 percent of fans wanted Bonds to break MLB's all-time home run record.[63] Tellingly, whereas 55 percent of black fans were rooting for Bonds, only 34 percent of white fans were doing so.[64] A later poll conducted by ABC and ESPN found an even starker contrast: 75 percent of black fans and only 28 percent of white fans were hoping that Bonds would surpass Aaron's mark.[65] This racial divide existed in perceptions of Bonds's achievements not only among fans but also among the media.

While mainstream white sportswriters did not raise the issue of race, black newspapers had been discussing it for quite some time. In 2003, Marcus Henry of the *New York Amsterdam News* wrote, "There are some in the media who choose to emphasize his sometimes surly attitude as opposed to his skill as a baseball player. But that shouldn't be a shock when one considers how much different black and white athletes are treated in the media. Rarely does anyone talk about Ty Cobb's racist views. Nor do they emphasize Mickey Mantle's problem with alcohol addiction or the allegations that Braves manager Bobby Cox is a wife-beater."[66] In 2005, Marvin Wamble wrote in the *New Pittsburgh Courier* that Bonds "had to be respected because of his skill, but sports reporters in general do not like athletes who display a hint of arrogance. This dislike is especially evident for African-American millionaire athletes who refuse to bow down to the Holy Pen."[67] In a 2006 piece published in the *Los Angeles Sentinel*, Maulana Karenga contended, "Certainly, at the heart of the hatred and hostility directed toward Barry Bonds now and Hank Aaron earlier are the issues of race and racism, summed up in [W. E. B.] Du Bois' cogent and compelling category, 'unforgivable Blackness.' Indeed, in a racist society, being Black in itself is unforgivable; being Black and excellent is intolerable, and being Black, excellent and defiant is outrageous. Hank Aaron is the first two; Barry Bonds is . . . all three."[68] In 2007, Earl Ofari Hutchinson argued in the *Chicago Defender*, "Bonds has run neck in neck with O. J. Simpson as the man much of the public loves to loathe for two tormenting reasons. One is race, and the other is Bonds. The two are not inseparable. A big, rich, famous, surly, blunt-talking Black superstar who routinely thumbs his nose at the media sets off all kind of bells and whistles in the public mind."[69] The black press clearly saw a racial component in the ways in which Bonds was being framed long before he approached Aaron or Ruth, calling into question whether Bonds's "playing of the race card" was neither new nor completely unheard of.

Despite the denials and Bonds's continued dominance even after the implementation of steroid testing, every discussion regarding Bonds's achievements seemingly ended with an asterisk and a question mark, especially when he returned to full form in 2006 after an injury-prone 2005. The lengths to which sportswriters and federal investigators would go to get Bonds soon became clear: in June, federal prosecutors attempted to pressure Diamondbacks pitcher Jason Grimsley to wear a wire to obtain incriminating evidence against Bonds.[70] Grimsley and Bonds had never been teammates, and Grimsley said that he did not know Bonds very well.[71] Until federal agents searched Grimsley's home, forcing him to admit that he used performance-enhancing drugs, most of baseball's steroid discussion centered on batters rather than pitchers. The singular focus on batters certainly has racial connotations, given that the vast majority of U.S.-born black baseball players are position players, while the number of U.S.-born black pitchers hovers in the single digits each year.

CHARGES—OFFICIAL AND OTHERWISE

In July 2006, after three years of trying, a grand jury failed to indict Bonds on charges of perjury, tax evasion, or any steroid-related matter. Wrote Jason Whitlock of the *Kansas City Star*, "Federal persecutors, oh, I mean federal prosecutors announced today that they will continue their Grand Jury witch hunt to put Bonds in jail for passing Babe Ruth on the home-run chart."[72] The zeal with which authorities have pursued Bonds is not surprising. As Patricia Hill Collins points out, "Since 1980, whatever measures are used—rates of arrest, conviction, jail time, parole, or types of crime—African American men are more likely than White American men to encounter the criminal justice system."[73] As a result, although white sluggers such as McGwire and Giambi and white pitchers such as Grimsley have admitted to using performance-enhancing drugs during their careers, authorities focus solely on a black man, Bonds.

Bonds entered the 2007 season poised to break Aaron's MLB career home run mark. The combination of Bonds's curmudgeonly personality and the specter of steroids took what should have been an awe-inspiring moment and infused it with vitriol. When Bonds tied Aaron's mark, baseball commissioner Bud Selig was in attendance but offered a puzzling reaction. As the ball flew out of PETCO Park in San Diego, Bonds was greeted with more cheers than boos; however, Selig had to be prodded to his feet by Texas Rangers owner Tom Hicks. Selig stood but then placed his hands in his pockets. Reports indicated that Selig did not even speak to Bonds when the slugger tied the record. When Bonds subsequently broke the record, Selig was not present.[74]

On August 7, 2007, when Bonds came up to bat in the bottom of the fifth inning, hometown fans offered an enthusiastic standing ovation. Bonds was already 2-for-2 with a double and a single, driving in two of the Giants four runs in the tied game. Cameras flashed every time Bonds swung the bat, and when the count moved to 3-2, the crowd chanted "Barry, Barry . . ." Bonds sent the next pitch over the right field wall for the 756th home run of his career. Bonds's son was waiting for him at home plate, and the emotional slugger pointed in the air in a tribute to his father. The entire stadium erupted in cheers as Bonds hugged his teammates and his family and waved to the crowd. After a taped message from Hank Aaron was played on the score- board, Bonds thanked the fans, his teammates, his family, and the opposing team; he broke into tears as he thanked his father.

ESPN's Jerry Crasnick celebrated the occasion, like so many other journal- ists, by writing, "If we can't embrace Bonds because of his personality, and we can't admire him because of the short cuts he took, why should anybody care that he's baseball's home run champion? The answer is, lots of people don't. Now that Bonds has No. 756 in the bank, most folks outside San Francisco wish he would just pack up his bats and size 8 hats and go away."[75] Mike Bau- man wrote on MLB.com that "Barry Bonds breaking Henry Aaron's record is not the worst thing that ever happened in baseball, but it is not a particularly glorious occurrence, either. . . . Henry Aaron is an authentic national hero. Barry Bonds is an authentic national suspect."[76] Reeves wrote, "What I feel today is not so much rage, as sadness. . . . I don't recognize that boy in the man who now owns sports' most coveted record."[77] Bonds was forty-three years old when he broke the record, so Reeves's reference to "that boy" has massive racial connotations. *Sports Illustrated*'s Rick Reilly wrote, "It's like a man robbing a bank and then having a giant party to watch him count the money."[78] During the postgame press conference, Bonds was asked if he thought the record was tainted. His answer: "This record is not tainted at all, at all, period."[79] Sportswriters continued to downplay Bonds's achievement and attach a homemade asterisk to his record.

THE NEW SHADOW BALL

Bonds ended the 2007 season with career marks of 762 home runs, 1,996 RBIs, 514 stolen bases, 2,558 walks, a .298 batting average, .444 on-base percentage, and a .607 slugging percentage. But even those impressive stats could not prevent Bonds's continued fall from grace. In November 2007, after four years, thousands of hours of investigation, and tens of thousands of dollars, federal prosecutors finally indicted Bonds on three counts of perjury and one count of obstruction of justice stemming from his 2003 grand jury testimony. With the trial scheduled to take place during the 2008 season, many observers wondered if Bonds would retire to focus on his legal troubles. That decision was taken out of his hands when the San Francisco Giants announced that they would not offer Bonds a new contract. By the start of the 2008 season, all traces of Bonds's legacy and historic chase had been erased from the ballpark that his on-field excellence helped build.

Author Pat Conroy notes that "baseball fans love numbers. They like to swirl them around their mouths like Bordeaux wine. Most statistics are modest, unassuming and without presumption. Other statistics have more body, and by their richness and bite, provide a substantial addition to the satisfaction and mystery surrounding the game."[80] Numerous volumes have been dedicated to the study of baseball statistics, allowing fans to compare and contrast their favorite players both past and present. By all statistical measures, Barry Bonds is one of the best players in the history of the game. But despite his numbers, many writers refuse to acknowledge his greatness.

After *Game of Shadows* was released, Selig asked former Maine senator George Mitchell to conduct an investigation into steroid use in MLB. After hearing about Mitchell's involvement, many observers suspected that the investigation was simply a ploy to enable baseball "to formally distance itself from Bonds's accomplishments."[81] After twenty months and an undisclosed amount of money, Mitchell issued his report: instead of hanging Bonds out to dry by himself, the Mitchell Report aired the dirty laundry of Roger Clemens, a player equal to Bonds in stature and curmudgeonly behavior.

Given the similarities between Clemens and Bonds, it stands to reason that sportswriters would treat the two superstars in a similar fashion. Such has not been the case. If Bonds is considered the best batter of his generation, Clemens is certainly its best pitcher. Clemens boasts seven Cy Young Awards and stands eighth all-time in career wins and second in career strikeouts. If Bonds has been framed as being less than civil toward sportswriters, teammates, and fans, Clemens is no Eagle Scout. At the same time, like McGwire, Clemens's behavior is not framed in the same manner. When discussing Clemens's surliness, sportswriters often joke about his exploits, even after he beaned Mets catcher Mike Piazza in the head during a regular-season interleague game and then threw the barrel of a broken bat in

Piazza's direction during a World Series game three months later. While film of both confrontations was played on an endless loop, the commentary was unexpected: Clemens was described as a "thrower of balls. And sometimes of bats. Both of which may be aimed at an opponent at any time."[82] The confrontations with Piazza are reduced to a punch line instead of being framed as potentially serious assaults. Finally, one of the criticisms leveled at Bonds is that his statistical dominance comes at a time when he should have been thinking about retirement, not taking his game to another level. Clemens, who is two years older than Bonds, earned his sixth Cy Young Award and led the American league in strikeouts at the ripe old age of thirty-nine. In essence, Clemens is equal to Bonds in terms of talent, age, and surliness, so if race is not a factor in how Bonds has been framed, then Clemens should receive similar treatment from sportswriters.

FINAL THOUGHTS

When Clemens's name was leaked prior to Mitchell's initial press conference, ESPN commentators and sportswriters afforded the pitcher a privilege that Bonds did not receive, engaging in a much more extensive discussion of how the evidence had been collected and whether it could be corroborated. Mitchell had no subpoena powers and could not compel any players, past or present, to cooperate with the investigation. According to Bryant, "Short on access and information, Mitchell's investigators aggressively pressured team trainers, managers and strength coaches to speculate about players and their possible use of performance-enhancing drugs."[83] Jonathan Littleman feigned concern that Mets clubhouse employee Kirk Radomski was "Mitchell's A–No. 1 source—a towel boy handed to him on a silver platter. That's it? One towel boy, one strength and conditioning coach, and existing government investigations out of Albany, N.Y., and BALCO. Not exactly Sherlock Holmes. Or Sam Spade."[84] ESPN.com's Lester Munson expressed similar skepticism: "The tough issue is what constitutes reliable information. . . . [Mitchell] is dealing with information and possibly some people involved in the sale or delivery of drugs."[85] In essence, while sportswriters ignored the illegal use of sealed grand jury testimony to convict Bonds in the court of public opinion, the use of testimony from federal snitches was egregiously troublesome.

Even as the Mitchell Report gave baseball a "white Barry Bonds,"[86] the role that race plays in how sportswriters frame Bonds is clear. Argued Ralph Wiley, "What Barry Bonds has done is show great merit in the game. Unfortunately when you are what is called 'black,' that can be inconvenient; often when you show merit, the rules on merit are changed to make them more obtuse."[87]

Differences clearly exist in how sportswriters have framed Bonds, McGwire, Giambi, and Clemens. This does not mean that every sportswriter who prints a harsh word about Bonds is a racist. According to Wise, "One can hate Barry Bonds and also spend Sundays singing 'We Shall Overcome' with the Harlem Boys Choir before reading select passages from *Go Tell It on the Mountain*."[88]

At the same time, it would be nearly impossible for race not to enter the discussion in some fashion. By framing Bonds as a surly, doping curmudgeon, sportswriters have obscured the role that race plays in how some media representatives discuss Bonds's accomplishments. Characterizing Bonds in this manner also guarantees that, as ESPN's Michael Wilbon points out, "No matter how many home runs he hits, if he hits 780, he's never going to be recognized as the greatest home run hitter in the game. He may not like that, it may not be fair, but that's the reality."[89] Because Bonds lacks the warm and fuzzy personality that sportswriters seem to require from black athletes, the steroid clouds follow Bonds, and the racial smog that permeates actions and perceptions means that Bonds will never receive the professional respect his on-field performance deserves.

NOTES

1. Bob Hertzel, "Vote Shows Bonds Had It All Despite Image," *Sporting News*, December 3, 1990, 40.

2. Dave Kindred, "Bonds Gets the Record but Not the Credit," *Sporting News*, October 15, 2001, 72.

3. Jim Reeves, "Bonds Cheated and Disgraced the Game and Hank Aaron," *Fort Worth Star-Telegram*, August 8, 2007, http://www.star-telegram.com/sports/story/194941.html (August 8, 2007).

4. Steven Travers, *Barry Bonds: Baseball's Superman* (Champaign, IL: Sports Publishing, 2002), 254.

5. Richard Lapchick, with Jenny Brenden, and Brian Wright, *The 2006 Racial and Gender Report Card of the Associated Press Sports Editors* (Orlando, FL: Institute for Diversity and Ethics in Sport, 2006), 5.

6. Ibid.

7. Ibid., 12.

8. Derrick Bell, "The Racism Is Permanent Thesis: Courageous Revelation or Unconscious Denial of Racial Genocide," *Capital University Law Review* 22, no. 1 (1993): 586–73.

9. Fred L. Pincus, "Discrimination Comes in Many Forms: Individual, Institutional, and Structural," in *Readings for Diversity and Social Justice*, ed. Maurianne Adams (New York: Routledge, 2000), 31.

10. John Thorn, Phil Birnbaum, and Bill Deane, eds., *Total Baseball: The Ultimate Baseball Encyclopedia*, 8th ed. (Wilmington, DE: Sport Media, 2004), 730.

11. Richard Goldstein, "Bobby Bonds, 57, a Star and the Father of Barry, Dies," *New York Times*, August 24, 2003, N35.

12. Ibid.

13. Ron Fimrite, "Remembering Bobby Bonds," *Sports Illustrated*, September 1, 2003, 59.

14. Ibid., 58.

15. Thorn, Birnbaum, and Deane, *Total Baseball*, 714–16.

16. Ibid., 730.

17. Jeff Pearlman, *Love Me, Hate Me: Barry Bonds and the Making of an Antihero* (New York: HarperCollins, 2006), 26–33.

18. Richard Hoffer, "The Importance of Being Barry," *Sports Illustrated*, May 24, 1993, 12–22.

19. Pearlman, *Love Me, Hate Me*, 76.

20. John Steigerwald, "Bonds Looks Like Another Al Oliver," *Pittsburgh Post-Gazette*, June 7, 1986, 13.

21. Bruce Keidan, "No Warm Bonds in This Clubhouse," *Pittsburgh Post-Gazette*, July 9, 1986, 11.

22. *SportsCentury* (ESPN), "Barry Bonds" (n.d.).

23. Tom Barnidge, "Paradoxical Bonds Reaches Pinnacle; Father's Shadow No Longer Engulfs Him," *Sporting News*, October 29, 1990, 15.

24. Hank Hersch, "30/30 Vision: Pittsburgh's Barry Bonds Sees Those Numbers Coming," *Sports Illustrated*, June 25, 1990, 59–61.

25. Joe Sexton, "Baseball: It's Not Always Yo, Ho, Ho but Pirates Sail Along," *New York Times*, June 12, 1992, 15.

26. *SportsCentury* (ESPN), "Barry Bonds."

27. Ulish Carter, "Will Pirates Ever Win Again?" *New Pittsburgh Courier*, October 17, 2007, C5.

28. Tim Keown, "Bonds Is Coming, Stewart Is Going," *San Francisco Chronicle*, December 9, 1992, B1.

29. Scott Ostler, "Caring a Lot, Knowing Little, about Bonds," *San Francisco Chronicle*, July 23, 1993, E1.

30. Mark Purdy, "Don't Tell Me Barry Bonds Isn't the Best Ever," *Sporting News*, May 17, 1993, 7.

31. Bruce Jenkins, "Playing to Barry Bonds' Drum Beat," *San Francisco Chronicle*, March 8, 1993, C14.

32. Bob Nightengale, "Bonds and Belle Will Cash in on Being Bad Boys," *Sporting News*, November 11, 1996, 35.

33. Jeff Pearlman, "Appreciating Bonds," *Sports Illustrated*, June 5, 2000, 50.

34. Tim Keown, "Bonds on Racism, Limos," *San Francisco Chronicle*, February 26, 2004, E5.

35. William Ladson, "The Complete Player," *Sporting News*, July 12, 1999, 12.

36. Bob Ley, "#6: McGwire and Sosa Chase Maris," *The Headliners* (Bristol, CT: ESPN, 2004).

37. Patricia Hill Collins, *Black Sexual Politics: African Americans, Gender, and the New Racism* (New York: Routledge, 2004), 166–67.

38. Dave Kindred, "The Class of '98," *Sporting News*, December 21, 1998, 14.

39. bell hooks, *Reel to Real: Race, Sex, Class at the Movies* (New York: Routledge, 1996), 54.

40. Todd Jones, "You Don't Have to Like Bonds to Appreciate Him," *Sporting News*, November 4, 2002, 12.

41. Rick Reilly, "He Loves Himself Barry Much," *Sports Illustrated*, August 27, 2001, 102.

42. Tom Verducci, "Pushing 70," *Sports Illustrated*, October 8, 2001, 43.

43. Dave Zirin, *What's My Name, Fool? Sports and Resistance in the United States* (Chicago: Haymarket, 2005), 244–45.

44. Michael Eric Dyson, *Open Mike: Reflections on Philosophy, Race, Sex, Culture, and Religion* (New York: Basic Civitas, 2003), 216.

45. George Lipsitz, "The White 2K Problem," *Cultural Values* 4, no. 4 (2000): 521.

46. *Nine Innings from Ground Zero* (DVD) (HBO, 2004).

47. Ken Rosenthal, "Bonds Excels Where It Counts: On the Field," *Sporting News*, July 2, 2001, 14.

48. Bruce Jenkins, "Unprecedented, Unappreciated," *San Francisco Chronicle*, October 8, 2001, D2.

49. Dyson, *Open Mike*, 216.

50. *Nine Innings from Ground Zero.*

51. Mark Fitzgerald, "Furor Follows AP Disclosure on McGwire," *Editor and Publisher* 131, no. 35 (1998): 10–12.

52. Steve Marantz and Michael Knisley, "American Hero," *Sporting News*, September 21, 1998, 20–21.

53. Jack McCallum and Richard O'Brien, "Swallow This Pill," *Sports Illustrated*, August 31, 1998, 14.

54. "Report: Bonds, Giambi, Sheffield Received Steroids," ESPN.com, March 2, 2004, http://sports.espn.go.com/espn/wire?section=mlb&id=1748917 (September 29, 2004).

55. *SportsCenter*, "Jason Giambi," ESPN, December 2, 2004.

56. Peggy McIntosh, "White Privilege: Unpacking the Invisible Knapsack," in *White Privilege: Essential Readings on the Other Side of Racism*, ed. Paula S. Rothenberg (New York: Worth, 2002), 97.

57. Tim Wise, "Home Runs, Heroes, and Hypocrisy: Performance Enhancers in Black and White," TIMWISE.org, June 13, 2007, http://www.timwise.org (August 17, 2007).

58. Lance Williams and Mark Fainaru-Wada, "What Bonds Told the BALCO Grand Jury," *San Francisco Chronicle*, December 2, 2004, A1.

59. Mark Fainaru-Wada and Lance Williams, *Game of Shadows: Barry Bonds, BALCO, and the Steroids Scandal That Rocked Professional Sports* (New York: Gotham, 2006).

60. *Pardon the Interruption*, "Will Test Clear Bonds' Name?" ESPN, September 27, 2004.

61. *Outside the Lines*, "Bonds' Image and Race," ESPN, February 27, 2005.

62. Ibid.

63. "Poll Shows Minorities Support Bonds HR Chase," ESPN.com, July 16, 2007, http://sports.espn.go.com/mlb/news/story?id=2938959 (March 1, 2010).

64. Marcus Henry, "Barry Bonds Continues to Slam the Ball while Media Slams Him," *New York Amsterdam News*, August 14, 2003, 44.

65. Pat Forde, "Sports World Incubator for Larger Discussions to Come," ESPN.com, May 24, 2007, http://sports.espn.go.com/espn/columns/story?columnist=forde_pat&id=2881430&sportCat=mlb (July 25, 2007).

66. Henry, "Barry Bonds Continues," 44.

67. Marvin Wamble, "No Brown on Bonds' Nose," *New Pittsburgh Courier*, March 16, 2005, C8.

68. Maulana Karenga, "Raceball, Baseball, and Unforgivable Blackness: Hank, the King, and Barry, the Man," *Los Angeles Sentinel*, June 1, 2006, A7.

69. Earl Ofari Hutchinson, "Don't Rush to Judgment on Bonds," *Chicago Defender*, 21 November 2007, 8.

70. Associated Press, "Grimsley's Attorney: Feds Asked Diamondbacks Pitcher to Wear Wire in Bonds Probe," AP Online, June 9, 2006, http://www.boston.com/sports/baseball/articles/2006/06/09/feds_wanted_pitcher_to_wear_wire_in_probe/ (March 1, 2010)

71. *Pardon the Interruption*, "Bonds Not Indicted," ESPN, July 20, 2006.

72. Ibid.

73. Collins, *Black Sexual Politics*, 80.

74. *Pardon the Interruption*, "Thoughts on Bud's Reaction," ESPN, August 6, 2007.

75. Jerry Crasnick, "Why Should Anybody Care?" ESPN.com, August 7, 2007, http://sports.espn.go.com/mlb/news/story?id=2950598 (March 2, 2010).

76. Mike Bauman, "Bonds Sparks Mixed Emotions, Not Joy," MLB.com, August 8, 2007, http://mlb.mlb.com/news/article_perspectives.jsp?ymd=20070808&content_id=2136800&vkey=perspectives&fext=.jsp (August 8, 2007).

77. Reeves, "Bonds Cheated."

78. Rick Reilly, "Giving Bonds His Due," *Sports Illustrated*, July 23, 2007, 76.

79. *SportsCenter*, "756," ESPN, August 8, 2007.

80. Pat Conroy, "Hank Aaron's Pursuit of an Immortal and His Magic Number," in *Total Baseball*, ed. Thorn, Birnbaum, and Deane, 309.

81. *SportsCenter*, "756."

82. Jeff Merron, "Hormonally Charged," ESPN.com, March 8, 2005, http://sports.espn.go.com/espn/page2/story?page=merron/050309&num=0 (March 19, 2005).

83. Howard Bryant, "Friction and Fractures Erode Faith in Mitchell's Investigation," ESPN.com, December 11, 2007, http://sports.espn.go.com/mlb/news/story?id=3142651 (11 December 2007).

84. Jonathan Littleman, "Mitchell's Best Source Was a Towel Boy," Yahoo! Sports, December 13, 2007, http://sports.yahoo.com/mlb/news;_ylt=AvYsAi12IKhPrITwSqtuqInZxLsF?slug=li-mitchellanalysis121307&prov=yhoo&type=lgns (December 14, 2007).

85. Lester Munson, "Legal Questions Abound in Anticipation of Mitchell Report," ESPN.com, December 6, 2007, http://sports.espn.go.com/mlb/columns/story?id=3142722 (December 11, 2007).

86. Dan Wetzel, "Clemens Is No Different Than Bonds," Yahoo! Sports, December 13, 2007, http://sports.yahoo.com/mlb/news?slug=dw-clemenssteroidsearly121307&prov=yhoo&type=lgns (December 14, 2007).

87. Ralph Wiley, "Sour Grapes," ESPN.com, March 4, 2004, http://sports.espn.go.com/espn/page2/story?page=wiley/040304 (October 27, 2004).

88. Dave Zirin, *Welcome to the Terrordome: The Pain, Politics, and Promise of Sports* (Chicago: Haymarket, 2007), 162.

89. *Pardon the Interruption*, "Will Barry Ever Play Again?" ESPN, August 2, 2005.

KIRBY PUCKETT
A Middle American Tragedy

—SHERRIE L. WILSON

INTRODUCTION

After Kirby Puckett's death at the age of forty-five in 2006, playwright Syl Jones wrote a play, called simply *Kirby*, about the Minnesota Twins center fielder. The play, which premiered at the History Theatre in St. Paul, Minnesota, in October 2007, traced Puckett's path from stardom, including his entry into the Major Leagues in 1984 and his induction into the Baseball Hall of Fame in 2001, to disgrace in the wake of a highly publicized divorce and allegations of domestic violence, infidelity, and sexual assault.[1]

Jones compared Puckett's life to a Greek drama, with a "rise, fall, exile [from Minnesota to Arizona] and posthumous redemption." The story "had this intersection of sports, race and mythology," and Jones "thought it was incredible theater and it would write itself."[2] Graydon Royce of the *Minneapolis Star Tribune* summed up the play's message: "Greek literature teems with tragic heroes, and Puckett's story has the broad strokes of legend: an explosive arrival in 1984; white-hot fame during two world championships; his stoic optimism and gratitude when glaucoma cut his career short in 1996; his fall from grace when ugly details of his sexual misconduct and divorce became public; and his death from a stroke at the age of 45, while in exile in Arizona. As in the classics, fate has given Puckett an eternal saga in place of a long life."[3] The playwright sought to portray all sides of Puckett. "It's not a biography of Kirby," Jones told the *Star Tribune*. "It is a work of fiction. But it won't succeed unless it rings true. There's an essence of truth."[4]

The play is set in Puckett's mind after his stroke, piecing together thoughts and memories that Puckett might have had as he reviewed his life.[5] Karl Gehrke of Minnesota Public Radio described the play as portraying "the difference between baseball and life." Indeed, during much of his career with the Twins, Puckett seemed to succeed at both, but his private life later unraveled. Jones wanted the audience to realize the dangers of worshiping heroes and placing athletes on pedestals.[6]

The play encapsulates the legend of Kirby Puckett—his rise, fall, and even his posthumous (if not local) redemption. The focus of this chapter is to examine these phases of Puckett's life, with an emphasis on three themes played out repeatedly in media coverage of Puckett—his image as an Everyman with an average, not necessarily athletic, body; his image as a typical midwesterner who fit in with Minnesotans despite racial differences; and his image as a star athlete who contributed to the community. The coverage of these themes in both Minnesota and national media differed distinctly during the three phases of Puckett's life.

ENTER KIRBY PUCKETT

The rise of Puckett's reputation began from the moment he set foot on a baseball field with the Twins in 1984. He led the team to World Series championships in 1987 and 1991 and was voted Baseball's Best Role Model and Friendliest Player in a 1993 *Baseball America* reader survey.[7] His popularity with Twins fans only seemed to grow after glaucoma suddenly forced him to retire as a player in 1996 and after his selection to the Baseball Hall of Fame five years later.

When Puckett woke up on March 28, 1996, a fuzzy black dot obscured his vision. The problems were traced to glaucoma, and the damage was permanent. Puckett was forced to retire immediately. The following September, the Twins and fans thanked Puckett for his contributions to the team with an hour-long pregame ceremony attended by more than fifty-one thousand people. The program included videos, speeches, and banners; Puckett told the crowd that he had "played in front of the best fans in the whole entire world."[8] Rick Shefchik of the *St. Paul Pioneer Press* called Puckett Twins fans' "all-time favorite player," praising his humility, hard work, and contributions to the community. Shefchik speculated that Puckett could be a productive member of the community for another thirty-five years. Mike Gelfand, a reporter who covered the Twins in the 1970s, said that the "best thing" Puckett did in his career was "allowing us to idealize him. People want to believe there are people out there better than they are. Maybe we ought to be thanking him. He always acted like a nice guy, and that's all you can ask. These days, a guy who takes care of his public image seems to be more the exception than the rule."[9]

In 2001, Puckett became a first-ballot Hall of Fame inductee, with 2,304 career hits, ten All-Star appearances, and six Gold Glove Awards. At the time of his induction, Puckett said, "I know the people [in Minnesota] are proud as hell. I've loved Minnesota since I first laid foot in it. I'm probably going to die in Minnesota."[10] Puckett became the Twins executive vice president for baseball, and his popularity led Minneapolis to name a street near the Metrodome Kirby Puckett Place.[11]

In 1999, the *Star Tribune* named Puckett Minnesota's most important sports figure of the twentieth century. The lead on the newspaper story read, "It's official. Kirby Puckett, a skinny kid from Chicago when he arrived in 1984, is a Minnesotan through and through."[12] Dave St. Peter, the Twins' senior vice president for business affairs said in 2001, "The last season [Puckett] played in was 1995, and doing market research revealed that in 1995, '96, '97, '98, '99 and in 2000, he was always the most popular player with the Twins, even though he hadn't played for us in six years."[13]

PUCKETT'S RISE TO POPULARITY

Puckett's popularity can be demonstrated through several themes that appeared repeatedly in media coverage: his image as an Everyman with an average, cuddly body; his image as a typical midwesterner who fit in with Minnesotans; and his image as a star athlete who contributed to the community. In the coverage of Puckett's rise to baseball stardom and Hall of Fame induction, these themes bore a positive tone.

Puckett as Everyman

The Minnesota media consistently portrayed Puckett as a down-to-earth Everyman with whom fans could identify. Author Chuck Carlson, one of several Puckett biographers, called him the "embodiment of the American dream." Puckett "was no physical specimen at 5-foot-8 and 200 pounds (depending on what scale you used, that is). He readily, even gleefully admitted that he was no Rhodes scholar and had no desire to be one. Kirby Puckett was a baseball player. From start to finish. Nothing more, nothing less."[14] A 2003 *Sports Illustrated* article painted Puckett as "adorable, chubby and bald, Everymanish—'a cantaloupe with legs,' as Jim Murray described him. Even his name! Absolutely euphonious, a joy out of Dickens."[15] Similarly, in coverage of Puckett's Hall of Fame induction, *Star Tribune* writer Jim Souhan called Puckett an "amalgam of Superman and Everyman," popular with fans because they saw him both sweat and laugh.[16]

Tied to this theme were descriptions of his body as being that of an average person rather than of a star athlete. For many of his playing years, and definitely after his retirement, Puckett was overweight, which seemed to make him all the more appealing to the public. According to *Star Tribune* sportswriter Jay Weiner, "From the moment Kirby Puckett burst onto the

Minnesota scene, he was more than likeable. He was positively embraceable. Besides his obvious skills of hitting, running, and throwing, this roundish man knew how to adjust to his surroundings, how to invite smiles, and how to stir emotions."[17] Another newspaper writer said Puckett's "smile made him lovable and his girth made him huggable."[18]

In 1993, Puckett wrote a children's book, *Be the Best You Can Be*, that demonstrated his role as a hero for young people. Puckett commented about his size, "Lucky for me, size doesn't matter much in baseball. . . . Being your best means to accept who you are and to make the most of what you have. To succeed you have to believe in the body and talents God gave you."[19]

Puckett as a Minnesotan

Another media theme depicted Puckett as a typical midwesterner who fit in well with Minnesotans, most of whom are white. Issues involving race seldom surfaced in the media's coverage of Puckett, and Puckett seldom raised racial issues. His love of baseball and his strong on-field work ethic seemed to endear him to Minnesotans. He was one of them.

Minnesotans loved Puckett because he chose to live in the state and married a local woman, Tonya Hudson. Fans saw these decisions as particularly significant because he one of the few African Americans on a team in a state with a small minority population. As sportswriters Frank Deford and George Dohrmann, wrote, "He was held up as Exhibit A Homey, not only for other African Americans who would join the Twins but also for those hired by the Vikings and, later, the Timberwolves."[20] Fans adored Puckett because his love of the game and loyalty to the Twins seemed to rise above the financial focus of many players. By 1989, Puckett had the highest salary in baseball, and in 1992, a poll showed that 81 percent of fans wanted the Twins to pay Puckett whatever salary was necessary to keep him from moving to another team. At the 1992 Democratic National Convention in New York, a delegate from Minnesota proclaimed it "the state of Walter Mondale, Hubert Humphrey and Kirby Puckett."[21]

Puckett delighted fans during off-season Twins' marketing caravans in rural areas of the Upper Midwest. He had a way of "flattening out differences, of minimizing tensions" in an age when rising sports salaries and free agents sometimes disillusioned fans. Puckett's popularity did not translate to higher African American attendance at Twins' games, however. This was a consequence, according to Weiner, of long-standing tensions between the Twins and Minnesota's minority population that had developed largely from the actions and statements of onetime team owner Calvin Griffith.[22] During a

1978 speech to the Lions Club in Waseca, Minnesota, Griffith claimed, "I'll tell you why we [the Twins] came to Minnesota. It was when we found out that you only had 15,000 blacks here. Black people don't go to ballgames, but they'll fill up a rassling ring and put up such a chant that it'll scare you to death. . . . We came here because you'll got good, hardworking white people here." These comments came in 1978, after two of the Twins top black players, Larry Hisle and Lyman Bostock, had left as free agents; Rod Carew followed soon thereafter.[23]

Six years later, Puckett arrived in Minnesota. Minnesotans seemed to love him as they had no other African American athlete. "Perhaps it was his non-threatening manner," Weiner wrote. "Perhaps it was his palpable lack of anger at a time when young, black males were characterized as especially angry and unemployed. Perhaps it was his pure joy of playing the game and his ability to block out distractions."[24]

During a conversation about Puckett's lack of emphasis on racial issues in baseball, he asked Weiner, "Who would I be mad at?"[25] When Puckett began playing with the Twins, the team had only two other black players, Ron Washington and Darrell Brown, and Puckett replaced Brown in the starting lineup. While understanding racism in society, Puckett saw racial progress on a team that recognized players' contributions no matter their race. Weiner concluded that fans should not scold Puckett for his lack of social activism: "For better or for worse, Puckett was, simply, a baseball player and a friendly fellow, but really nothing more. He preferred it that way. He knew his limitations. He seemed happy with himself." Despite his involvement with charities, Puckett never became a community leader.[26]

In April 1986, Puckett was the only African American on the Twins' twenty-five man roster. (The only other black Twins player was Alex Sanchez, from the Dominican Republic.) During batting practice at the Metrodome, Angels star Reggie Jackson asked reporters, "Why aren't there colored boys on [the Twins]. It's a shame, an absolute shame. . . . You got players [on the Twins] who can't even play and there are colored boys who need work. . . . You have Kirby Puckett and that's it."[27] The comments provoked no public response from Puckett. Sixteen years later, however, Puckett told Weiner that Jackson had spouted off about race and then left town. According to Puckett, he told Jackson, "'I'm the only black man on this team but my teammates never treated me any differently.' I was just here to play baseball."[28] Given the Twins' negative history with black players, Weiner said, "Puckett almost inadvertently fell into a slot that needed to be filled: the role of the engaging, going-along-to-get-along black employee. It is not as if he consciously decided to play that role. He was simply a perfect fit for a state that has always had difficulty facing its racism." Black scholars and sports observers whom Weiner consulted said that Puckett "made black players palatable for a lot of Minnesotans."[29]

Puckett at times made subtle comments about social issues, although the public sometimes missed his actions. When he arrived at the ballpark and announced that he and Tonya had just adopted a daughter, some of his teammates were surprised at the speed of the process and wondered about a waiting period. Puckett's response: "Not [a waiting period] for black babies. Black babies you can adopt the same day."[30]

Should Puckett have used his popularity with Minnesotans to address issues of race? Perhaps, but he clearly did not feel comfortable in the role of politician or philosopher. Puckett was proud to be an African American and did not run from that identity, but his passion lay in playing baseball.[31] His approach helped him relate to white Minnesotans, which in and of itself served a positive purpose.

Puckett as a Community Contributor

The media's emphasis on Puckett's community service added to the public's positive perceptions about the baseball superstar. The annual Kirby Puckett Eight-Ball Invitational pool tournament raised money for the Children's Heart Fund. In addition, he was involved with the Make-a-Wish Foundation, which grants wishes to children with life-threatening illnesses.[32] During spring training in 1996, Puckett sat in the dugout with a Minnesota teenager who had bone cancer, talking with her, signing autographs, and giving her Twins memorabilia. Puckett found the experience deeply moving: "If I'd stayed out there five more minutes, I'd have been crying. Words can't really express something like that. We're in a position to make a difference in other people's lives. I've always said I wanted to somehow give something back." According to Carlson, Puckett's community service "gave the Twins their soul."[33]

After glaucoma ended Puckett's playing career, he launched a personal crusade to inform the public about the need for regular eye exams to screen for the disease, which disproportionately hits African Americans.[34] Puckett helped make the national "Don't Be Blindsided!" glaucoma-awareness campaign sponsored by Pharmacia and Upjohn a success.[35]

These actions complemented the positive attitude with which Puckett seemed to face the premature end of his baseball career. An article in *People* reflected his optimism: "Don't cry for Kirby. I'm not gonna let one bad thing destroy all the good in my life." Puckett was excited about life and wanted to spend more time with his family, and he did not "want pity. I've had a fairy-tale life. I'll be able to see my kids grow up, admire those fish I plan to catch. I can change the furniture in this room, but I can't change my vision. I won't let that get me down. My heart's beating, my left eye is doing well. My life is great."[36]

Some journalists speculated that Twins fans throughout the Upper Midwest made Puckett into a larger-than-life figure. Steve Rushin, a Minnesota native and *Sports Illustrated* writer, noted, "I think it's fair to say that Puckett was, for a time, not only the most popular person in Minnesota, but the most popular Minnesotan ever. . . . To fans and press alike, he symbolized all that was good about professional athletes, even if our faith wasn't merited."[37] But Rushin's comments came after circumstances in Puckett's private life had begun to mar his public image. The larger-than-life figure the media had helped to create began to plunge off his pedestal.

PUCKETT'S FALL

Just months after Kirby Puckett's induction into the Hall of Fame, he and Tonya announced that they were divorcing. A private investigator had told Tonya that Kirby had conducted affairs with several women: according to a police report, when she confronted him about the matter over the telephone, he threatened to kill her. Tonya Puckett told police that her husband had previously choked her with an electrical cord, placed a pistol against her face as she held their daughter, and locked her in the basement. She also accused him of using a power saw to cut through a door to get to her.[38] Kirby and Tonya Puckett's marriage officially ended in late December 2002. Their divorce settlement required Kirby Puckett to pay monthly child support and other expenses for his two children, aged ten and twelve.[39]

In March 2002, Laura Nygren, a woman who said she had carried on an affair with Kirby Puckett for eighteen years, obtained a temporary protection order barring him from contacting her. She said that Puckett had shoved and threatened her after learning that she had talked with Tonya.[40] Nygren told the media that Kirby Puckett thrived on "women who had low self-esteem, were overweight, on welfare and had kids. It's safe for him. He thinks we're thankful because nobody else will have us." According to Nygren, the locations where she and Puckett had sex included hotels, the Metrodome parking lot, and his Twins office.[41]

Later that year, Puckett was accused of pulling a woman into the men's restroom of a suburban Twin Cities restaurant and groping her. He was charged with false imprisonment, a felony, and fifth-degree criminal sexual conduct, a gross misdemeanor. A misdemeanor assault charge was later added to the list.[42] According to Weiner, during the weeklong trial in the spring of 2003, witnesses frequently referred to Puckett as that "big, fat black guy." The former player, "in size fifty-two suits, sat Buddha-like in the courtroom. This was no game. This was real life." Even though the jury acquitted him, some jurors said they thought he had done something wrong, even if it did not rise to the level of criminal charges. His reputation had been tarnished.[43]

The sexual assault charges created a rift between Puckett and the Twins. After the charges were filed, the Twins did not renew his contract as a vice president, though organization officials said that the decision had not resulted from the charges. Puckett turned down a lower-level job with the organization. After the verdict, the Twins issued a statement: "From the beginning, we understood the seriousness of the allegations against Kirby. This chapter of his life has been very difficult for Kirby, his family, friends and fans, and we are glad that today it has closed."[44]

In one of a series of stories published by the *Star Tribune* after Puckett's death, his friend Dwayne Harris described helping pack up the memorabilia in Puckett's Metrodome office in December 2002. Other Twins employees stayed away as Puckett reminisced and packed boxes. "It was a hard day," Harris said. "He just wanted to get out of there. [Puckett] said, 'I can't believe they don't want me anymore.'" Puckett thought the Twins had abandoned him because no one from the organization attended his trial. In May 2003, Puckett returned to the Metrodome for the induction of announcer Bob Casey, who had befriended Puckett when he first came up to the Majors, into the Twins Hall of Fame. Later that summer, the Twins tried to renew discussions with Puckett, but friends said he was too bitter to return.[45]

Because of Puckett's popularity, his tragic fall from grace hit Twins fans hard. To the Twin Cities media, Puckett's trial represented the state's version of the O. J. Simpson trial.[46] When the *St. Paul Pioneer Press* published a December 2002 article about the allegations against Puckett, he declined to comment: "You don't have to give me fairness. You write what you write. I've got nothing to say. You write your story. You do your job, man. You do what you got to do."[47] Then, on March 17, 2003, *Sports Illustrated* ran "The Rise and Fall of Kirby Puckett."[48] On the magazine's cover, "his overweight face, punctuated by his drooping and blind right eye, stared out at us, juxtaposed with a photo of him as we remember him: svelte, angelic, youthful."[49] An outcast in his adopted home state, Puckett sought refuge in Arizona.

The media coverage of Puckett's fall reiterated the themes that had appeared during his years of popularity, but they took on a distinctly different tone. The imperfect body that had endeared him to fans became a source of negative commentary about his poor health and failure to take care of himself. According to the *Chicago Sun-Times's* Carol Slezak, Puckett did not "seem so cuddly anymore, not after standing trial for sexual assault."[50] As their divorce neared finalization, Tonya expressed concern about Kirby's health: "I want him to get his life together. I really worry about him a lot. He breathes very heavy. He's put on weight. It's not just a matter of him getting his weight down. It's a psychological thing. It's getting his mind together."[51]

After Puckett retreated from public life, he became frustrated with the concern about his weight and health. Puckett loved to eat and party, and his friends grew concerned.[52] When he moved to Arizona with girlfriend Jodi Olson, Puckett lacked an incentive to lose weight and had little structure to his life. In September 2005, friends estimated that he weighed at least 310 pounds. "His arms and legs were still as powerful and thick as tree trunks, but his stomach was round and his face puffy. His bad right eye, the one blinded by glaucoma, was folded nearly shut." Some of those who knew him wondered whether the weight problems resulted from depression over leaving baseball, but others said the problem was simply that he loved to eat. Puckett often told friends he would not live past fifty. Friends who tried to confront Puckett about his weight had little success. One friend purchased a health club membership for Puckett, but he worked out only once.[53]

After his death, a *Star Tribune* writer opined that in Puckett's last days, he "no longer looked like the man who had hurled himself against the Metrodome Plexiglas, rising as if that famous derriere—what he called the 'Puck Pack'—was filled with helium. As a player, he worked incessantly in spring training to shed his winter pounds, to set an example for his teammates. As a citizen, he had no such incentive, no such outlet."[54]

Puckett's acceptance by Minnesotans was also called into question given the negative tone in the media coverage of his fall. Puckett's popularity with Twins' fans had seemed to transcend race, and although the coverage of Puckett's legal problems did not focus extensively on race, the media did discuss the questionnaire given to prospective jurors, which asked about racial attitudes and negative experiences with blacks.[55]

In addition, Puckett's popularity came under criticism in the media coverage of Puckett's failings. When the *Sports Illustrated* article was published right before the beginning of the trial, SI.com asked writer Frank Deford his opinions about Puckett. Although Deford had previously heard negative reports about Puckett, the writer was shocked because the allegations contradicted the usual impression of Puckett. According to Deford, fans felt betrayed and "a little foolish. That's a big theme of this story—the fans were taken. They gave their hearts away and it turned out the man to whom they gave their hearts was not so deserving. Even if Puckett is acquitted of the sexual assault charges brought against him, it's still very clear that he's not the person everyone thought he was. But a fascinating aspect of the story reflects on how fans get so carried away with their heroes."[56]

The *Sports Illustrated* article took almost a cynical tone toward Puckett, noting that after his retirement, he became just "fat little Kirby Puckett," which "meant being able to spend more time with his mistress of many years, who nobody seems to have known existed, because Kirby was, of course, an ideal family man—even though, truth be told, he wasn't even an ideal scoundrel, because he also cheated on his mistress of many years with a passel of other sad and lonely women. And you thought the fans were duped. She was so shocked at his perfidy, the mistress of many years, that she began to seek comfort in commiseration with the wife."[57] Tom Powers of the *St. Paul Pioneer Press* called the *Sports Illustrated* article "condescending" when it suggested that Minnesotans loved Puckett so much because the state lacked "star power" and because Puckett lifted "everyone's ultrashaky sense of self-esteem." Powers did not think fans had been "duped."[58]

Whether Minnesotans had been "duped" remains a matter of opinion, but Puckett's fall brought numerous media pleas for the public not to worship sports heroes. After Tonya Puckett's allegations against her husband began to leak out, many fans wondered whether the claims were true. One caller to the *Star Tribune* said, "If you can't believe in Kirby, who can you believe in?" But, as Dan Barreiro wrote, the public too often assumes that the qualities an athlete displays during games transfer into private life. Fans want to believe in a "sports fairy tale." The public should not assume that the best athletes make the best role models.[59]

Similarly, the Puckett case inspired Slezak to write about not expecting perfection from star athletes, who should not be expected to be superhuman: "The key to maintaining a solid relationship with your sports hero is separation. Admire his hitting, his defense, his hustle. Marvel at his ability to deliver in the clutch. Dream of one day being as good as him. Just keep it on the field. That way, you're less likely to be disappointed. And he'll be less likely to let you down."[60]

The references to Puckett's charity work also took on a negative tone after the allegations against him surfaced. At one point, Puckett's attorney, Chris Madel, tried to use Puckett's contributions to the community as a defense: "The only reason why Kirby Puckett was charged today is because he is a famous person. . . . It seems strange to me that this is the way the county attorney thanks Kirby Puckett for all he has done for the state of Minnesota." Hennepin County attorney Amy Klobuchar responded that she was just doing her job and that after his alleged behavior in the restaurant, "he was no one's hero."[61]

Moreover, Tonya Puckett had helped to shape Kirby Puckett's reputation as a humanitarian and a role model. After the couple's divorce, she told a reporter, "I feel like Kirby went out and played ball and made a living. My job was raising the children and being a wife and doing everything to build him up in the community and make [charitable events] happen."[62] She was behind the establishment of the Kirby and Tonya Puckett Scholarship Program at the University of Minnesota with a $250,000 endowment, and she did much of the work for the annual pool tournament.[63]

Nygren backed up these claims that Tonya was responsible for Kirby Puckett's charity work: he had told his longtime mistress that he hated charity work.[64] Puckett often complained to Nygren about having to do community service. On one occasion, when he was leaving Nygren to go see a sick child, he told her, "I don't give a s——. It's just another kid who's sick."[65] After his divorce, Puckett ended his involvement with the pool tournament.[66]

REDISCOVERING KIRBY PUCKETT

On March 5, 2006, Puckett suffered a stroke at his home in Scottsdale, Arizona. He was airlifted to a hospital, where he had several hours of surgery. A news story that was part of a *Star Tribune* series written after Puckett's death described the scene at the hospital as a gathering of "the two halves of Kirby Puckett's life—baseball, and after baseball." His fiancée, Jodi Olson, and her family congregated at one end of the hallway, while Tonya Puckett and his two children gathered at the other end. His siblings, former teammates, and friends visited the hospital, too. They came together to pray over his bedside. On March 6, he died.[67]

Puckett's death at such a young age was viewed as a sad ending to a legendary career. Puckett's July 1996 statement that "Tomorrow is not promised to any of us" was remembered at the time of his death. Souhan wrote, "Puckett's tomorrows served as painful reminders of his yesterdays. Puck's poetry became prophecy, and that is the stuff of tragedy."[68]

After Puckett's death, *St. Paul Pioneer Press* columnist Bob Sansevere wrote, "Larger-than-life characters aren't supposed to grow old before our eyes. Or become frail. Or make mistakes. Or have an aura that dims. More than anything, they're not supposed to die at a young age. When that happens, there is a sorrow that hovers like a giant shroud over the land where the character became larger than life. It is like that now in Minnesota. Kirby Puckett is dead. Those are the four most depressing words I have ever strung together."[69]

When Puckett died, much of the media coverage seemed to shift from the negative to his baseball accomplishments as well as his contributions to the Twin Cities area and to the sport. Much has been written about Puckett since his death, and Puckett's image continues to evolve. To a certain extent, posthumous coverage has exonerated him.[70] In that respect, the media has seemed to come full circle. During his rise, Puckett was portrayed as a cross between a larger-than-life superhero and the guy next door. During his fall, he was an overweight womanizer who had lost his Minnesota values. After his death, media portrayals returned to a more positive tone, perhaps out of respect to the fond baseball memories that Puckett still invoked among Twins fans. If Puckett had lived longer, perhaps he could have returned to Minnesota to reclaim more fully his reputation. The tragedy of Puckett's life is that he never had an opportunity to do so.

NOTES

1. Graydon Royce, "Tragic Hero; A New Play Explores the Mythic Reality of Kirby Puckett, Whose Life Played Out Like a Greek Drama," *Minneapolis Star Tribune*, October 12, 2007, 1F.

2. Ibid.

3. Ibid.

4. Ibid.

5. Karl Gehrke, "Kirby Puckett's Modern Tragedy on Stage," Minnesota Public Radio, October 11, 2007, http://Minnesota.publicradio.org/display/web/2007/10/10/puckettplay/ (14 June 2008).

6. Ibid.

7. Bob Sansevere, "The Secret Life of Kirby Puckett," *St. Paul Pioneer Press*, December 19, 2002.

8. Jim Caple, "Kirby Takes a Seat; Minnesotans Let Kirby Puckett Have It—a 51,011-Fan Salute—and Are Rewarded in Kind," *St. Paul Pioneer Press*, September 8, 1996, 1C.

9. Rick Shefchik, "Puckett Proves Again He's One in a Million; 'Kirby's Salute' Pays Tribute to Fans," *St. Paul Pioneer Press*, September 7, 1996, 1A.

10. Tom Powers, "Puckett Gives Maz Reason to Smile," *St. Paul Pioneer Press*, August 6, 2001, 1C.

11. Walter Leavy, "Kirby Puckett: On a New Mission," *Ebony*, October 1997, 174–78.

12. Patrick Reusse, "Millennium; Top 100 Sports Figures; Introducing No. 1: Kurrr-bee PUCK-it!" *Minneapolis Star Tribune*, December 25, 1999, 12S.

13. Jim Souhan, "Kirby Puckett; A Lasting Legacy; Defying All Odds, Popularity Rises after Retirement," *Minneapolis Star Tribune*, August 5, 2001, 5S.

14. Chuck Carlson, *Kirby Puckett: Baseball's Last Warrior* (Lenexa, KS: Addax, 1997), 177–78.

15. Frank Deford and George Dohrmann, "The Rise and Fall of Kirby Puckett," *Sports Illustrated*, March 17, 2003, 58–69.

16. Jim Souhan, "Personality Plus; Kirby Puckett Making Mischief; Kirby Puckett Making History. He Won Over Fans and Teammates with Heroics Spiced by Humor," *Minneapolis Star Tribune*, August 5, 2001, 4S.

17. Jay Weiner, "Kirby Puckett: All Player All the Time," in *Swinging for the Fences: Black Baseball in Minnesota*, ed. Steven R. Hoffbeck (St. Paul: Minnesota Historical Society Press, 2005), 191.

18. Sansevere, "Secret Life."

19. Kirby Puckett, as told to Greg Brown, *Be the Best You Can Be* (Minneapolis: Waldman House, 1993), 18.

20. Deford and Dohrmann, "Rise and Fall."

21. Ibid.

22. Weiner, "Kirby Puckett," 193–94.

23. Ibid., 200, citing *Minneapolis Tribune*, October 1, 1978, A1.

24. Ibid., 194–95.

25. Ibid., 195.

26. Ibid., 195–96.

27. Ibid., 201, citing *Minneapolis Star Tribune*, April 28, 1986, 1D.

28. Ibid.

29. Ibid., 201, 202.

30. Tom Powers, "There's a Lot Behind Puckett's Grin," *St. Paul Pioneer Press*, July 16, 1996, 3F.

31. Weiner, "Kirby Puckett," 212.

32. Rachel A. Koestler-Grack, *Baseball Superstars: Kirby Puckett* (New York: Chelsea House, 2007), 61.

33. Carlson, *Kirby Puckett*, 35.

34. Leavy, "Kirby Puckett."

35. Jennifer A. Webb, "Kirby Puckett Dies; Baseball Great Championed Glaucoma Awareness," *Ophthalmology Times*, April 15, 2006, 7.

36. Margaret Nelson, "With No Regrets," *People*, March 3, 1997, 67–69.

37. Steve Rushin, "The Puck Drops," SI.com, March 11, 2003, http://sportsillustrated .cnn.com/inside_game/steve_rushin/news/2003/03/11/puckett (June 14, 2008).

38. Bob Sansevere, "Pucketts Getting a Divorce; Popular Ballplayer's Wife Reports Threatening Phone Call," *St. Paul Pioneer Press*, January 12, 2002, 1A.

39. Jim Adams, "Pucketts' Divorce Finalized by County Judge," *Minneapolis Star Tribune*, December 31, 2002, 3B.

30. Mike Wells, "Hennepin County: Woman Gets No-Contact Order against Puckett," *St. Paul Pioneer Press*, March 28, 2002, 8B.

41. Sansevere, "Secret Life."

42. Amy Mayron, "Hennepin County: Puckett Jury Selection on Deck," *St. Paul Pioneer Press*, March 23, 2003, 1C.

43. Weiner, "Kirby Puckett," 192.

44. Amy Mayron, "Puckett Cleared of Sexual Assault; 'I'm Glad It's Over,' Former Twins Star Says," *St. Paul Pioneer Press*, April 4, 2003, A1.

45. Richard Meryhew, "After the Game; The Kirby Puckett We Never Knew; A Minnesota Hero's Hard Fall from Grace," *Minneapolis Star Tribune*, October 30, 2006, 1A.

46. Weiner, "Kirby Puckett," 192.

47. Sansevere, "Secret Life."

48. Deford and Dohrmann, "Rise and Fall."

49. Weiner, "Kirby Puckett," 192.

50. Carol Slezak, "Don't Expect Perfection," *Chicago Sun-Times*, April 7, 2003, 103.

51. Sansevere, "Secret Life."

52. Meryhew, "After the Game; The Kirby Puckett We Never Knew; A Minnesota Hero's Hard Fall from Grace," 1A.

53. Richard Meryhew, "After the Game; The Kirby Puckett We Never Knew; Finding a Family, Losing His Health," *Minneapolis Star Tribune*, October 31, 2006, 1A.

54. Jim Souhan, "Kirby Puckett, 1960–2006; A Baseball Tale of Joy Spirals into a Tragedy," *Minneapolis Star Tribune*, March 7, 2006, 1A.

55. Jay Weiner, "Puckett Jury Is Set for Day One; The Opening Statements Are Today in the Sex-Assault Case against the Former Twin," *Minneapolis Star Tribune*, March 27, 2003, 1B.

56. "Puckett Had Everyone Fooled," SI.com, March 11, 2003, http://sportsillustrated .cnn.com/inside_game/frank_deford/news/2003/03/11/deford_q_a (June 14, 2008).

57. Deford and Dohrmann, "Rise and Fall."

58. Tom Powers, "Fans Weren't Wrong for Adoring Puckett," *St. Paul Pioneer Press*, March 14, 2003, 1D.

59. Dan Barreiro, "Puckett Case Is a Good Lesson," *Minneapolis Star Tribune*, January 20, 2002, 1C.

60. Slezak, "Don't Expect Perfection," 103.

61. Jim Adams and Randy Furst, "Puckett Is Charged in Sex Case; He's Accused of 2 Crimes, Including Felony, at Bar," *Minneapolis Star Tribune*, October 19, 2002, 1A.

62. Sansevere, "Secret Life."

63. Ibid.

64. Ibid.

65. Deford and Dohrmann, "Rise and Fall."

66. Sansevere, "Secret Life."

67. Richard Meryhew, "After the Game; The Kirby Puckett We Never Knew; Life and Death on His Own Terms," *Minneapolis Star Tribune*, November 1, 2006, 1A.

68. Souhan, "Kirby Puckett, 1960–2006," 1A.

69. Bob Sansevere, "We Want to Believe Superheroes Never Die," *St. Paul Pioneer Press*, March 7, 2007, 1D.

70. See, for example, Hal Bodley and Bob Nightengale, "'He Taught Us to Play the Game Like It's Your Last,'" *USA Today*, March 7, 2006, 6C; Gordon Wittenmyer, "Puckett Was 'At His Happiest'; Fiancee, Former Wife Recall the Last Days of the Legendary Twin," *St. Paul Pioneer Press*, March 8, 2006, 1A; David Hawley, "One More Cheer; Thousands Join Friends, Family, and Former Teammates to Celebrate Puckett's Life and Love of the Game," *St. Paul Pioneer Press*, March 13, 2006, 2P; Bob Nightengale, "Twins Opener Hails Fallen Star Puckett," *USA Today*, April 12, 2006, 4C; "No Disagreement Here on the Shape of Puckett's Legacy," *St. Paul Pioneer Press*, March 13, 2006, 1C.

DON'T BELIEVE THE HYPE

The Racial Representation of Mike Tyson in Three Acts

—THABITI LEWIS

Don't crucify me for who I am and I tell the world who I am. . . . I would love to be Tiger Woods. I would love to be Will Smith. I would love to be Michael Jordan. I could have played the game and, "Oh, I'm somebody I'm not," but I'm just not that kind of person, because I'm very uninhibited. I've got to be in the mix. I've got to be Tyson.

—IRA BERKOW, 2002

INTRODUCTION

The deep bass and lyrics of rap music announce the fighter's entry. Sometimes he is accompanied by the sonic force of the rhythms of Public Enemy's hit song, "Welcome to the Terrordome."[1] Other times, the belligerence of DMX's "What's My Name?" blares into the crowd to announce his entrance.[2] As it plays, a chiseled sweaty figure descends from a tunnel, clad in only a white towel with a hole ripped in the middle for his head to poke through, black boxing trunks, boxing gloves, black shoes, no socks, and a vicious stare. He has a Jack Dempsey–style haircut parted to the left and gold teeth reminiscent of Jack Johnson. His taut musculature looks determined and angry. The man's physique is immaculate; every aspect of his body, from his calves to his neck, is hard muscle—an iron figure.

Once Mike Tyson enters the ring, it becomes clear that he is a minimalist, a gladiator concerned only with the task before him. The only bling is his gold teeth and the colorful championship belt affixed around his waist or over the shoulders of his assistants. His figure offers a striking contrast to his opponents, whose trunks, shoes, and robes are often quite colorful. The other contrast is that Tyson is a bundle of nervous energy, pacing his corner and anxiously waiting for the bell so he can uncoil rage, seemingly only concerned with devouring his prey so that he can relieve his pent-up frustrations. All who enter the ring fear the rage of Mike Tyson.

"Welcome to the Terrordome," a favorite Tyson hip-hop song early in his career, is primarily instrumental and full of the bass, sonic boom, explosive force, and rage that mirrored his ring performance. Each riff of the music's bass provides a thunderous blow, ripping eardrums the way Tyson ripped into his opponents' bodies. His boxing display was akin to the sonic boom and chaos of multiple sounds—bells, whistles, guitars, screams, raw force, and rage—synonymous with hip hop music and culture of the late 1980s and early 1990s. So, while "Welcome to the Terrordome" promised "a journey into sound,"[3] Tyson promised fans and opponents a journey into rage, power, and the fury of his fists. In addition, the group performing this music, Public Enemy—brash, smart, and inventive enough to usher rap music out of dance mode—was like Tyson, electric and original. Indeed, this music was an appropriate background beat for the lyrical performance of terror that Tyson displayed in the ring.

Although he resonated with the hip-hop of the era while his distinctive peekaboo boxing style was reminiscent of the 1950s, he also emphasized a nearly robot-like discipline, dedication to craft, intense concentration, the necessity of extreme confidence, and superb art. Yet his execution of his art was improvisational perpetual motion, bobbing and weaving left and right with fluid defense and offense, not unlike the rhythms of hip-hop music, epitomizing its emphasis on innovation.

Tyson, the New Age heavyweight, was a unique conflation of grit, aesthetics, and style that paid homage to a previous era while embracing his own generation. His voracious knowledge of boxing history was central to his representation and performance, as his first narrative shaped initial public perception of him. He was the prodigy who ate, slept, and drank boxing. It consumed him; all who faced him in the ring were consumed with fear because of the myth of the vicious rage and power of "Iron" Mike Tyson, the unbeatable destroyer.

But in the shadows always lurked another side of Tyson, and the music that carried him into the ring echoed his life and fragile emotions. His ring entrance was part performance, part attempt to inscribe his identity. Indeed, he never let the world forget that he was a poor black kid from Brownsville. Tyson is typical of most tragic figures in that he contributes significantly to his own plight. Listening to "What's My Name" (another Tyson favorite) reveals a dangerous man on the edge:

> If you want it we got it
> Come and get it nigga we wit it
> All you gotta do is set it baby
> Ryde or die
> What'cha niggas want, uh, uh
> What'cha niggas want.[4]

These are more than mere words. The lyrics are drenched in a dangerous nihilism, challenging not only his opponent in the ring but the world. It is a declaration embodying Tyson and a generation whose disposition represents the same nihilism, anger, and in-your-face bare bones hard-core "take me as I am" sentiment.

In the ring, Tyson's in-your-grill (face) style of simultaneous defense and offense that slipped opponents' punches then exploited errors with counter-punches that made something of nothing exemplified core hip-hop creeds. Like the culture and its accompanying music, his ring strategy required the extreme self-confidence needed to move close enough into an opponent's space to make Tyson's unique skills work; his control over the space in the ring for his benefit resonated with a hip-hop culture consumed with control-ling public spaces that routinely displaced them. And Tyson, a poster child for his displaced generation, controlled all the space in the boxing ring for more than half a decade.

Once within the very public space of the boxing ring, Tyson, like hip-hop, usually delivered thunderous uncompromising body shots and sonic hooks to the head that resulted in stylized first round knockouts reminiscent of a DJ laying a beat and a B-boy making just the right break to those beats. Ironically, despite his high nasal voice, his postfight interviews revealed an articulate young man whose lyrical skills, analysis of his performance, and knowledge of boxing history created just the right balance for a perfect performance.

PRODUCTION NOTES ON TYSON'S RACIAL REPRESENTATION

It is difficult to write about Tyson because he is such a public figure, an icon, and at times a caricature of himself. The public feels it knows Tyson and assumes that no additional narrative is necessary. Few people are unaware of Tyson or some version of his story: his first, brief marriage and painful divorce from Robin Givens; his subsequent marriages and divorces; and the struggle over him between Bill Cayton and Don King. In fact, there is little debate that he is a tragic figure who creates a great deal of his own misfortune. The world has watched in horror, in outrage, in humor, and in disgust for two decades as Tyson's life spiraled downward like a bad drama. Also, there is no dispute that he has a history of violence and mentally unstable behavior.

However, racial representations of Tyson have ebbed and flowed over time. People often ignore how his representation became more racially moti-vated after he switched managers. This process hastened the shift in his public image from hero to villain and finally to fool—all of which, truth be told, held true when he was with his white handlers. Still, the world has viewed him intently and occasionally with empathy. Tyson's image is so public and complex that it is difficult to discuss him without suffering the resistance or disgust of many who feel they already know him. Therefore any discussion of Tyson is daunting because details of his reputation precede him. It has been shaped by a mountain of magazine articles, Web sites, YouTube clips, books, and most recently a film, simply titled *Tyson*.[5]

Still, the role of race in shaping his very public identity remains under-explored. Before accepting the hype of the good kid tainted by the bad black man, it is important to scrutinize the racial dynamics surrounding the changes in this narrative. Why is it that when surrounded by his entirely white entourage, Tyson emerges a hero, but when his entourage is entirely black, he becomes a villain? Tyson was always the same figure: a hell-raiser, boxer, convicted rapist, kid from Brooklyn who never had anything and does not know how to act. But in his first act, the world consumed a narrative of him as a dedicated boxer who loved to raise pigeons and was placed on the right track. The media depiction of him shifted as he changed hands from his white managers or father figures (Jim Jacobs, Cayton, and Cus D'Amato) to the hands of King, the evil black hustler.[6]

Few observers have critically examined the racial legitimization and racial acceptance Tyson received because of his association with Cayton, Jacobs, and D'Amato; their presence alone initially made the media and a vocal white audience embrace Tyson as a hero. Equally overlooked are the racist under-pinnings of the notion that his affiliation with King hastened his public down-fall and tainted his image. His many transgressions suddenly became news.

Here, in three acts, I explore the centrality of race and its impact on the performance of sport celebrity in our society. I also examine Tyson's compel-ling attempt to wrestle with the overtly racial construction of his image and his attempt to claim mastery over his body—a Promethean cultural appro-priation of sorts—in what can be seen as akin to a "final act" in his struggle.

The racial representation of black athletes as villains in sport is nothing new. American sport culture has a history of being a site of battle over the racial image of people of color, starting with Jack Johnson, whose crime was being too uppity and dating white women, and continuing through Muham-mad Ali (before he was stricken with Parkinson's disease), whose crime was being uppity and joining the Nation of Islam, to Barry Bonds, who is simply too uppity. Tyson's racial representation is therefore far from an isolated case: such representations have occurred regularly in American sport culture.

Johnson, the first black heavyweight champion, struggled against the racial ropes of reputation. Throughout his life (and after), he has been labeled

everything from a coward and a beast to a womanizing criminal. Yet, the U.S. Congress recently took up a resolution intended to clean up Johnson's tarnished legacy. Ironically, conservative, white senator John McCain, is urging/directing the nation's first black president, Barack Obama, to pardon Johnson's unjust 1913 conviction for transporting women across state lines for immoral purposes.[7] Black (and a few white) Americans and politicians have spent decades trying to erase the act of racism that sent Johnson to prison on trumped-up charges, his only crime being his "unforgivable blackness."[8] But McCain's request for a pardon is big news. The effort acknowledges that Johnson's career and reputation were destroyed as a consequence of his success in the boxing ring and his relationships with white women.

The attempt to pardon Johnson exemplifies the power of race in how individuals are represented. McCain's act shows that the recuperation, repackaging, and recovery of black sports bodies can be performed by a range of people motivated by various interests. Ironically, Tyson's reputation was marred once he separated from white men, while Johnson's will be revived because white men have made a commitment to recover it. This reexamination of Tyson's reputation reveals the impact of contemporary racial representations of black athletes as villains and fools in the aftermath of black athletes' struggles of the 1960s and 1970s.[9]

An appropriate lens through which to view the public gaze of Mike Tyson and his performance in three acts is Orrin E. Klapp's *Heroes, Villains, and Fools: The Changing American Character* (1962). Klapp points out that heroes are winners, and Tyson was indeed an electrifying winner and thus a hero to be emulated and respected. However, after the end of his involvement with Cayton and Jacobs, Tyson reemerged as a villain, a public threat, though he might easily have been originally characterized in the same way. In the latter stages of his career, when his ring dominance diminished, he became a figure of ridicule—a fool. According to Klapp, heroes act as leaders in times of adversity; they are winners, are splendid performers, and are socially acceptable, and they state themes of a socially approved ethos. In a word, they are figures we want to emulate.[10] The pre-King Tyson, while a splendid performer and winner, was only socially acceptable because of his affiliation with white father figures who conveyed that they had tamed the wild beast.

But villains are the exact opposite. They threaten the welfare of independent groups. They are rogues, troublemakers, and rebels who violate order and usurp power. The villain "often serves society, for example, as a scapegoat or safety valve for aggression, or as a perfected hate-symbol building morale for law enforcement and other actions."[11] Such figures are strangers—suspicious,

isolated monsters. Tyson's behavior fit this category in each act of his life. But the fact that he became a villain only after his camp became primarily black confirms notions of black immorality and negativity as well as "generalized forms of deviant behavior that have structural significance" in terms of race in American society.[12]

Fools, in contrast, represent institutionalized clowning. They are figures of ridicule who disarm people. And there are three kinds of fools: the incompetent fool (the initial perception of Tyson in the final act); the clever fool who needs outlets for his aggression (again, Tyson); and the nonconforming types whom we ridicule as deviants and outsiders.[13] And to be sure, the clever fool with a touch of nonconformity sums up Tyson in his most recent iteration.

ACT 1: THE NEW BLACK HERO

The Tyson to whom the public was initially introduced wore trunks and black shoes with no socks, but he did not enter the ring to rap music. He was the twenty-year-old "Kid Dynamite" or "Iron Mike" who on November 22, 1986, scored a second-round knockout over Trevor Berbick to win the WBC title to become the youngest heavyweight champion. By 1988, Tyson had beaten James "Bonecrusher" Smith, Tony Tucker, Tyrell Biggs, and Michael Spinks to emerge as the undisputed heavyweight champion, officially the most feared man in boxing. The first time I heard of Tyson, my friends described him as unbeatable, a no-nonsense, muscled guy who stood in the middle of the ring waiting to knock out Marvin Frazier in the first minute of the first round. He was a primal force of destruction.

There is a well-worn narrative that Tyson was a bad kid turned good by D'Amato, who, with his partner, Camille Ewald, cared for the young Tyson. D'Amato reformed the boy, giving him his own bedroom for the first time in his life and a home in a nine-bedroom house in the Catskill Mountains. According to legend, Tyson was thirteen when he was discovered by Bobby Stewart, a former professional boxer who ran the boxing program at the Tyron School for Boys. (In reality, Tyson sought out Stewart.) The two-hundred-pound, five-foot, eight-inch Tyson captured Stewart's attention, and Stewart became Tyson's first trainer and introduced him to D'Amato.[14]

Tyson, as the story goes, trained religiously, was a good kid, obeyed the rules—at least most of the time. He was obsessed with boxing and pigeons, boxing traditions, and boxing history, and he loved D'Amato like a father. The story was refined into the fable of Cus and the Kid.[15] D'Amato joined with Cayton and Jacobs to make Tyson a hero, a model of what it took to

be champion, including humility and a willingness to succumb to the better angels of good white folks who built his character, his boxing skills, and his confidence.

While this construction contains some truth, absent from this narrative are the details regarding how his origins shaped the early Tyson and affected every stage of his life. Tyson grew up amid perpetual family crisis. His mother was an alcoholic, his father abandoned the family, and severe poverty reigned. Less attention is devoted to the fact that Tyson, although bigger than most kids his age, was quite passive and was often beaten up as a consequence of his lisp. When the man-child discovered his power, however, he became vicious, wreaking havoc without concern for the feelings of his victims. He stopped going to school. He joined a gang, drank, smoked cigarettes, stole from fruit stands, beat up kids for fun, became a pickpocket, and stole gold chains from the necks of women at bus stops. The world learned about these aspects of his past to underscore what a wonderful job D'Amato and company had done in reforming this vicious sociopath.

This narrative was so romantic and sold so well that Tyson was depicted as a man who became a fighter to right the wrongs committed against his person, family, neighborhood, class, and race. The image of him as a hero was complete. He was a winner, a splendid performer and socially acceptable. His ethos was socially approved.[16]

In the first act of Tyson's public life as hero, his historical personal demons, his sociopathic tendencies, and his psychological scars are ignored. While there is some mention of his low sense of self-worth resulting from his feelings of being abandoned and unloved, the focus is on how D'Amato helped to reform Tyson and then boxing gave him a purpose and confidence. But there was always a Tyson whose negative self-image issues were never resolved because D'Amato knew that he was old and dying. Jacobs also knew that D'Amato was ill and dying, so the two men had to hurry up and make Tyson a champion. Although Tyson the fighter was cultivated and honed to near perfection, Tyson the person was abandoned, his numerous flaws left to languish by those who knew but had neither the time nor perhaps the concern to stop and help him balance his fragile psychological and emotional state.

Even after D'Amato and company "saved" Tyson, he returned to his old neighborhood to rob people; he also tried to molest an ex-trainer's young daughter. But the public did not hear about such incidents. The public also did not learn that D'Amato allowed Tyson to sign a contract that gave Cayton and Jacobs a huge cut of the fighter's earnings. For Tyson's fight against Spinks, Cayton and Jacobs received five million dollars. Jacobs and Cayton also received 66 percent of all income from Reel Sports, which primarily filmed and distributed Tyson fights; 33 percent from licensing Tyson's fight films to foreign television markets; and 20 percent of his commercial endorsements.[17] Also missing from the D'Amato reform narrative is the information that Tyson's friend, trainer, and surrogate father handed him over to Jacobs and Cayton to repay a debt: Jacobs had long given D'Amato a monthly stipend of roughly one thousand dollars to support his Catskill gym and his house expenses.[18] Tying the hugely profitable Tyson "into a series of agreements that gave [Jacobs and Cayton] control over every aspect of his career"[19] is not the act of an angel. The shady business surrounding Tyson's ties to this group are overshadowed by a narrative of selfless white paternalism that rescued Tyson from the evils of Brownsville and of himself.

In fact, the construction of the young Tyson in the ring was a performance. While Tyson certainly struck an imposing figure, the fact that he fought each month added to his lore as a destruction machine with an unquenchable desire to mete out pain. Equally overshadowed is the fact that Tyson's performance was enhanced by his opponents, most of whom were big and slow, tailor-made to allow his speed, style, and strength to produce first-round knockouts and construct an aura of invincibility. His early ring persona presented a striking figure that masked his inner fears. This performance alone usually won most fights before the bell rang. Tyson was the perfect attraction: beastly and vicious yet humble and gentle in the hands of his cuddly old father figure. This racial representation was palatable to the white viewing public; it reified old stereotypes but assured them that he was under the "proper" control.

Understanding the heroic early Tyson requires understanding what the marketing of his performance in the ring reflected. In making the mythical monster of Tyson—Tyson "the Destroyer"—Jacobs and Cayton also played to all the worst stereotypes of black men in American social history. Under their management and mythmaking, he became less human and more monster. Although they humanized him in some public spaces, they often used their white presence—and his white entourage—to put America at ease regarding this volatile black figure. The message was that D'Amato, Cayton, and Jacobs were the ultimate ringmasters, able to control their lethal and terrifying young prospect. The white public had nothing to worry about. While Tyson was managed, trained, and surrounded by white men, he was considered the sport's most exciting performer and arguably the greatest of all time. By 1987, D'Amato, Cayton, and Jacobs had made Tyson—and themselves—wealthy.

Indeed, the early Tyson story offers great theater. The loving trainer and father figure dies before the fighter wins the title, which he dedicates to his mentor. The dominant narrative shows a loving and supportive network of white figures who care for the undisputed champion of the world, making him a likeable person. People were drawn to Tyson, falling over themselves to associate with the genial, bright young man with a gap-toothed smile. The young Tyson appealed to Main Street, and he became a spokesman for Pepsi, Kodak, and Nintendo and for the New York Police Department, the Internal Revenue Service, the Federal Bureau of Investigation, and the Drug Enforcement Administration. Meanwhile, the violent outbursts were swept under the rug—people were paid to keep quiet about Tyson's indiscretions.

ACT 2: THE VILLAIN

What kind of role model would I be if I forgot where I came from?
—MIKE TYSON

As is the case with most plays, major crises emerge by the second act, creating significant chaos. The first such incident in this particular drama was Tyson's brief marriage to and painful divorce from Robin Givens. In addition, rumors held that he moved between states of passivity and rage. He left Cayton and joined King, the hustler who allegedly cared only about how much money Tyson could make. King purportedly saved Tyson from the clutches of Givens and her mother by helping him switch all his bank and brokerage accounts, totaling nearly fifteen million dollars, back into Tyson's name. King also helped persuade Givens to agree not to seek or accept money.[20] He embraced Tyson at his weakest point during the Givens fiasco, while Cayton explained that he was unwilling to do so.[21] Steve Lott, an assistant to Cayton and Jacobs, confirmed in a *New York Times* article the sentiment that Tyson's affiliation with blacks led to his downfall: "From 1984, from the time Mike turned pro, to 1988, Tyson was a national hero. . . . Then Mike came under the influence of Givens and her mother, and then Don King, and everything went downhill from there."[22]

In 1988, Tyson's life "suddenly" spun out of control. Jacobs died of leukemia in March. Tyson secretly signed a deal with King in May. He got into a street fight with Mitch "Blood" Green outside a Harlem clothing store early one August morning. He wrecked his car in September and fired trainer Kevin Rooney in December. All these incidents are said to have resulted from

Tyson's affiliations with King and the other nefarious black associates who tainted the fighter's good character.

Despite this chaos, Tyson continued to win fights, and all opponents feared him. Except, that is, 42–1 underdog James "Buster" Douglas, who knocked Tyson out in the tenth round of a February 11, 1990, bout in Tokyo. This single blemish set Tyson on a frantic quest to reclaim the title from Evander Holyfield in November 1991.

But in July, Tyson attended the Miss Black America contest and allegedly raped participant Desiree Washington in his Indianapolis hotel room. He was subsequently indicted and convicted, and on March 26, 1992, Tyson began serving a six-year sentence at the Indiana Youth Center in Plainfield, Indiana. He was released on March 25, 1995.

According to the media narratives, while under King's stewardship, Tyson became villainous, domestically violent, a rapist—in short, the typical bad black man.[23] But a careful examination shows that Tyson was always psychotic, always robbing and fighting people, always a misogynist. The only thing that changed was that Tyson separated from his white masters, removing the blinders that had prevented the media from seeing that he was just a typical black bruiser. Once he started hanging out with boyhood friends such as Rory Holloway, incidents like the one with Green became examples of the "real" Tyson emerging from the deep dark basement. He lost ground as a role model for youth, the marker for athletic heroism in the modern world.[24]

Under King's management, Tyson had the illusion of freedom to do whatever he wanted; his white managers had not granted him the same freedom because they feared he would behave badly. The new, more politicized and racially conscious albeit misguided Tyson reemerged in the news and in tabloids as irresponsible and outlandish, lacking his previous work ethic. Media reports claimed that boxing was no longer the center of his life, a shift in focus that explained his loss to the mediocre Douglas.

King and the rest of Tyson's black entourage, it was reported, caused Tyson's social and economic demise. This narrative reflects the realities of racial prejudice, and a double standard emerges. King allegedly cheated Tyson out of his money, but the financial misdeeds of D'Amato, Cayton, and Jacobs are overlooked.

King is also depicted as having persuaded Tyson to embrace a new problack persona, antiwhite and hateful. King teaches young Tyson, who was formerly surrounded by whites, "The white man ain't nothing."[25] Upset with the media depictions of the new problack Tyson, King pays Spike Lee fifty thousand dollars to develop a minidocumentary for HBO prior to Tyson's fight with Alex Stewart. The documentary, filmed in black and white, shows Tyson remembering, "We're two black guys from the ghetto and with hustle and they don't like what we're saying. We're not, like, prejudiced anti-white. We're just pro-black. . . . They always change the rules when black folks come into success. Black success is unacceptable."[26] The Tyson of the second act is indeed problack, but when he broaches the realities of race and the unfair double standards that it demands, he receives only additional disgust, ridicule, and unpopular treatment in the media.

A year after his release from prison, a rusty Tyson recaptured the WBA title from an unheralded Bruce Seldon, only to lose it to Evander Holyfield less than a year later. Then the world watched in horror as Tyson bit Holyfield's ear in the second round of their rematch and was disqualified. Tyson had cried out, but no one was listening. He did not want to box anymore; and as luck would have it, this act earned him a one-year ban from the ring.

When he returned, he continued to spin downward, taking a beating from Lennox Lewis and finally quitting after another humiliating loss. The Iron Mike myth had long dissipated. The chanters, the hangers-on, and the leeches were now gone, along with most of his money. In the end, Tyson's racial representation emerges as a cautionary tale, a Shakespearean tragedy about what happens when Caliban turns against the good white hand that feeds him. Tyson became a villain in mainstream media—a nigger unleashed—but remained a hero among the members of the hip-hop generation and much of the black community representing the modern-day Stack-o-Lee.

With the assistance of media, Tyson unleashes a new voice that sought to be empowered. At the core of lived performance is valuing life lived daily and doing what feels natural. It is, in fact, unlike the Tyson of the first act, but his life and his ring aesthetics are perceived as thug and gangsta. What does it say that Tyson, whose ring aesthetics resonated with the general public and hip-hop heads after he left Cayton and Jacobs, is perceived as dull and angry? Inside Tyson's squeaky voice, we at times hear eloquent, passionate expressions of his personal demons and the frustrations of a young black man seeking love who is also being asked to perform for so many people—too many divergent things.

DMX's "What's My Name" captures the conflicted Tyson persona:

> I stay flippin'
> One minute I'm cool, the next minute I'm up on a nigga, rippin'
> That's my style
>
> . . .

> I've lost my mind
> And I'm about to make you lose yours too
> From far away one time.[27]

It is Tyson laying himself bare, a declaration that he is unpredictable, being driven crazy, and down for whatever, ready to "Ryde or die." His performance inside and outside the ring is as unpredictable, angry, and nihilistic as DMX's persona in the lyrics to the song.

Tyson's very public association with hip-hop, the music of the streets (narrowly viewed in popular culture as one-dimensional expressions of rage) compounded his new bad-man reputation largely because of the culture's emphasis on "doing you" or "keeping it real." And Tyson's life and ring performance personified all of the above. Tyson is hip-hop in the sense that he is perpetual innovation, and even his privileged life cannot evade the social realities that plague the dispossessed of his generation.

Tyson's racial representation became very negative and violent after his white entourage vanished. The media and public displayed outrage. Therefore, to completely understand his plight is to acknowledge the intricacies and fragility of identity—the prevalence of race. All identity—how we see ourselves and how others see us—is socially created. In sport culture, the media have the power to create what society perceives to be truth. Indeed, identity is created through relationships that lead us to understand ourselves as heroes, villains, fools, fathers, mothers, teachers, and so forth. In Tyson's case and in a sophisticated world of technology, he emerged in news stories, on the Internet, in film, and on television as primarily villain or fool. His actions were those of a man trying to thwart the imposed identities that imprisoned his identity. In an act of self-preservation, Tyson redrew the boundaries of his body; although he was on the ropes, he fought back against his perceived enemies for control of his body.

ACT 3: ACT LIKE YOU KNOW

On December 15, 2008, I conducted an Internet search for photos of Mike Tyson. Among my choices was a photo of a pudgy man in a white dress shirt and tan slacks standing center stage at the Game of the Year videogame awards in Las Vegas. The man appears somewhat listless, but I keep looking because he looks familiar. This man is not quite six feet tall, portly, clearly overweight, and balding. Perhaps he is a programmer who has spent his entire life in front of a computer. I decide it is a mistake and move to view additional photos.

The next photo is of the same man, only in this photo he is turned to his right, revealing a bizarre and outrageous tattoo on the left side of his face. "Oh shit," I blurt out, "It's Mike Tyson!"

Literary critic Houston A. Baker Jr. formulates the concepts "mastery of form" and "deformation of mastery."[28] "Mastery of form" is a means through which black people establish for themselves a literary voice that revises the socially produced minstrel distortions of black people and transforms them into art, a "Promethean cultural appropriation."[29] This deformation unmasks the minstrel and boldly reveals the folk, or "the territory within their own vale/veil."[30] While on the surface he came across as a fool, Tyson worked to establish an original voice in his final act, revising the minstrel production of Iron Mike Tyson by masking his face (with a tattoo) and former body (in fat). In the final analysis, people will have to acquaint themselves with the "territory within" Tyson's "vale/veil."

The Tyson of 2009 contrasts dramatically with the mythical Iron Mike who struck fear into opponents and the world without throwing a punch during the 1980s and 1990s. The figure posing for pictures reflects the malleable reality of Tyson's life. Perhaps the change in the shape of his body is his attempt to remold himself in his own image, precisely what he often lamented his handlers had forbidden him from doing.

In many ways, Tyson has struggled with the same existential crisis that has plagued many African American comedians since the minstrel shows of the nineteenth century: trying to negotiate the line between character and caricature, acting an angry fool and being one. The first time I saw Tyson's tattooed face, I laughed and thought to myself, "This boy is truly acting a fool; he has lost his mind." Perhaps not, because this new masked villain is not easily recognizable as the Tyson the world has come to know, hate, or love. As Tyson has acknowledged, "I know at times I come across like a Neanderthal or a babbling idiot, but I like that person. I like to show you that person because that's who you all come to see."[31]

On deeper reflection, the tattoo on his face might seem to be an attempt to mask his former self or a cover to hide him from the world. He might also be mocking his public image as a monster by making himself visibly appear monstrous, thus repelling people while providing himself the peace and isolation he seems to desire. It is also quite possible that I hear not my laughter at Tyson but Tyson's laughter at the world that thought it knew him so well. One thing is certain: it takes pugnacity and some real swagger to walk around with such a tattoo on one's face. In fact, it takes a heavy dose of swagger to deform the former Tyson with this new Mike.

Tyson's actions could also be read as asserting mastery of his image and of his body. In this regard, the tattoo and fat new self represent a reclaiming of sorts. Conversely, his new image is a response to the careful invention and scripting of his body for nearly two decades. His mastery of form destroys the former image, which he never really controlled. Perhaps he wants to repel the hordes of people who have always surrounded him. But since this is Tyson, it is also quite possible that he was simply bored. However, he seems consciously to be trying to murder the former reification of the violent bad black man that became his public persona and to be doing so on his own terms.

CURTAIN CALL

I know that basically I'm not wanted here. Americans are not civilized people.
—**MIKE TYSON**

Again, Tyson is far from a sympathetic figure, and I have no interest in making him one here. By most standards, he is a social psychopath, as his actions indicate. But Tyson's life nevertheless exemplifies the unfair racial representation of athletes of color. Each of the three acts reveals how race is played out and how it affects public perception and media coverage of athletes. Thus, the events of Tyson's unfinished final act represent signs of improvisational reinvention—reclamation and mastery over self. Always a commodity, his body controlled by many individuals and entities, Tyson is now offering a performance that attempts to establish his own voice and to make his body in his own image.

The media continue to portray Tyson as transformed from Iron Mike the hero to Tyson the fool, having devolved from striking opponents with sonic punches to biting opponents' ears and leg; cursing out the New Jersey Athletic Control Board; serving nine months in prison for a 1998 assault after a car accident; losing to lowly Kevin McBride in 2005; and, finally, the ultimate jester, conducting bizarre sparring exhibitions in Las Vegas. These are examples of Tyson the fool, fodder for comedy—the object of our public gaze and amusement. But perhaps we should not believe the hype that Tyson is a complete fool; Tyson might be having the last laugh.

Tyson (2008), a documentary film directed by James Toback, is a perfect measure of this final act.[32] Although the film is at times unfocused, Tyson delivers poetically articulate monologues as he chronicles his life. He tells his story in his own high-pitched voice, with no one else to drown out his meaning. The film forces people to remember Tyson more for being a superb boxer than for his litany of ill behavior. And while the film might lack balance (absent are the points of view of those whom Tyson has wronged and whom he claims have wronged him), he is asserting control, at least to some extent, of the narrative of his image. He also spoofs himself in the 2009 comedy *The Hangover*.[33]

As part of his third act, the reshaped Tyson also promotes the gaming sites FortuneFun.com and Casino Fortune and the Nintendo game Mike Tyson Punchout. This pudgy, iconic figure adorned with tattoos of Che Guevara, Arthur Ashe, and Mao (images that suggest that Tyson has more depth than many observers want to admit) seems to be finding creative ways to engage in the deformation of mastery. The new Tyson literally mocks, with a neominstrel mask, the former distortions he helped to create. His new body expresses a defiling of the "iron" image—defiance, killing Mike, reclaiming his body, and presenting the new Mike Tyson. With his new body, he signifies or reveals the territory within his vale in bold fashion, making his new self fun and somewhat sympathetic.

The new self has received some much-needed counseling and rehabilitation. Whatever one wants to believe of the new Tyson, however, his career offers proof that American sport culture is a site for racial performance where persons of color are made or unmade in public as hero, enemy/stranger, or antisocial thug through the power of racial representations.

NOTES

1. Public Enemy, "Welcome to the Terrordome," *Fear of a Black Planet* (Def Jam Recordings, 1990).

2. DMX, "What's My Name?" *And Then There Was X* (Island Def Jam Music Group, 2000).

3. Public Enemy, "Welcome to the Terrordome."

4. DMX, "What's My Name?"

5. *Tyson* (DVD) (Sony Pictures, 2008).

6. Conversations with historian Davarian Baldwin helped me to shape some of this thesis regarding the dynamics of the racial representation of Tyson and black men in sport culture from a historical perspective. Further, our discussion led me to reflect on the racial implications keeping notions of race stagnant with brutish images of "Negroes unleashed" and particularly on how this image was tied to Tyson after King became his manager and promoter.

7. Frederic J. Frommer, "McCain Seeks Pardon for First Black Champ," *Associated Press*, April 1, 2009.

8. *Unforgivable Blackness: The Rise and Fall of Jack Johnson* (DVD) (PBS Paramount, 2005); Geoffrey C. Ward, *Unforgivable Blackness: The Rise and Fall of Jack Johnson* (New York: Vintage, 2006).

9. Thabiti Lewis, *Ballers of the New School: Race and Sport in America* (Chicago: Third World Press, forthcoming), esp. chapter 1, outlines American culture as a site of racial performance where persons of color are made or unmade in public. This book dissects media representations of persons of color as enemy, stranger, and thug.

10. Orrin E. Klapp, *Heroes, Villains, and Fools: The Changing American Character* (Englewood Cliffs, NJ: Prentice-Hall, 1962), 27–28, 35.

11. Ibid., 50, 51.

12. Ibid., 65.

13. Ibid., 69.

14. Montieth Illingworth, *Mike Tyson: Money, Myth, and Betrayal* (New York: Carol, 1991), 9–10.

15. Ibid., 82.

16. Gary Smith, "Tyson the Timid, Tyson the Terrible," *Sports Illustrated*, March 21, 1988, 72–84.

17. Illingworth, *Mike Tyson*, 81–82.

18. Ibid., 13–14.

19. Ibid., 81.

20. Ibid., 294–97.

21. Ibid., 292–93.

22. Ira Berkow, "Tyson Remains an Object of Fascination," *New York Times*, May 21, 2002, D1–D4.

23. Richard Hoffer, "Destined to Fall," *Sports Illustrated*, February 17, 1992, 24–31. See also Lewis, *Ballers*, 46.

24. Berkow, "Tyson Remains," D3.

25. Ibid.

26. Illingworth, *Mike Tyson*, 126.

27. DMX, "What's My Name?"

28. Houston A. Baker Jr., *Modernism and the Harlem Renaissance* (Chicago: University of Chicago Press, 1989), 15–17.

29. Ibid., 33.

30. Ibid., 50.

31. Berkow, "Tyson Remains," D1.

32. *Tyson* (DVD).

33. *The Hangover* (Warner Bros. Pictures, 2009).

LOST IN TRANSLATION
Voice, Masculinity, Race, and the 1998 Home Run Chase
—SHELLEY LUCAS

INTRODUCTION

After being exalted for their athletic performance and sportsmanship in the 1998 home run chase, Mark McGwire and Sammy Sosa slowly lost their place on the pedestal reserved for baseball heroes and, specifically, in this case, home run sluggers. A succession of controversies, allegations, investigations, and exposés have pelted away at the base onto which Big Mac and Slammin' Sammy have been hoisted during the feel-good 1998 season. This chapter will explore the elevation of Sosa and McGwire during the 1998 season and the subsequent denigration of the two players' reputations. Although these two men shared the spotlight during the home run chase and have since had their sporting achievements tainted by similar allegations of steroid use, the discourses surrounding them have diverged in significant ways. During the 1998 season, for example, McGwire was exalted as a father, a family man, and an advocate for child abuse prevention, while Sosa was routinely highlighted for his comedic persona, good-natured relationship with the press, and devotion to his mother in the Dominican Republic. When confronted with suspicions of steroid use in the ensuing years, both men suffered a loss of voice—a loss featured prominently in mainstream media. Yet this loss of voice generated different meanings for each player. A collective disappointment in McGwire registered in media coverage of the steroid speculation and investigations, while derision and disdain dominated many reports about Sosa. I explore the relationship between their loss of voice and masculinity, race, power and privilege. An analysis of mainstream media coverage shows that similar to the home run chase, media discourse concerning the suspicion of illegal performance-enhancing drugs highlighted Sosa's racial identity, while McGwire's racial identity remained unnamed.

THE 1998 HOME RUN CHASE

In 1998, St. Louis Cardinal Mark McGwire and Sammy Sosa of the rival Chicago Cubs battled each other (and a few others, early on) in a season-long home run hitting competition. As the season progressed, both men were on track to break Roger Maris's record of sixty-one home runs in a season, set thirty-seven years earlier. To make a long season short, both McGwire and Sosa broke Maris's record, but McGwire finished on top with seventy home runs to Sosa's sixty-six. The two players were the subject of much media attention, not just for their batting performance but also for their good-natured relationship and sportsmanship as the competition heated up and the pressure intensified. McGwire and Sosa were lauded for saving baseball and rejuvenating America's pastime, and the home run chase was credited with providing a national diversion from a presidential impeachment inquiry. At the conclusion of 1998, Sosa and McGwire received numerous accolades and awards from sports-related organizations and publications. Sosa was named the National League's Most Valuable Player, and both the *Sporting News* and *Sports Illustrated* named McGwire and Sosa Sportsmen of the Year.[1] The two men were also recognized for their humanitarian and philanthropic efforts: McGwire reportedly made a million-dollar-a-year commitment to assist abused children, while Sosa helped raise funds and contributed to relief efforts for the Dominican Republic and neighboring countries in the aftermath of Hurricane Georges. Moreover, at the 1999 State of the Union address, Sosa sat next to First Lady Hillary Clinton, an honor intended to acknowledge his baseball skills and his philanthropy. He also received the Humanitarian of the Year award at the 1999 ESPY awards. The home run hysteria surrounding these two players continued the next season, albeit at a reduced pitch. McGwire ended the 1999 season with sixty-five home runs, two more than Sosa. Just a few years later, however, a series of public confessions, criminal investigations, and government inquiries began that would cast dark shadows on the good feelings and memories of 1998. Various events added to the speculation that the home run chase had been tainted by the use of illegal performance-enhancing substances, and media coverage of these events frequently included references to Sosa, McGwire, and the 1998 season.

- In May 2002, *Sports Illustrated* printed an article in which former player Ken Caminiti admitted to using steroids and estimated that 50 percent of players used steroids, stoking concerns about recent hitting records and the use of illegal performance enhancers in baseball.[2]
- In June 2003, Sosa got caught using a corked bat, leading some observers to question whether he had cheated to hit sixty or more home runs three times.
- In the fall of 2003, Barry Bonds, Jason Giambi, Benito Santiago, and Gary Sheffield testified before a grand jury as part of a federal investigation of the Bay Area Laboratory Cooperative (BALCO) for the distribution of steroids.

- In February 2005, Jose Canseco's book, *Juiced*, hit the shelves, creating a media frenzy as current and former players and league officials were asked to comment on Canseco's allegations of widespread steroid use.[3]

Several weeks after the release of Canseco's controversial tell-all, McGwire and Sosa were among a group of players subpoenaed to testify before the U.S. House Committee on Oversight and Government Reform about steroid use in baseball. In the wake of that testimony, Major League Baseball commissioner Bud Selig appointed former U.S. senator and federal prosecutor George Mitchell to investigate the illegal use of performance-enhancing drugs in the sport. After a twenty-month investigation, the Mitchell Report was released in December 2007: the document linked eighty-six players to illegal steroids and other performance-enhancing drugs.[4] The House Committee later held two days of hearings to further explore the Mitchell Report findings. Although public, political, and governmental scrutiny of Major League Baseball, its policies, and particular players continues, much of the recent discourse about McGwire and Sosa is linked to the 2005 congressional hearings.

METHODS

The examination of these players' very public fall is based on a qualitative analysis of mainstream media sources retrieved from searches run on Lexis-Nexis and SportDiscus databases, with additional clippings acquired and collected over the time period studied. As a consequence of the magazine's widespread circulation and prominence, *Sports Illustrated*'s coverage of the home run chase and ensuing investigations is cited extensively, although a variety of newspapers, magazines, and radio and television transcripts were also identified and reviewed. Because of the overwhelming number of newspaper reports and the commonalities identified in the initial review of sources, I narrowed my focus and drew more heavily from reports in larger newspapers. Three common themes emerged from this analysis: masculinity, voice, and race as they pertain to dominant discursive constructions of Sosa, McGwire, and their home run prowess.

Though their 1998 performances elevated both Sosa and McGwire to star status, Michael L. Butterworth found that print media coverage of the home run chase and these two athletes was decidedly uneven.[5] In media representations, McGwire was constructed as a mythic hero by focusing on his size and strength and by positioning him as the rightful front-runner. This positioning was supported by the marginalization of Sosa, in large part by racializing Sosa with overtly narrow narratives and stereotypes, and leaving McGwire's whiteness unnamed.

Race was also a notable factor in *Sports Illustrated*'s coverage of the home run chase.[6] Throughout the season, *Sports Illustrated* featured McGwire's role as a devoted father and family man while denying Sosa that same fatherhood role (until nearly the end of the season) by failing to mention that he had a family. *Sports Illustrated*'s story angles were suspect, particularly in light of an earlier special report on irresponsible fatherhood that profiled numerous athletes, almost exclusively nonwhite (and mostly African American), who had fathered out-of-wedlock children and often refused or challenged paternity and child-support orders.[7] *Sports Illustrated* missed an opportunity to challenge racial stereotypes of black men (Sosa's dark skin color would mark him as a "black Latin" player) as hypersexual, immoral, and irresponsible by neglecting to identify Sosa as a father and a husband.[8] Instead, *Sports Illustrated*'s coverage of Sosa cast him in a perpetual childlike state, with repeated references to his childhood and his mother and stories emphasizing his clownish and happy-go-lucky behavior—racial stereotypes of a harmless Sambo or coon. This depiction of Sosa represents a blend of African American and Latino stereotypes; indeed, these stereotypes overlap.

Throughout their history in U.S. baseball, Latin players have been stereotyped as quick-tempered, ignorant, lazy, passive, inferior, moody, and oversensitive,[9] all traits that were ascribed to Sosa at different times in his career. Jane Juffer argues that television coverage of Sosa resulted in a new stereotype, the "good, unselfish, modest but fun-loving Latino," which contrasted the earlier historical image of the selfish hotdog.[10] Similar trends in media coverage emerged in the ensuing decade, as McGwire remained unmarked by race. His masculinity stayed central to narratives about him, and his hero status was underscored by the disappointment registered after his 2005 testimony and his 2010 admission that he had indeed used steroids. Coverage of Sosa again accentuated his difference, primarily in racialized terms.

MARK MCGWIRE

McGwire's fall from grace was steeper and faster than Sosa's because McGwire had further to fall. He had won the home run chase, his whiteness and nationality contributed both to his hero status and to the limited attention paid to his androstenedione (andro) use in 1998, and he had retired from baseball in 2001 and could not redeem himself with future athletic performances.[11]

Growing suspicions about widespread steroid use in baseball had led to finger-pointing at McGwire and other power hitters, but his appearance at the 2005 congressional hearings caused great damage to his reputation. The focus on his physical size, his emotions, and his voice painted a picture of a diminished man that contrasted sharply with the heroic and humanitarian image promulgated in 1998.[12]

Media coverage and commentary related to the March 17, 2005, House committee hearings often included physical descriptions of McGwire's body size and body language, frequently referring to his physique seven years earlier. For example, McGwire was described as "less mammoth"[13] than when he played baseball; National Public Radio's Scott Simon noted that "McGwire looked dramatically thinner than the man whose Popeye arms had once swatted 70 home runs. Just sitting down to the hearing table in an ordinary-sized suit led credence to the suspicion that he'd swelled his muscles with steroids."[14] Such comments evoke the media fascination with McGwire's size and strength during the 1998 season, a facet of media attention that Butterworth argues was a key factor in the construction of McGwire as a hero. According to Butterworth, "The construction of McGwire as an archetypal hero according to his size and strength created the image of an individual carrying the weight and burden of an entire community."[15]

Another aspect of McGwire's character to be revisited after the hearing was his display of emotion—specifically, crying. In two feature stories published during the 1998 season, *Sports Illustrated* drew attention to the fact that McGwire was a big strong man who was not afraid to show his emotions.[16] Much was made of the fact that he broke down in tears during a press conference as he announced the establishment of a foundation to help abused and neglected children. These articles seemed to demonstrate and affirm McGwire's masculinity, which incorporated size, strength, and athleticism, as well as communication skills, sensitivity and emotional depth, factors not commonly associated with hegemonic masculinity. Quite a different picture emerged following the 2005 hearing. McGwire's tears were again the subject of media attention, but this time his emotional response was presented as a sign of weakness. Reports noted that McGwire was emotional during his opening statement: a *New York Times* story reported him as "choking up and appearing close to tears."[17] A later column recalled that "McGwire seemed contorted with tension, his face flushed red, his eyes watering up."[18] The *Washington Post* reported that he "seemed timid when compared with the sheer power and dominance he showed hitting those 70 home runs in 1998."[19] Another sportswriter alluded to a common image associated with McGwire in 1998 in an effort to illustrate the changed man who appeared at the hearing: "Once baseball's Paul Bunyan, [McGwire was now] deflated and weeping."[20]

While reporters had plenty to say about McGwire's body language and what it might communicate, McGwire himself was noted for what little he had to say. He ducked the question of steroid use, stonewalled the questioners, and stammered some responses. According to one sportswriter, "His tragic verbal denouement—'I'm not here to talk about the past'—has since defined him, even more than his own name does."[21] *Sports Illustrated*'s Rick Reilly, who had previously written a feature story extolling McGwire's masculinity, later called him out on account of his diminished size, emotions, and voice: "You looked small and weak. You were the Incredible Shrinking Man up there. They say getting off steroids will do that to your body. Can it do that to your morals, too? ... Be that big man again. *Tell the truth.*"[22] As these comments suggest, after the hearing, McGwire was largely defined by his loss of voice, not by his traditional masculinity.

The descriptions of McGwire's demeanor and appearance painted the picture of a smaller, weaker man, very different from the rugged individualist and heroic figure featured in 1998 media coverage. The discourse surrounding his downfall was steeped in more of a tone of disappointment than was associated with discussions of Sosa. According to media reports and media constructions, baseball fans preferred that McGwire break Maris's home run record. One *USA Today* poll found that 79 percent of those surveyed were rooting for McGwire, compared to only 16 percent for Sosa, and media stories consistently posited McGwire as the front-runner and Sosa as the runner-up.[23] McGwire occupied a higher pedestal and had a heavier burden to shoulder as the mythic hero who saved baseball and the nation. The 2005 crush of media coverage portrayed a man who had now succumbed to the weight and burden of the baseball community and its fans.

SAMMY SOSA

Sosa's plunge was longer than McGwire's and full of twists and turns, and ups and downs. He is the only player to hit more than sixty home runs three times (1998, 1999, and 2001), but he was caught using an illegally corked bat in 2003. His thirteen years with the Chicago Cubs ended badly at the conclusion of 2004 (fans booed him), and the Cubs traded him to the Baltimore Orioles, for whom he played in 2005. He was later subpoenaed to testify at the congressional hearing: he had an attorney read prepared sworn testimony and brought along an interpreter, earning rebukes in the press.

Sosa's offensive performance declined steadily after 2001, raising suspicions that he had previously used steroids but no longer did so. Sosa did not play professional baseball in the United States in 2006 but returned the next season to play for the Texas Rangers. On June 20, 2007, he became only the fifth player to hit six hundred career home runs, joining Hank Aaron, Barry Bonds, Willie Mays, and Babe Ruth. This achievement generated much discussion, disdain, and doubt among sportswriters, who downplayed his chances of being inducted into the Baseball Hall of Fame despite his membership in that exclusive club.

Sosa's congressional testimony garnered more media attention after he hit his 600th home run than it did at the time. Although media coverage of the 2005 hearing generally mentioned Sosa, much more attention was directed at the details of McGwire's testimony.

According to a *New York Times* story about the hearing, "Sammy Sosa could have been McGwire's co-star if the committee had pressed him about his denial that he ever used steroids. But the representatives, who were so eager to go after McGwire and later Commissioner Bud Selig and Donald Fehr, executive director of the union, demanded little of Sosa."[24] As in 1998, McGwire occupied the starring role while Sosa was cast in a secondary role.

What led to the belated backlash? According to the *Washington Post*, Sosa "brought an interpreter and a lawyer who read his statement for him despite the fact that those of us who know him from the baseball beat realize that he is perfectly fluent in English."[25] The *New York Times* suggested that Sosa "copped a language-barrier plea before Congress,"[26] a common assessment that would become more prevalent when discussions of Sosa's Hall of Fame chances arose. Sportswriters took on an especially derisive tone after Sosa reached the six hundred home run milestone in 2007, as this auspicious occasion sparked debate about whether he would be voted into the Baseball Hall of Fame. Becoming a member of this exclusive club made it even more likely that Sosa will need to be seriously considered for induction. The baseball journalists who reported on Sosa's home run are, for the most part, the same ones who will have the option of voting for him.

Sosa's use of an interpreter and lawyer was perceived as a personal affront by the members of the press who regularly covered Sosa. The *Chicago Sun-Times* accused Sosa of "advancing the absurd notion that his English was poor."[27] According to *USA Today*, "Though fluent in English, Sosa wanted us to believe there was a barrier that limited his help."[28] A *San Francisco Chronicle* reporter commented that Sosa's "mark on the game might be more about suddenly forgetting the English language on Capitol Hill than becoming the fifth player to reach 600 homers."[29] These expressions of incredulity accompanied references to his "no hablo ingles"[30] testimony and biting comments about Sosa's ability to lobby for his Hall of Fame induction two years later: "Funny, but his command of two languages sounded pretty good after swatting No. 600."[31]

This was not the first time that the media had assessed Sosa's English-language skills. During the home run heydays of the late 1990s, Sosa's use of English was a big part of his fan- and media-friendly personality, although his fluency was questionable. He was described as "charming the baseball empire in his second language, English"[32] and "merrily mangling his adopted lingo."[33] Sosa's personality helped turn his "language handicap" into an asset, according to a sports marketer.[34]

By 2005, sportswriters also expressed frustration at Sosa's refusal to accommodate media requests and/or his silence in response to their questions, thereby making their jobs more difficult. Complaints that he "lost his voice"[35] and was "far too evasive"[36] offered a stark contrast to his glory days in the late 1990s, when Sosa had seemed to enjoy the attention and welcomed media requests. McGwire, conversely, was reportedly much less comfortable with the attention and often responded brusquely to media requests until later in the home run race, when Sosa was credited with getting McGwire to loosen up. However, once the allegations and investigations started to pile up, Sosa became less responsive to requests from the press and less likely to make himself available. In such instances, Sosa's voice continued to penetrate, even when he chose to mute it. The press relayed this "loss of voice" and gave it power and volume by naming it. With this act of resistance, Sosa's silence became louder than words.

The attention directed to this one aspect of his assimilation into U.S. culture comes without any reflection or acknowledgment that learning a second language is a major obstacle for many Latin or other foreign-born players.[37] The mainstream media's intense focus on Sosa's decision to use a written statement rather than testifying in his second language (English) indicates a callous disregard for the difficulty he and other Latin players have faced when coming to the United States to play baseball. Sosa arrived in the United States at age seventeen without speaking English. The discourse about Sosa's sudden loss of voice (or the preferred voice, English) elides the history of Latinos in baseball and their struggles and does not reflect the history of media coverage that has been unkind, impatient, and patronizing to Latin players. Fellow Dominican ballplayer Pedro Martínez expressed frustration with the media's treatment of Sosa following the corked bat incident, noting that people laughed at the way Sosa spoke English: "At least he's trying. It is not like [members of the media] are trying to become bilingual and talk to us and make it easier for us."[38] Implicit in Martínez's observation is the fact that the overwhelming majority of sports editors, reporters, and columnists are white (94.7 percent, 86.7 percent, and 89.9 percent respectively)[39] and presumably speak English as their first language. A study of more than three hundred Associated Press newspapers found that Latinos accounted for only 2.8 percent of editors, 1 percent of columnists, and 2.7 percent of reporters; on Opening Day 2004, however, it is estimated that more than 25 percent of all Major Leaguers were foreign-born Latinos, and in 2005, 44 percent of all players in organized baseball were U.S.- or foreign-born Latinos.[40] Through their positions of power and privilege as white members of the media, journalists impart meaning and magnitude to Sosa's voice. Whether he is cast as charming or chafing, the focus on Sosa's use of English clearly marks him as the Other.

Media coverage of Sosa's testimony and his 600th home run mark him as both included and excluded from the national pastime. Juffer argues that for many television viewers in the late 1990s, Sosa "represents the simultaneous integration and distancing of the Latino immigrant: he speaks for Chicago as long as he wears the Cubs' uniform, but dressed in street clothes, he is back in the Dominican Republic, welcoming them to his country, his real home."[41] Though Juffer was referring to Sosa's appearance in a tourism advertisement, I extend her analysis to understand the representations and rhetoric directed at Sosa in the mid-2000s. Sosa spoke for the United States and Major League Baseball when he wore his Cubs' uniform in 1998. He was warm, welcoming and charming in the media spotlight, he deferred to the white, U.S.-born McGwire as "the man," and his graciousness in the home run chase was deemed a salve for the nation's and baseball's worries and wounds. But dressed in a suit and tie at the congressional hearing, accompanied by a lawyer and an interpreter, he was the Other: the non-English-speaking immigrant, the dark-skinned impostor, not an American hero or a savior of baseball but rather a saboteur.

The likelihood that he would receive serious consideration for inclusion into the Hall of Fame after hitting his 600th home run elevated the level of discourse about the significance of Sosa's language proficiency and by extension his status as Other. Of course, his possible place in the Hall of Fame is not contingent on his language skills but is based on a complex calculation of his baseball performance and suspicions of steroid use. However, given the current lack of concrete evidence against Sosa, some members of the press have used their power to suggest that his language skills are a meaningful factor to consider.

CONCLUDING REMARKS

The media discourse surrounding Sosa and McGwire's fall from grace and their place in baseball history says as much about them as about journalists. This discourse brings together issues of race, masculinity, privilege, and power, all of which are intimately connected to voice. McGwire's masculinity was highlighted in the media to the exclusion of his racial identity, while Sosa was marked by his race with little attention to his masculinity. For both athletes, an emphasis on voice—what they said or did not say and how they said it—were linked to representations of masculinity and race.

McGwire's silence was epitomized by his ubiquitous remark, "I'm not here to talk about the past." His silence was all the more noticeable because he had been placed upon a pedestal as a mythic (white) hero, and as such, much was expected of him that day on Capitol Hill. McGwire's testimony was embodied in repeated references to markers of hegemonic masculinity, including physical size, emotional control, and body language. Conversely, Sosa's silence was located in his inability, read more typically as unwillingness, to speak English and the scorn he faced for having his lawyer read prepared testimony while Sosa sat in silence. These moments of silence suddenly increased in volume after Sosa hit his 600th career home run, as members of the mainstream press reminded readers of his testimony as well as of Sosa's immigrant status and re-marked him as the Other.

A gulf exists between player and press, power and privilege. Whose voices have the most power in these scenarios, and what do these voices tell us? The silences attributed to McGwire and Sosa spoke volumes, at least in the eyes of members of the media. The power of the press allows journalists to voice their views and perceptions. Though these writers seek to illuminate issues and athletes of interest and concern, they often tell stories about themselves as well. For example, some sportswriters admitted their culpability in the home run hysteria by failing to notice, write about, or question the increasing body sizes that accompanied the increasing home run tallies. Others expressed angst about the seemingly impending Hall of Fame votes for Sosa and/or McGwire, while still others relished the opportunity to block Sosa's induction, barely hiding their disdain and their perception that he had both escaped detection for presumed steroid use and manipulated the U.S. government by pretending to not speak English when subpoenaed.

ESPN.com's Howard Bryant argues that McGwire has been treated differently than Bonds in the court of public opinion not because Bonds is black but because McGwire "happens to be white, and it started with the decided lack of bloodlust to pursue him after he folded before Congress."[42] Bryant's comments about McGwire are especially germane: "Too many fans and members of the press, especially, willfully deluded themselves with the McGwire myth, built by them because of their shared whiteness, their belief in his false purity. To turn on McGwire would be to admit he took steroids in '98, that the whole thing was a testosterone-fueled act. Unlike with Bonds, whose record-breaking years of 2001 and 2007 came long after the public had learned the joke was on them, it was too hard for them to outright reject McGwire. The legend became fact, so they printed the legend."[43] Just as McGwire's fall was tempered by this concept of shared whiteness with the media, the derisive coverage of Sosa's 600th home run and, by extension, his 2005 testimony revealed the racial divide between members of the nearly exclusively white press and the rapidly increasing population of Latinos in America's national pastime.

Sportswriters operate from positions of power and privilege. Many of them are members of the Baseball Writers' Association of America and will vote on future Hall of Fame members—their jobs accord them a public venue in which to voice their opinion on McGwire's and Sosa's place in history. The athletes also maintain a measure of control over what they say and do not say, but these acts of resistance, these moments of silence, do not often go unheard.

POSTSCRIPT

Nearly five years after his infamous proclamation that he "was not here to talk about the past," McGwire broke his oath of silence and announced, "It's time for me to talk about the past and to confirm what people have suspected."[44] Through an "orchestrated barnstorming confessional"[45] on January 11, 2010, McGwire admitted to using steroids and human growth hormones at various points in his baseball career, including during the 1998 home run chase. Similar to the media coverage of the 2005 congressional hearing, references to his current physical size (e.g., smaller than his playing days) and emotional control (e.g., breaking down into tears during his confession) were common. For the most part, his confession does not seem to have resurrected his reputation.[46] Despite earlier pleas to "tell the truth" (e.g., *Sports Illustrated*'s Rick Reilly), McGwire's silence on certain details continues to define him. His refusal to concede that steroids benefited his hitting performance and his silence on the details of how, when, and where he obtained the substances have led many in the media to dismiss his confession as a self-serving career move.[47] Finally, McGwire's confession has led to a new round of speculation by sportswriters about his chances of being inducted into the Baseball Hall of Fame. Although McGwire eventually found his voice and confessed to drug use, he did not speak loudly or clearly enough for some in the sports media, and those writers will have the last word when they cast their votes.

NOTES

1. Dave Kindred, "The Class of '98," *Sporting News*, December 21, 1998, 10–16; Tom Verducci, "Stroke of Genius," *Sports Illustrated*, December 21, 1998, 44–53.

2. Tom Verducci, "Totally Juiced," *Sports Illustrated*, June 3, 2002, 34–48. According to research by Bryan Denham, McGwire was subject to more media attention than Sosa following the *Sports Illustrated* exposé. McGwire was referenced in 24.2 percent of the 231 articles selected to meet the criteria for Denham's data set, fewer than Jose Canseco (50.2 percent) and Barry Bonds (25.5 percent), but more than Sosa (16.5 percent). See Bryan E. Denham, "*Sports Illustrated*, the Mainstream Press and the Enactment of Drug Policy in Major League Baseball," *Journalism* 5 (2004): 51–58. Without conducting a quantitative analysis of the media coverage of the 2005 hearings, I have found that McGwire's presence elicited more media attention than did Sosa's.

3. Jose Canseco, *Juiced: Wild Times, Rampant 'Roids, Smash Hits, and How Baseball Got Big* (New York: Regan, 2005).

4. George J. Mitchell, *Report to the Commissioner of Baseball of an Independent Investigation into the Illegal Use of Steroids and Other Performance Enhancing Substances by Players in Major League Baseball*, December 13, 2007, http://files.mlb.com/mitchrpt.pdf (April 14, 2010).

5. Michael L. Butterworth, "Race in 'The Race': Mark McGwire, Sammy Sosa, and Heroic Constructions of Whiteness," *Critical Studies in Media Communication* 24 (2007): 228–44.

6. Shelley Lucas, "Who's Your Daddy? Fatherhood, Race, and the Home Run Chase" (paper presented at the annual meeting of the North American Society for the Sociology of Sport, Cleveland, November 3–6, 1999).

7. Grant Wahl and L. Jon Wertheim, "Paternity Ward," *Sports Illustrated*, May 4, 1998, 62–71.

8. For an overview of race stereotypes, see Abby L. Ferber, "The Construction of Black Masculinity: White Supremacy Now and Then," *Journal of Sport and Social Issues* 31 (2007): 11–24.

9. Samuel O. Regalado, *Viva Baseball! Latin Major Leaguers and Their Special Hunger* (Urbana: University of Illinois Press, 1998).

10. Jane Juffer, "Who's the Man? Sammy Sosa, Latinos, and Televisual Redefinitions of the 'American' Pastime," *Journal of Sport and Social Issues* 26 (2002): 353.

11. See C. L. Cole and Alex Mobley, "American Steroids: Using Race and Gender," *Journal of Sport and Social Issues* 29 (2005): 3–8; Bryan E. Denham, "On Drugs in Sports

in the Aftermath of Flo-Jo's Death, Big Mac's Attack," *Journal of Sport and Social Issues* 23 (1999): 362–67.

12. One result of the overwhelming media attention during the 1998 season was that people became more aware of two public health issues associated with McGwire: child abuse prevention and andro use. Journalists had discovered andro, a testosterone-producing supplement, in McGwire's locker in August, and although this finding created some controversy, the substance was not banned by Major League Baseball at the time. A year later, McGwire announced that he had stopped taking andro because he did not want children to emulate him by using it. Research indicates that media coverage of McGwire during the home run chase positively influenced the public's knowledge, beliefs, and attitudes about child abuse prevention and andro, concluding that McGwire "did promote awareness of Androstenedione, a desire to learn more about it, and a desire to try it" (William J. Brown, Michael D. Basil, and Mihai C. Bocarnea, "The Influence of Famous Athletes on Health Beliefs and Practices: Mark McGwire, Child Abuse Prevention, and Androstenedione," *Journal of Health Communication* 8 [2003]: 54). Legislators presumably sought to spotlight such influences with the March 2005 hearings, which were designed to call out professional athletes for their failure to serve as positive role models for impressionable young athletes. The audience included family members of teens who had committed suicide after using anabolic steroids.

13. Murray Chass, "In Last At-Bat, McGwire Is Uncomfortable Again," *New York Times*, March 20, 2005, 9.

14. Scott Simon, "Congress Holds Hearing on Steroid Use in Major League Baseball," *Weekend Edition Saturday*, National Public Radio, March 19, 2005.

15. Butterworth, "Race," 235.

16. Tom Verducci, "Man on a Mission," *Sports Illustrated*, March 23, 1998, 76–84; Rick Reilly, "The Good Father," *Sports Illustrated*, September 7, 1998, 32–45.

17. Duff Wilson, "McGwire Offers No Denials at Steroid Hearings," *New York Times*, March 18, 2005, A1.

18. George Vecsey, "For Two, a Day of Recognition; For One, a Day of Reckoning," *New York Times*, January 10, 2007, D1.

19. George Solomon, "Up on the Hill, Baseball Finds a Mountain of Trouble," *Washington Post*, March 20, 2005, E02.

20. S. L. Price, "The Liars Club," Sports Illustrated.com, December 26, 2005, http://vault.sportsillustrated.cnn.com/vault/article/magazine/MAG1115060/index.html (March 27, 2008).

21. Howard Bryant, "Don't Forget Mark McGwire on Barry Bonds' Day in Court," ESPN.com, December 7, 2007, http://sports.espn.go.com/mlb/columns/story?columnist=bryant_howard&id=3145754 (December 27, 2007).

22. Rick Reilly, "Choking Up at the Plate," *Sports Illustrated*, March 38, 2005, 76.

23. Butterworth, "Race," 235.

24. Chass, "In Last At-Bat," 9.

25. Thomas Boswell, "Players of Stature, Feats of Clay," *Washington Post*, March 18, 2005, D01.

26. Vecsey, "For Two, a Day of Recognition," D1.

27. Jay Mariotti, "A Missing Person's Report; Lots of Players' Names Mentioned in Mitchell's Steroid Study, but, as If by Magic, Sammy Sosa Once Again Eluded the Snare," *Chicago Sun-Times*, December 6, 2007, A79.

28. Jon Saraceno, "Having It Both Ways: Sosa Wants to Take Glory and His Secret to the Grave," *USA Today*, June 22, 2007, 2C.

29. John Shea, "Sosa's 600 Homers Need Translation for Hall Voters," *San Francisco Chronicle*, June 24, 2007, D6.

30. See John Klein, "Steroid Scandal May Cost Sosa Votes, Too," *Tulsa World*, July 1, 2007, B1; Mark McGuire, "To Hall with Cheaters? Sosa's Situation Different among Steroids-Era Sluggers," *Albany (New York) Times Union*, June 22, 2007, B1.

31. Saraceno, "Having It Both Ways," 2C.

32. George Vecsey, "Sports of the Times: Many Joys of a Home Run Lovefest," *New York Times*, September 8, 1998, D1.

33. Steve Rushin, "Sam the Ham," *Sports Illustrated*, September 14, 1998, 35.

34. Juffer, "Who's the Man?" 351.

35. Murray Chass, "Powerful Issues Shadow Orioles' Aging Sluggers," *New York Times*, July 5, 2005, D3.

36. Saraceno, "Having It Both Ways," 2C.

37. See Adrian Burgos Jr., *Playing America's Game: Baseball, Latinos, and the Color Line* (Berkeley: University of California Press, 2007); Regalado, *Viva Baseball*.

38. Burgos, *Playing America's Game*, 248.

39. *The 2006 Racial and Gender Report Card of the Associated Press Sports Editors* covered more than 300 Associated Press newspapers. This study included 5,100 people and reported on the staff positions of sports editors, assistant sports editors, columnists, reporters, copy editors and designers, and support staff/clerks. With the exception of the support staff/clerks category, all of the positions were occupied by white males at percentages ranging from 86.7 to 95. A follow-up study conducted two years later showed hardly any change in these five positions. In the 2006 study, there were no Latinos represented in the sports editor or columnist position, and only .5 percent of the reporters (11 of 2,128) were Latino. See Richard Lapchick, with Jenny Brenden, and Brian Wright, *The 2006 Racial and Gender Report Card of the Associated Press Sports Editors* (Orlando, FL: Institute for Diversity and Ethics in Sport, 2006); Richard Lapchick, with Eric Little, Ray Mathew, and Jessica Zahn, *The 2008 Racial and Gender Report Card of the Associated Press Sports Editors* (Orlando, FL: Institute for Diversity and Ethics in Sport, 2008).

40. Burgos, *Playing America's Game*, 244.

41. Juffer, "Who's the Man?" 349.

42. Bryant, "Don't Forget."

43. Ibid.

44. Tyler Kepner, "McGwire Admits Steroid Use in 1990s, His Years of Magic," *New York Times*, January 12, 2010, B10.

45. William C. Rhoden, "Baseball Needs More Talking and Less Tears," *New York Times*, January 13, 2010, B14. McGwire's confession was publicized via a statement released to the Associated Press, an hour-long interview with Bob Costas on the MLB Network, and interviews with select other media outlets.

46. For example, see Selena Roberts, "Coming Clean: It's Complicated," *Sports Illustrated*, January 25, 2010, http://images.si.com/vault/article/magazine/MAG1165035/2/index.htm#top (March 25, 2010); Lynn Zinser, "Skepticism Follows McGwire's Tears," *New York Times*, January 13, 2010, http://www.nytimes.com/2010/01/13/sports/13leading.html

(March 25, 2010); Joe Posnanski, "It's Time to Forgive Mark McGwire," SI.com, January 12, 2010, http://sportsillustrated.cnn.com/2010/writers/joe_posnanski/01/12/posnanski .mcgwire/index.html (March 25, 2010).

47. Three months before his public confession, McGwire was announced as the hitting coach for his old team, the St. Louis Cardinals. From that moment on, speculation mounted about whether he would come clean about his presumed steroid use. His confession has been interpreted as a way for him to start that job with a clean slate.

BRANCH RICKEY
Moral Capitalist
—ROBERT F. LEWIS II

INTRODUCTION

During most of his career, Branch Rickey was, according to Robert Peterson, "the most successful front-office operator in baseball."[1] Like the moguls who dominated the movies in the 1930s and 1940s, Rickey's success largely depended on an oligopolistic environment similar to the Hollywood studio system that had Rickey counterparts such as Louis B. Mayer and Darryl F. Zanuck exploiting their studio "teams" of "players" without legal or worker challenge. Both the MLB and studio oligopolies are considerably less dominant today as a result of legislation and union interventions, and the public as well as the players have benefited from these diffusions of power.

In his later years, Rickey could not achieve what he did throughout most of his career. A 1922 Supreme Court decision affirming MLB's antitrust exemption provided legal protection for his exploitative activities by assuring perpetual subordination of players. Rickey exercised virtually complete control over his players, "enabled by the overwhelming power of the perpetual reserve system," which remained in effect for almost two decades beyond his MLB executive tenure.[2] With free agency and arguably the most powerful union in the country (as well as a more critical media) working against MLB executive dominance today, Rickey's bombastic controlling style would not succeed. Therefore, it is unlikely that he would currently enjoy the high general esteem bestowed by the baseball and larger community if his career had begun a half century or so later. His generally positive reputation perseveres primarily because of his signing of Jackie Robinson. That event, which MLB continuously and almost compulsively celebrates, overshadows his dubious methods and accomplishments in an era of virtually unencumbered executive exploitation.

Rickey's strong personality, evangelical religious zeal, teaching ability, and entrepreneurial business acumen, supported by his competent son-assistant, would now perhaps be more suitable attributes for a Billy Graham/Oral Roberts career. A TV evangelist retains the operational and personal freedom that used to be available to MLB executives and movie moguls. But the current MLB environment would not give Rickey the license he needed to excel. Rickey had a strong moral component as well as the ability to make money, both of which are suitable for an evangelist. Equipped with an aphorism for every occasion, Rickey generally took the offensive: "A moderate is a moral pickpocket."[3] Always willing to lecture an audience, like an evangelist, he tended to make profound assertions to justify any of his actions and sometimes shifted from one extreme to the other.

As an articulate, forceful moralist, Rickey as a TV evangelist could have rallied his flock on current religious issues. One can envision the archconservative Rickey today as an ardent right-to-lifer. In 1943, *Time* magazine observed that the Dodger president "talks like an evangelist in a voice that exploits the whisper as aptly as the roar."[4] A potential fatal flaw, however, in this new, fabricated role—as well as in the prior real life—is reflected in John C. Chalberg's observation that preacher Rickey was "not above thinking he was above it all."[5] Some failed TV evangelists as well as other public figures have had that egocentric flaw. As a result of significant postmortem research, notably reflected in Lee Lowenfish's recent biography, Rickey's current reputation has become more problematic.

The new Rickey might have to forsake his perennial cigar (sometimes used as a prop to help him collect his thoughts), but the image of oversized hat raked back, bushy eyebrows, Churchillian bow tie, booming incessant voice, and (in later years) cane would help make this "moral capitalist" iconic in today's media environment. Modern versions of his private plane and chauffeured car would still serve as appropriate embellishments for the capitalist aspect of his image, while his background and forceful style would demonstrate his strong moral sense of right and wrong. Scott Simon notes that Rickey was "one of life's great unscripted actors."[6] In the current investigative journalism environment, however, Rickey the evangelist or baseball executive would likely not fare as well on the public stage.

While his vulnerability existed in kinder media days, it was less destructive to his image. The media tended to chide but not excoriate him. In covering Rickey during his tenure as the Dodgers' president, noted sportswriter Red Smith punned, "Rickey is a man of many facets—all turned on."[7] Sportswriters labeled Rickey's Dodger office the "Cave of the Winds."[8] One agent complained, "Sometimes I thought if you asked him what time it was, he would tell you how to make a watch."[9] Simon observes, "He could give baseball minutiae the same weight as matters of state—which could lend him an appearance of ridiculousness."[10] Rickey "was never one to keep his advice to himself."[11] Indicative of his prolific persona is the collection of 131 containers of his writings in the Library of Congress.[12]

As John Monteleone notes, Rickey was "a man of ultimate paradoxes, a capitalist/moralist/competitor/do-gooder/visionary/reactionary all rolled into one."[13] Such a description would also fit Graham or Roberts. As a moral capitalist operating in a protected oligopoly, Rickey defied the Peter Principle (man rises to his level of incompetence) for three decades by achieving greater success the higher he rose in the MLB hierarchy, until business complications, competition, and failing health overcame him in the 1950s.[14] Then the Peter Principle prevailed as Rickey continued to rely on old ideas and approaches in a changing environment. He still pontificated, though less effectively in writing than in speech. Baseball writer Roger Kahn called Rickey's 1965 autobiography "trivial and pretentious," criticizing Rickey's self-serving manner and outdated commentary.[15] Lowenfish's biography effectively captures the paradoxes and the fall from grace of the "ferocious gentleman."

Rickey was a better (but not very good) field manager than player and a great off-field executive because he used his paradoxical characteristics in a successful leadership role. At an executive level, that combination of traits kept his opponents—other team executives in trade activities, media in interviews, players in salary discussions—at a tactical disadvantage and enabled Rickey to achieve his objectives most of the time. Neil Sullivan contends that the key to Rickey's success was "the ability to integrate the disparate elements of his personality and to nurture players who mirrored his own pragmatic daring."[16] With such conflicting attributes, however, he also made significant business errors, notably objections to advertising beer or televising games ("Baseball does not fit the television screen")[17] with the Dodgers. The errors occurred more often later in his career as the game became more complicated and his earlier cumulative advantages waned.

Sociologist Richard Watts's description of the economic "cumulative advantage" or "rich get richer" effect applied to Rickey during his successful stints with the St. Louis Cardinals and Brooklyn Dodgers. Watts observes that if one object or idea happens to be more popular or successful than another at just the right time and place, it will tend to become more popular or successful, generating significant long-term differences between it and its competition.[18] Rickey's quick maneuvering following MLB's decision to allow clubs to buy Minor League teams in the early 1920s enabled the Cardinals to develop, through a newly created "farm system," a cumulative advantage that lasted for two decades. Though he used an exploitative process that signed recruits for little or no money, Rickey the moral capitalist always rationalized that he was giving his players an opportunity for a better life. Rickey the TV evangelist would likely rationalize that enticing his flock to send him money would aid God's work and enable followers to achieve heavenly rewards—while lining his own pockets.

PARADOX AND POWER

Joseph S. Nye Jr., dean of the Kennedy School of Government at Harvard, has developed a geopolitical "smart power" model that helps to frame Rickey's paradoxical use of morality and capitalism. Nye first describes power as "the ability to influence the behavior of others to get the outcomes one wants."[19] Rickey's strong personality, moral certitude, and oratorical acumen enabled him to possess and use such power. The MLB reserve clause gave him license to use that power continuously.

In his model, Nye simply divides power into two contrasting subcategories, hard and soft. For Nye, "hard power" is typically military or economic in the form of threats (sticks) or inducements (carrots). Outside Nye's geopolitical context, however, hard power tends to be economic. With a capitalist focus on money and a moralist focus on right, supported by the reserve clause license, Rickey badgered players into salary submission and leveraged his organizational strength into profitable trades.

"Soft power," Nye observes, "is the ability to get what you want through attraction rather than coercion or payments. It builds on the appreciation for a country's culture, political ideals, and policies."[20] In MLB's "country," which is supported by its own culture, ideals, and policies, the articulate and manipulative Rickey generally persuaded fans, media, and other executives by giving them what they thought they wanted—winning teams, story lines, surplus ballplayers.

To Nye, "smart power" is ultimately neither hard nor soft but both, varying in proportion according to the situation. Rickey adjusted the hard economic power of a moral capitalist and the soft power of a marketing moralist in varying degrees in his ongoing activities. Ultimately, however, his continued overreliance on hard power contributed to his downfall as his moral suasions became more transparent and his relative economic clout diminished in a more competitive environment. Nye makes a similar observation about recent U.S. geopolitics in arguing for more use of soft power to achieve international stability. Although one can view Rickey as more articulate than George W. Bush (a former MLB team owner), the two men share an ultimately hazardous moral arrogance.

THE MORAL FOUNDATION AND THE CAPITALIST CALLING

Born in Little California (later called Stockdale), Ohio, on December 20, 1881, Wesley Branch Rickey came from devoutly religious stock, including one of the principal founders of the Methodist Church in America, for whom he was named.[21] His mother, Emily, to whom he was devoted until her death in 1935, served as his primary religious and educational influence, telling or reading him stories with moral lessons. His father, Frank, was a pious New Testament Christian who supplemented his farming occupation with evangelical activities and thus served as an external role model for his children. Rickey's middle name, by which he was known, had scriptural roots in Isaiah 11:1 and John 15:2.[22] Using the religious tree metaphor, his parents reinforced their son's connection with God. From his parents' examples and teachings came his unwavering confidence in a sense of right and wrong.

Those parental religious influences enabled Rickey to adopt a moral approach in his public demeanor and use it skillfully to achieve his business ends for most of his career. Befitting his given first name, Rickey subscribed to the message in "The Use of Money," a 1760 sermon by John Wesley, founder of Methodism, and incorporated into his conduct its lessons of individualism, enterprise, and charity. Biographer Murray Polner observes that James H. Finney, an Ohio Wesleyan University student who taught Rickey in elementary school, relied on that sermon and other Wesleyan teachings to build self-esteem among rural boys.[23]

Decrying the popular religious view that money was "the grand corrupter of the world, the bane of virtue, the pest of human society," Wesley asserted that "love of money is the root of evil, not money itself." The challenge, he argued, was to use money well.[24] "The Use of Money" incorporated three rules: gain all you can, save all you can, and give all you can. The first rule encouraged pursuit of success but tempered it with the admonition to avoid hurting others in the process. The second warned against superfluous spending on self and indiscriminate giving to family. The third reinforced humanity's position as a steward rather than a proprietor of possessions and urged people to share wealth according to God's Word.[25] While Rickey publicly claimed to follow those rules, he often simply behaved like an amoral capitalist by unduly hoarding or excessively spending money in his baseball activities. Wesley's sermon would have served Rickey the TV evangelist as well.

As he matured, overcoming a childhood stutter, Rickey solidified his moral foundation by earning two undergraduate degrees at Methodist-run Ohio Wesleyan and by coaching and teaching in his spare time. Rickey was a teetotaler who refused to play baseball on Sunday, even during his brief Major League career, in tribute to his religious beliefs and his parents. When he became an executive, he claimed that he did not attend Sunday games or drink alcohol, earning himself a nickname, the "nonalcoholic Rickey," a word play on a popular gin drink.[26] Lee Scott, a Dodger traveling secretary, asserted that his boss occasionally violated his rules for personal conduct as well as other moral precepts, noting, "Branch Rickey is full of crap."[27]

To whet his capitalist appetite, Rickey earned a law degree at the University of Michigan and attempted to establish a practice in Boise, Idaho, with two Ohio Wesleyan fraternity brothers. That failure prompted his further pursuit of baseball as a career. His upbringing helped establish him as a moral capitalist, with its inherent conflict between moral goodness and amoral profit, as he progressed in the business of baseball. When he bestowed on Rickey the nickname "the Mahatma," after Mohandas K. Gandhi, sportswriter Tom Meany likened the Dodger president to author John Gunther's description of the Indian leader as "an incredible combination of Jesus Christ, Tammany Hall, and your father."[28] That nickname implied recognition of Gandhi's best and worst qualities, including an overbearing pomposity and an insufferable certainty.[29] It provided amoral dimensions to earlier Rickey moral monikers, "Preacher" and the "Deacon." MLB commissioner Kenesaw Mountain Landis, a perennial Rickey adversary, implicitly acknowledged the moralist-capitalist paradox by calling him "that sanctimonious so and so."[30]

When Rickey signed Jackie Robinson and assigned him to the Dodger farm club in Montreal for the 1946 season, *Look* magazine accused him of excessive moralizing. Rickey promptly called a press conference to defend his action on social and economic rather than moral grounds: "I mentioned something [about morality] in order to remove it out of the many causes for what I did. I mentioned it because I don't want it to linger in your mind as the reason why I did it."[31]

Robert F. Burk observes that Rickey's primary motive in the signing was that of a capitalist: "Having identified blacks as the untapped source of first-rate, inexpensive playing talent, he had concluded that they could secure pennants and profits for his long-struggling franchise while also killing off the gate rivalry posed by the Negro Leagues."[32] Nevertheless, Rickey was universally lauded as a champion of civil rights. Noted sportswriter Grantland Rice effused at the time, "Next to Abraham Lincoln, the biggest benefactor of the Negro is Branch Rickey."[33] Perhaps acknowledging his primary business motive, Rickey refused to accept awards for stimulating broader integration: "It would be a shame to take credit for that."[34] Out of baseball temporarily ten years after his signing of Robinson, however, Rickey, defended his integrationist actions on moral grounds and argued that immediate integration was the only defensible position for America.

To the paradoxical Rickey, baseball was both a business and a civil religion.[35] Chalberg observes that Rickey usually had multiple motives for his actions.[36] Lowenfish notes that Rickey described his ideal baseball team as "a band of ferocious gentlemen," combining the competitive zeal to win at all costs with a moral demeanor.[37] Like Connie Mack, Rickey dressed in street clothes as a field manager and followed Mack's and John McGraw's lead in insisting that his players dress and conduct themselves well in public but play aggressively on the field.[38] Lowenfish reinforces the paradox by calling Rickey a ferocious gentleman as well.

This moral zeal reflects the influence on Rickey of philosopher William James's essay, "The Moral Equivalent of War." Noting humanity's conflicted relationship with war—spiritual nurture versus abhorrence of bloodshed— James argues that modern man can achieve the positive spiritual results through war on "Nature," through conscription directed at peacetime efforts to improve quality of life. He lauds priests and doctors as having developed a martial type of character without actual war. Citing H. G. Wells's observation that a military organization is the most peaceful of activities, James expresses appreciation for its order, discipline, tradition, service and devotion, physical fitness, unstinted exertion, and universal responsibility—"absolute and permanent human goods."[39]

To Rickey, baseball was a moral equivalent of war conducted by his ferocious gentlemen. For him, baseball was primarily an individual game, so winning was simply the result of organized individual effort. In military metaphor, baseball was a series of individually waged battles orchestrated in the team/unit context of a war game. In his impassioned speech to Cardinal players before the first game of the 1931 World Series against the Philadelphia Athletics, he exclaimed, "The greatest attribute of a winning ballplayer is a desire to win that dominates."[40] As a TV evangelist, he could implore individuals actively to seek redemption through deeds within a morally supported community/congregation.

As he preached taking the high ground in competition, Rickey rationalized his often duplicitous business maneuvers by tying them to moral principles. One aspect of his procedural makeup was frequent conflicts between what he would say and what he would do in like circumstances, but he could usually articulate a plausible resolution, thereby projecting a characteristic of TV evangelists.

Polner notes that a trademark of Rickey, the frequent trader, was "the sweeping praise and unequivocal raves about baseball players he wanted to send away."[41] Rickey also profited from those sales. In 1928, player sales added thirty-five thousand dollars to his already high sixty-five thousand dollar salary.[42] That practice reinforced a Rickey strategy of "addition by subtraction,"[43] in which he helped the club by eliminating players who could no longer contribute effectively. As Dodger president in 1948, Rickey sold six hundred thousand dollars worth of excess players, stockpiled through aggressive recruiting during World War II, and received 10 percent as a bonus, as he did for players he sold throughout his executive career in St. Louis and Brooklyn.[44]

Asserting his risk-oriented business acumen as well as his ability to judge player performance progression, he observed, "It is better to trade a player a year too early than a year too late."[45] Reinforcing that risk-taking approach was his general maxim, "Never surrender opportunity for security."[46] The personal financial incentive presumably enhanced his tendency to overrate his trade bait, but Rickey rationalized that such deals were good for his club and gave his traded players a greater opportunity to play. This behavior demonstrated moral capitalism in action and conformed to his interpretation of Wesley's money use rules.

During the celebrated signing of Robinson, Rickey cited Giovanni Papini's *The Life of Christ* in directing the Negro signee's behavior. Influenced by Papini's description of Jesus as a nonviolent person, Rickey concluded that this characteristic was critical to successful integration.[47] "I'm looking for a ball player with guts enough not to fight back," he told Robinson.[48] Rather than condoning alternative behaviors of fighting or fleeing, he implored Robinson to continue to play but turn the other cheek to the verbal and physical abuse he would likely face as the first known African American MLB player in six decades. Robinson reportedly responded, "I have two cheeks, Mr. Rickey. Is that it?"[49]

Conversely, Rickey reverted to a legalistic position in refusing to compensate the Kansas City Monarchs when he signed Robinson without their permission while Cleveland owner Bill Veeck paid the Newark Eagles for signing Larry Doby, who, like Robinson, was not specifically bound to his Negro

League team by written contract. Rickey also justified his legal position on moral grounds: the Negro Leagues were disorganized and largely funded by the illegal numbers rackets. Ironically, the Monarchs had no connection with the rackets and were regarded as the best run of the Negro teams.[50]

Rickey also paid Robinson only a thirty-five hundred dollar signing bonus and a below-market salary, reinforcing his position as "El Cheapo," a nickname bestowed by New York sportswriter Jimmy Powers.[51] During a six-month media-reported feud with Powers, Rickey demonstrated that he "was actually highly sensitive to criticism,"[52] which helped account for his generally poor media relations. Rickey and Powers eventually reached a less-than-pleasant truce as Dodger performance improved. Nowhere was Rickey's parsimonious trait more apparent than in salary negotiations. Robinson teammate Gene Hermanski complained, "Mr. Rickey had a heart of gold and he kept it," while Eddie Stanky observed, "I got a million dollars worth of advice and a small raise."[53]

While Rickey appeared unusually cheap, his farm system player signings as well as his treatment of Robinson and subsequent black players signaled a trend that MLB executives followed for decades in their financial treatment of blacks and Latinos. It conformed to what sociologist Edna Bonacich calls the "split-labor theory": "As capitalism develops, the price of labor-power tends to rise, leading capital to seek cheaper labor-power."[54] MLB player salaries were escalating in the postwar era. In Bonacich's analytical context, Rickey followed the imperialist practice of "super exploitation" of powerless classes, beginning with farm boys and then later with blacks and Latinos. This practice, she notes, is rooted in Western European colonial capitalism. Rickey and other MLB executives acted as neocolonialists focused on economic rather than territorial gain.

In so doing, Rickey and other MLB executives created a financial surplus, a portion of which could be used to pay elite players, thereby exacerbating what became a class bias with significant racial connotations. Bonacich concludes that such an approach "helps to stabilize the system by keeping the working class fragmented and disorganized."[55] This uneven and oppressive financial treatment of players eventually provoked the solidification of the players' union under Marvin Miller and the implementation of free agency. A disgruntled Ralph Kiner, reflecting on his relationship with Rickey when both were with the Pittsburgh Pirates, asserted that Rickey "did more than any other person to bring about the union," which paved the way for free agency.[56]

Rickey's farm system was an early example, followed in modified form by exploitation of the Negro Leagues and the Caribbean, of MLB's neocolonialism. Ghanaian president Kwame Nkrumah defined the term in 1961 as the last act of imperialism, continuing the colonial tradition by capitalism-based economic means rather than by territory-based political or military means.[57] Neocolonialism is also an example of Nye's hard power. Nevertheless, Rickey justified his exploitative actions on moral grounds, as other neocolonialists and colonialists often did. TV evangelists tend to do the same with their colonies/congregations.

In Rickey's baseball world, the Minor League teams were the colonies that processed the player resources for use by the Cardinals in selling their finished product to the local fans as well as building a broader fan base, aided by the development of radio, in the frontier colonies. Such soft power manipulation is what Allen Guttmann calls "cultural hegemony" rather than "cultural imperialism," because the process allows for some active selection and selective retention by the dominated clubs and fans.[58] Cultural hegemony was even stronger in the later Negro and Caribbean neocolonial activities that Rickey initiated.

Nkrumah also asserted that neocolonialism works to the detriment of the exploiter as well as of the exploited because of the victims' inherent resistant reaction to the oppressor.[59] MLB suffered modestly from significant Minor League contraction, particularly in the South, after the Robinson signing, but later incurred major losses of power through the player union bargaining, final-offer salary arbitration, and free agency that countered MLB's imperialist abuse of monopsodic power. Edward Said observes that in global neocolonialism, a hybrid culture results from the interactive conflict of power and legitimacy.[60] Current MLB culture reflects such hybridization.

Rickey's ultimate defense of his actions was an unwavering generalized reliance on what he called reason, albeit sometimes contrived or conflicted by moral assertions. On his desk, he kept a quotation from nineteenth-century Scottish theologian William Henry Drummond: "He that does not reason is a bigot; he who cannot reason is a fool; and he who dares not reason is a slave."[61] With his highly developed moral confidence and stentorian demeanor, Rickey usually overwhelmed his audience, whether or not the "reasoning" was sound. Rickey's reliance on reason, supported by his verbal skills, helped him to succeed as a moral capitalist resolving the paradox and would have well served him as a TV evangelist.

ST. LOUIS AND THE FARM SYSTEM

Rickey launched his career as an MLB executive in St. Louis, initially with the Browns, but generally rose more significantly with the Cardinals. Complicating that progression were periodic setbacks resulting from ongoing vendettas with commissioner Kenesaw Mountain Landis and Cardinal owner Sam Breadon. Those conflicts both improved and diminished Rickey's reputation in the MLB community. It publicly peaked and stumbled with the Brooklyn Dodgers, then declined conclusively with the Pittsburgh Pirates.

By the time he joined the Browns as owner Robert Lee Hedges's thirty-one-year-old protégé in 1913, Rickey had failed in his careers as a baseball player and lawyer and had tired of college coaching. Hedges soon installed Rickey as the field manager for the cellar-dwelling Browns, though Rickey would later say that he never wanted to be a field manager.[62] After an innovative Florida spring training session in 1914, the Browns rose to fifth place; a year later, the team finished sixth after acquiring future Hall of Famer George Sisler, whom Rickey had coached at the University of Michigan and had recommended signing. Harold Parrot, Rickey's traveling secretary with the Dodgers, later observed, "Nobody could ever match his talent for putting a dollar sign on a muscle."[63] In keeping with the religious motif, Rickey carried what pundits called his Bible, a notebook where he recorded player observations and conversations with coaches and scouts.[64]

Hedges, however, tired of the financial drain of the Browns and sold them to the owner of the local Federal League team when that league collapsed after the 1915 season. Although under contract to the Browns for 1916, Rickey was replaced as manager, moving to the bankrupt Cardinals as its president. Thus began a twenty-five-year mutually successful but tempestuous partnership with Breadon, another strong-willed but profane businessman, who achieved majority control of the club in 1919.

Shortly thereafter, with considerable difficulty, Rickey persuaded Breadon to get a bank loan to purchase future Hall of Famer Jesse Haines, the last nonfarm player the Cardinals would buy until the mid-1940s. Recognizing the difficulty of that purchase and the cost of bidding against other Major League teams for Minor League talent, Rickey developed the first formal working agreement with a Minor League team. The Cardinals would recruit players and supply them to that team, which would, in turn, develop the players and return them to the Cardinals. Resenting the conventional bidding war for Minor League talent, Rickey later acknowledged that cost had driven his establishment of the farm system.[65]

The working agreement concept likely started informally in the late nineteenth century with the Cincinnati Reds and its owner, John T. Brush, who also owned the Indianapolis Hoosiers in the minor Western League. Beginning in 1895, the Reds loaned players to the Hoosiers for individual development as well as to improve the Minor League team. The practice generalized and matured into "syndicate baseball," which involved cross-ownership and player control between Major and Minor League teams. In an effort to balance competition, MLB leaders banned the practice in 1914.[66]

When the 1921 National Agreement among MLB clubs overturned the 1914 decision and again permitted them to buy Minor League teams, Rickey quickly extended the working agreement concept into what he called the "production and duplication" system, a term that lacked the panache of "farm system,"[67] the eventual label. His system was a collection of owned or affiliated Minor League teams that housed and developed players signed by Cardinal scouts, often at tryout camps held in various MLB "frontier" locations in the Midwest, South, and Southwest. At the time, St. Louis was both the most western and most southern MLB city. Rickey strategically exploited its geographical position.

By 1928, the Cardinals had held dozens of those camps, owned seven Minor League teams, and controlled 203 Minor League players. By then, the Cardinals were not only debt-free but handsomely profitable, largely from selling excess players.[68] By 1940, two years before he moved to the Dodgers as a result of his continuing feud with Breadon, the Cardinals owned thirty-two Minor League clubs and had working agreements with eight others. The system involved more than 600 players and was sometimes called "Rickey's chain gang,"[69] reflecting his hard power neocolonial organization. When Rickey strategically increased recruiting while with the Dodgers during World War II, sports pundits referred to those players as "Mother Rickey's Chickens," in keeping with the established farm metaphor.[70]

The Cardinals' farm system could have grown even larger had it not been for the intervention of Commissioner Landis, who had continuously objected to the concept because he thought it unduly restricted players from achieving their individual potential. Compounding this objection was the behavioral conflict between the profane Landis and the religious Rickey, whom the skeptical commissioner described as a "hypocritical Protestant bastard wrapped in those minister's robes."[71] A harbinger of that relationship was Landis's first ruling as commissioner on February 22, 1921, which invalidated Rickey's claim on Minor League first baseman Phil Todt.[72]

With support of the National Agreement, Rickey moved aggressively to extend his farm system and further to aggravate Landis. Much later, after a thorough investigation of the Cardinal system, Landis found that St. Louis controlled two teams in the Three-I (Illinois, Indiana, Iowa) League and therefore violated MLB rules. In what became known as the Cedar Rapids Decision because that team had not registered its St. Louis relationship with

MLB, Landis punished Rickey by declaring seventy-four Cardinal system players free agents on March 23, 1938. That incident foretold the departure of Rickey from the Cardinals because the often irrational Breadon was both embarrassed at the commissioner's finding and dissatisfied that Rickey had failed to fight the decision.[73]

In 1942, Rickey's last year with the Cardinals, St. Louis Minor League teams won one or both halves of their season races in every significant minor league.[74] The parent club won the pennant, adding to its 1926, 1928, 1931, and 1934 championships, and continued to win in 1943, 1944, and 1946 with the Rickey-built machine. With recruiting and development costs lowered through economically leveraged scale, efficiency, and exploitation, the Cardinals assembled the 1934 world championship team for only forty thousand dollars, according to an estimate by the *Sporting News*.[75] Sportswriter Joe Williams observed that Rickey "was the first to demonstrate the wisdom and practicality of going to the source for material and bringing it along by degrees and in quantity."[76]

Indicative of the Cardinals' success during his tenure was the comparative performance of the rival New York Giants, led by future Hall of Famer John McGraw, during implementation of the farm system. Never wishy-washy, McGraw assailed the farm system as "the stupidest idea in baseball."[77] He continuously fought adoption of a similar process for his team. The Giants had won four straight National League pennants in 1921–24, but despite their large-market financial resources, did not win again until 1933, after McGraw retired. Rickey observed, "You have two years to stay ahead of your competition when you come up with a new idea in baseball."[78] Thanks to McGraw's and others' delays, the Cardinals' cumulative advantage lasted considerably longer.

Fundamental to the farm system's success was a consistent developmental process used in spring training and maintained by the Major and Minor League teams throughout the season. Rickey justified investment in training: "What makes or breaks you is the ability to choose from among the in-between boys who will go on to make good."[79] He believed that systematized training not only improved performance but also better enabled management to choose those most likely to succeed. With a controlled processing system, his baseball factories produced players who shared a philosophy, training, and camaraderie fostered during their progressions through the minors.

Training included newly developed techniques and equipment, many created by Rickey himself. An early simple Rickey creation was the "visible strike zone," which used strings and poles to frame the zone so that pitchers could see the area to which they were throwing. He also introduced the "sliding pit," enabling players to practice sliding techniques with less risk of injury. Later, with the Dodgers, he was responsible for development of a batting tee, like the one used by youngsters in T-ball today, to correct batters who "overstrided" during their swings. With technical support from General Electric, he produced an "electronic umpire," the precursor of the current radar gun used to measure pitch speed. Perhaps his most valued creation was an early version of the current pitching machine, which made batting practice more efficient.[80]

As usual, Rickey had a pithy expression to justify his actions: "Luck is the residue of design."[81] The culmination of his training design, which resulted in his success in Brooklyn, was Dodgertown, a converted World War II naval air base in Vero Beach, Florida, that Rickey bought and converted in 1948 (for farm teams) and 1949 (for the Dodgers as well) to a training facility. Used by Dodgers for sixty years, it became the model not only for Major and Minor League teams[82] but also for the baseball academies that MLB teams began developing two decades later in the Caribbean. Dodgertown gave Rickey, the teacher-preacher, a captive player audience that he controlled from reveille to evening lectures (which often went over players' heads).[83] A modern Rickey would be preaching to his captive TV congregation.

To enhance the evaluation process, Rickey pioneered in the field of statistical analysis that has become fundamental to baseball management and fans today. His emphasis on "base and out" (numbers of bases a batter advanced runners versus outs caused) efficiency records preordained the current sabermetrics.[84] While with the Dodgers, he became the first MLB executive to hire a statistician—Allan Roth in 1947.[85]

Rickey based his neocolonial process on an "out of quantity comes quality" principle, a wholesale signing strategy using speed as a proxy for athletic ability in an untrained talent pool.[86] Using a sixty-yard dash as an initial screen, Rickey considered legs, arm, and power the three basic criteria for prospect evaluation. He provided a simple weighting: two points for legs and one each for arm and power.[87] He further contended that "a man is born with power," which therefore could not be created or even added through training.[88] While modern consensus disagrees, Rickey's conclusion arguably could have spurred the use of performance-enhancing drugs.

In signing a prospect, the Cardinal scout would often use a "desk contract," so called because the scout kept the contract in his desk and usually did not give the recruit a copy. By giving little or no compensation to the signee, the scout incurred minimal financial risk while taking the recruit off the market and assigning him to a Minor League team for further evaluation and development if warranted. Rickey developed his system so extensively with the Cardinals and the Dodgers—and profitably sold the considerable player surplus—that, by 1949, about three out of eight MLB roster players had been Rickey-system products.[89]

Rickey's exploitation of player recruits mirrored that of global neocolonialists and current multinationals: using economic leverage to extract human resources at low costs. Like those internationalists, Rickey morally rationalized his treatment of player recruits by strongly asserting that he had improved their standard of living. "I offered millhands, plowboys, high school kids a better way of life."[90] Again, he used his rhetoric and reason to resolve his moral capitalist conflict. Like other neocolonial ventures, these exploitative efforts engendered resistance among those affected.

BROOKLYN AND THE NEGRO LEAGUES

In the final year of his St. Louis contract, which Breadon refused to renew, Rickey achieved symmetry in his World Series record. In 1926, in their first-ever postseason appearance, the Cardinals upset the powerful New York Yankees, and in 1942, Rickey's last team again humbled a favored Yankee team that had won six of the seven previous AL pennants. That Cardinal team also provided the nucleus for pennant winners in three of the next four years.

The following year, Rickey moved to Brooklyn, where he replaced Larry McPhail, a protégé that Rickey had hired, fired, and helped land the Dodger presidency. McPhail had joined the army, and Rickey's son, Branch Jr. (nicknamed Twig), used his influence as Dodger farm director to help his father fill the vacancy. Twig, whom his father had lured from law school into baseball with the Cardinals before consenting to let him join McPhail ("the most grievous decision I ever faced")[91] in 1939, had begun growing the Dodger farm system.

With a wartime-depressed contract comparable to that with St. Louis— a forty thousand dollar salary plus the usual 10 percent bonus on player sales—Rickey shifted the farm system buildup into high gear. Unlike other MLB executives, who cut back on scouting and farm affiliations during the war, Rickey aggressively recruited players and increased the Dodgers' Minor League relationships to prepare for what he correctly thought would be a postwar boom in baseball popularity. Within three years, he and his "constant companion,"[92] Twig, had amassed twenty-seven Minor League teams, more than even the Cardinals, who had scaled back during the war.[93]

Combined with purging a Dodger team that was "dangerously vet-eranized,"[94] Rickey again set out on a risky course that, while incurring press and fan wrath, would again develop the cumulative advantage and elevate the Dodgers to an elite status that would last through their departure for Los Angeles after the 1957 season, seven years after Walter O'Malley forced Rickey out. Aided by his contrarian wartime recruiting strategy, Rickey repeated his farm system performance.

According to Rickey, however, building the farm system and removing aged veterans from the roster was not his first order of business as Dodger president: "The very first thing I did when I came into Brooklyn in late 1942 was to investigate the approval of ownership for a Negro player."[95] He sensed that changing wartime sentiment meant that the time for MLB inte-gration was approaching, but he had previously concluded that integration could not begin in the "stony soil" of St. Louis, a southern segregation-biased environment.[96]

The public Rickey was quick to provide a rationale for his actions and to proffer good copy. As Rickey was moving to implement his plan, he pub-licly claimed that he had been influenced by Gunnar Myrdal's *An American Dilemma* (1944). Rickey, the archconservative moral capitalist, apparently accepted the argument of the communist-leaning Myrdal that America had denied blacks the inherent rights of equality and democracy.[97] Again, Rickey demonstrated his ability to resolve his morality-capitalism paradox and pur-sue overtly incompatible objectives.

The moralist Rickey also claimed to have been motivated by an incident that occurred in 1903, when he coached the Ohio Wesleyan baseball team that included black first baseman Charles Thomas. In South Bend, Indiana, to play Notre Dame, Rickey learned from the hotel manager that Thomas could not have a room. Rickey, who had earlier overcome the University of Kentucky's refusal to play against Thomas, argued with the manager but was permitted only to house Thomas in his room. A dejected Thomas responded by rubbing his skin, trying to wipe off the black color. Rickey claimed to have had a "recurrent vision" of Thomas's reaction.[98]

No known Negro had played in MLB since the 1880s. Ironically, profes-sional baseball developed in the last half of the nineteenth century largely through the efforts of ethnic minorities who overcame Anglo-American prejudices. As the minorities gained power in the "melting pot," they assured that the pot would remain white. Since skin color became the differentiating criterion, some light-skinned Latinos and perhaps Negroes played, but the implicit ban continued. Rickey recruited some light-skinned Latinos for the Cardinals in the 1920s and for the Dodgers during World War II.

Relegated to their own teams and leagues, African American (and African Caribbean) players developed a strong market following not only through their popular barnstorming tours but also through the formalized Negro Leagues in the 1930s and 1940s. Players of that era more than held their own against MLB players in off-season exhibition games. Many MLB and Minor League team owners maintained financial leverage over Negro League teams, however, by charging a substantial share of the gate as rent for use of stadiums.

As commissioner, the bigoted Landis deflected any outside criticisms and attempts to integrate MLB by maintaining that no rule barred black players. In stating publicly that any club was free to sign a player of color, Landis relied on the owners who shared his prejudice. The advent of World War II and Landis's death in 1944 facilitated Rickey's integration strategy, which was grounded in a neocolonial desire to secure cheap talent.

The reason-oriented Rickey devised and carefully implemented a six-step plan that resulted in the signing of Jackie Robinson to a Minor League contract on August 28, 1945, and his MLB debut on April 15, 1947:

1. Gain backing of Dodger directors and stockholders.
2. Pick a Negro who would be the right man on the field.
3. Pick a Negro who would be the right man off the field.
4. Get a good reaction from the press and the public.
5. Secure backing from Negro leadership.
6. Facilitate acceptance by teammates.[99]

In his initial January 1943 meeting with George McLaughlin of Brooklyn Trust, which controlled the Dodgers, Rickey gained permission to expand scouting and to include Negroes in that recruiting market.[100] He later claimed that the team spent twenty-five thousand dollars to find the right Negro.[101] By forming a Brooklyn Brown Dodgers team in the new black United States League in 1945, he gave himself public license to research black players as well as to criticize the established Negro American and Negro National Leagues.[102] He included Caribbean players in the search but rejected them because of language and cultural complications, though he later revived that approach with the Pirates. Robinson was suggested by Wendell Smith, a black *Pittsburgh Courier* sportswriter who had long advocated MLB integration.[103]

Aided by mounting public pressure for postwar integration, Rickey moved aggressively ahead of his MLB competition. Within six months of the Robinson signing, Rickey stole three other players—Roy Campanella, Don Newcombe, and John Wright—from the Negro Leagues without compensating the players' previous teams because, Rickey alleged, no written contracts existed. In 1947, he paid the Memphis Blue Sox fifteen thousand dollars for the contract of his fifth signee, Don Bankhead, who on August 26 became the first black pitcher known to appear in the Majors in the twentieth century.[104] The prejudiced MLB owners continued to refrain from such pursuits, reinforced by a 15–1 (only Rickey dissenting) vote against integration in 1946. Once again, Rickey gained a head start and developed cumulative advantage.[105]

Two months before Robinson's Brooklyn debut, Rickey met with local black leaders as part of his reasoned integration plan and pleaded for calm rather than overtly celebratory support for the player, an approach summarized in the slogan, "Don't Spoil Jackie's Chances."[106] Rickey moved spring training from Florida to Cuba, with exhibition games in Panama, to avoid most of the traditional southern resistance. He relied on Leo Durocher, the Dodger manager, to quell a spring training teammate backlash against Robinson, thereby completing implementation of the plan. Although the volatile Durocher sporadically caused problems for Rickey during their long relationship, the manager adroitly maneuvered the players into line. Ironically, just before the season started, Landis's replacement as commissioner, Happy Chandler, suspended Durocher for a year for gambling, but the Dodgers remained unified in their support of Robinson.[107]

Although boxing had been integrated for most of the century and African Americans had already entered professional football and basketball, Rickey's signing of Robinson has been generally hailed not only as a major cultural breakthrough in baseball and other sports but also as a strong impetus for racial integration throughout the United States. It preceded *Brown v. Board of Education* by nine years and the 1964 Civil Rights Act by twenty. In their analysis, Anthony R. Pratranis and Marlene E. Turner call Rickey's initiative "the first, largely successful affirmative action program in human history."[108] Yet more than a dozen years passed before all MLB teams integrated. Today, while baseball is the most racially diverse of sports, that diversity is more attributable to the added participation of Latinos and Asians than to blacks, whose percentage on MLB rosters peaked at 27 percent in 1975 but dropped to 8 percent in 2008, about half their percentage in the U.S. population as a whole.[109]

For Rickey, the Robinson signing, still celebrated extensively by MLB, served as the capstone of his Dodger career. While he built a juggernaut that dominated the National League for the next decade, he lost an escalating internal battle with O'Malley for control of the team. O'Malley, who called Rickey a "psalm-singing faker," focused on the bottom line, not on the field of play.[110] Rickey contributed to his own demise through such actions as extravagant spending on the Dodgertown project, a financially imprudent takeover of the Brooklyn Football Dodgers, reactionary resistance to television, and moral objections to beer advertising.[111]

Following the death of partner John L. Smith, O'Malley secured his 25 percent of Dodger stock and squeezed Rickey out of the operation, thereby prompting Rickey to sell his stock, albeit with some clever maneuvering, and leave. Friend John Galbreath, head of the Pittsburgh Pirates, found a potential buyer who drove up the price O'Malley paid for the stock, then gave Rickey a five-year contract to run the Pirates at one hundred thousand dollars a year, with a guaranteed fifty thousand dollars per year renewal for the next five years.[112] With a private plane and a pilot and a license to bring along a staff, including Twig, Branch emerged well from his Dodger demise, particularly given that his seventieth birthday was approaching.

PITTSBURGH AND THE CARIBBEAN

Rickey's time with the Pirates, however, suggests that he should have retired after his Dodger reign. He inherited a team that had finished in the cellar—in part, ironically, because of trades that he had made in Brooklyn in which Pittsburgh surrendered Billy Cox and Preacher Roe in exchange for ineffective also-rans. Rickey embarked on his usual strategy of paring the roster of veterans and building the farm system, including the creation of a fall instructional league in 1951 to speed the development process. In 1953, after Rickey overcame owner, press, and fan resistance to trade Kiner, Rickey quipped to the popular future Hall of Famer, "We finished last with you and we can finish last without you."[113] And it was true: after a seventh-place finish in 1951, Pittsburgh remained at the bottom of the standings for the remainder of Rickey's five-year tenure as president.

Declining health played a role in Rickey's performance. Having been diagnosed in 1945 with Ménière's disease, an inner-ear imbalance that left him subject to attacks of dizziness, he was hospitalized on five separate occasions from 1950 to 1952 but generally disregarded physician advice to slow down. Polner asserts, however, that Rickey had a more fundamental problem that his son and staff failed to acknowledge or seek to correct: "The truth was that the old wizardry had become obsolete." Rickey's player-assessment skills also seemed to deteriorate, as indicated by his trading and signing results. His once innovative recruiting and development practices had become common-place. He had to compete with richer teams in the open market, attempting to do so by investing two hundred thousand dollars of his own money in the club. And he had run out of new ideas.[114]

He ramped up an old idea that he had not yet exploited with the Cardinals and Dodgers: Caribbean recruiting. Clark Griffith, the longtime owner of the Washington Senators, had initially begun recruiting Cubans in 1911 with Cin-cinnati, resumed in the 1930s, and accelerated the process during World War II to fill a roster depleted by wartime military service. Those recruits were light-skinned and avoided MLB's color ban. When Rickey began his integra-tion strategy, he considered Cuban players but stopped because of language/culture issues and because he could not find an ideal candidate.

In an effort to gain a competitive edge for the Pirates, he extended his minority recruiting strategy to the Caribbean (not just Cuba) and Mexico. Rickey recalled that the Dodgers had an outstanding Puerto Rican pros-pect, Roberto Clemente, and drafted him for the Pirates in November 1954. Impressed by the future Hall of Famer, Rickey reportedly told his longtime associate, Howard Haak, "You're going to Cuba and the Dominican this sum-mer. If there's any more of those creatures down there, I want 'em."[115] Using Rickey's "out of quantity comes quality" approach, a stopwatch, and desk con-tracts, Haak traveled extensively throughout the Caribbean for the next fifty years, and he was responsible for "truly open[ing] up Latin America to the big leagues."[116] That experience became another example of MLB hard power neocolonialism stimulated by Rickey but more successfully implemented by other teams, which were more sensitive to the cultural nuances of recruiting and developing foreign players. In short, other teams used more soft power.

Galbreath replaced Rickey with Joe L. Brown as general manager after the 1955 season and made him "senior consultant" for the remaining five years, though he was effectively out of a job. Branch Rickey thus did not directly benefit from the Caribbean strategy, but the Pirates' farm director, Twig Rickey, learned Spanish and helped to assure that the Caribbean pursuit would continue. Although Brown proved a very successful general manager, Rickey's upgraded farm system and Caribbean recruiting contributed to Pittsburgh's 1960 World Series championship and its stronger position over the next decade. Pittsburgh's Caribbean recruiting efforts were less effective than Rickey's Cardinal farm system or Dodger integration strategies because other teams quickly followed suit. Today, about 40 percent of the players on MLB and Minor League rosters are Latinos.[117]

EPILOGUE

During his last five years as a consultant with the Pirates, Rickey assumed the role of elder statesman, though separately as moralist and as capitalist. The moral Rickey supported the formation of the Fellowship of Christian Athletes; lectured on values, civil rights, race relations, and anticommunism; and served on a government commission on employment policy. The capitalist Rickey helped form the American Baseball Cap Company to produce helmets for players. After arguing unsuccessfully for MLB expansion, he helped to develop plans for a third Major League (the Continental League) and accepted its presidency.

Although the Continental League never reached fruition, it did provoke MLB to add four new teams and continue geographic expansion, thereby acquiescing to Rickey's (and others') pleas. In so doing, MLB preserved its monopolistic hold on players through the reserve clause. Ironically, Rickey, whose career had been significantly enhanced by the clause, argued against it in his third league pursuit, in which he proposed that teams pool their television revenue. This idea would have significantly reduced the revenue gap between MLB's large- and small-market teams.[118]

Branch Rickey concluded his career as an MLB executive by coming full circle, returning to the Cardinals as a consultant in 1962, the year Robinson entered the Hall of Fame and a year after Twig Rickey died of complications related to diabetes. The senior Rickey's final tenure in St. Louis lasted only two years, enabled by an uneasy truce with GM Bing Devine that allowed Rickey to offer opinions, though they usually were not heeded. Owner Gussie Busch replaced Devine with Bob Howsam during the 1964 season and had Howsam fire Rickey,[119] who then retired and wrote a self-serving and conspicuously outdated memoir, *The American Diamond: A Documentary of the Game of Baseball*, his only published work. Sportswriter Roger Kahn called the volume "trivial and pretentious."[120]

Although widely acclaimed in baseball and civil rights circles as a capitalist and a moralist, Rickey's final years were more talk than action. While his farm system, racial integration, and Caribbean initiatives contributed greatly to MLB's overall success, they also enhanced the hard power neocolonialism that MLB practiced until the player union coalesced and countered it. Often-irrational battles with Landis, Breadon, and O'Malley also tempered

Rickey's achievements. As reflected in the Pirates' performance, Rickey's post-Dodger years had more failures than successes. They reflected the late-career tendency of successful individuals to rely on past approaches, bolstered by sycophantic associates, rather than continuing to do what had made them successful: think outside the box and build productively on others' ideas. His success had also stemmed from his creative resolution of his moralist-capitalist paradox. In his final years, he divided rather than combined morality and capitalism by operating in the separate arenas of charity and business and no longer achieved the synergy from that dynamic tension.

Rickey encountered criticism throughout his career, but his dominating personality overcame it sufficiently to enable him to perform capably, a process that might not have been possible in today's stronger media market. His paradoxical moral capitalist approach, weakened by environmental changes, punctuated by the criticism, and reinforced by later research, now positions the once exalted Rickey as a flawed success who should not be as universally revered as he currently is.

Following Rickey's death on December 9, 1965, eleven days before his eighty-fourth birthday and two years before his election to the Hall of Fame, Arthur Daley, an esteemed sportswriter for the *New York Times*, claimed that Rickey's influence on the game was second only to that of Alexander Cartwright, who drew up baseball's first formal rules in 1845. Daley eulogized Rickey as "a genius, a man who could have attained the top rank in any business or profession. Baseball is fortunate that this extraordinary person chose to channel his talents in this direction. So dominating a figure was Rickey that he altered the course of its history."[121] But although Rickey made positive contributions to baseball, his dominance delayed changes needed to stabilize the game in the more competitive environment that emerged after his tenure.

NOTES

1. Robert W. Peterson, *Only the Ball Was White* (Englewood Cliffs, NJ: Prentice-Hall, 1970), 183.

2. Lee Lowenfish, *Branch Rickey: Baseball's Ferocious Gentleman* (Lincoln: University of Nebraska Press, 2007), 547.

3. Ibid., 119.

4. Harvey Frommer, *Rickey and Robinson: The Men Who Broke the Color Barrier* (New York: Macmillan, 1982), 199.

5. John C. Chalberg, *Rickey and Robinson: The Preacher, the Player, and America's Game* (Wheeling, IL: Harlan Davidson, 2000), 71.

6. Scott Simon, *Jackie Robinson and the Integration of Baseball* (Hoboken, NJ: Wiley, 2002), 81.

7. John Monteleone, ed., *Branch Rickey's Little Blue Book: Wit and Strategy from Baseball's Last Wise Man* (Wilmington, DE: Sport Media, 2004), 148.

8. Lowenfish, *Branch Rickey*, 325.

9. Frommer, *Rickey and Robinson*, 169.

10. Simon, *Jackie Robinson*, 70.

11. Chalberg, *Rickey and Robinson*, 6.

12. Ibid., 14.

13. Ibid., 15.

14. Laurence J. Peter and Raymond Hull, *The Peter Principle* (New York: Morrow, 1969).

15. Chalberg, *Rickey and Robinson*, 217.

16. Neil J. Sullivan, *The Dodgers Move West* (New York: Oxford University Press, 1987), 24.

17. Branch Rickey, with Robert Riger, *The American Diamond: A Documentary of the Game of Baseball* (New York: Simon and Schuster, 1965), 204.

18. Duncan J. Watts, "Is Justin Timberlake a Product of Cumulative Advantage?" *New York Times*, April 15, 2007, http://www.nytimes.com/2007/04/15/magazine/15wwlnidealab.t.html (April 15, 2007).

19. Joseph S. Nye Jr., *Soft Power: The Means to Succeed in World Politics* (New York: Public Affairs, 2004), 2.

20. Ibid., x.

21. Murray Polner, *Branch Rickey: A Biography*, rev. ed. (Jefferson, NC: McFarland, 2007), 14.

22. Lowenfish, *Branch Rickey*, 15–16. Isaiah 11:1 reads, "And there shall come forth out of the stem of Jesse, and a Branch shall grow out of the roots." John 15:2 reads, "Every branch in Me that beareth not fruit He taketh away; and every branch that bears fruit He prunes, that it may bear more fruit."

23. Polner, *Branch Rickey*, rev. ed., 18–20.

24. John Wesley, "The Use of Money," sermon 50, *The Works of John Wesley*, ed. Albert C. Outler (Nashville, TN: Abingdon, 1985), 2:267–68.

25. Ibid., 268–79.

26. Lowenfish, *Branch Rickey*, 201.

27. Frommer, *Rickey and Robinson*, 93.

28. Lowenfish, *Branch Rickey*, 325.

29. Simon, *Jackie Robinson*, 83.

30. J. G. Taylor Spink, *Judge Landis and Twenty-five Years of Baseball* (New York: Crowell, 1947), 232.

31. Monteleone, *Branch Rickey's Little Blue Book*, 111–12.

32. Robert F. Burk, *Much More Than a Game: Players, Owners, and American Baseball since 1921* (Chapel Hill: University of North Carolina Press, 2001), 96.

33. Jonathan Fraser Light, *The Cultural Encyclopedia of Baseball*, 2nd ed. (Jefferson, NC: McFarland, 2005), 786.

34. Polner, *Branch Rickey*, rev. ed., 4.

35. Ibid., 10.

36. Chalberg, *Rickey and Robinson*, 3.

37. Lowenfish, *Branch Rickey*, 8.

38. Ibid., 125.

39. William James, "The Moral Equivalent of War," in *Memories and Studies* (New York: Longmans, Green, 1924), 288.

40. Lowenfish, *Branch Rickey*, 214.

41. Polner, *Branch Rickey*, rev. ed., 93.

42. Lowenfish, *Branch Rickey*, 181.

43. Monteleone, *Branch Rickey's Little Blue Book*, 12.

44. Polner, *Branch Rickey*, rev. ed., 191. In the original edition, Polner identified the year as 1947, not 1948. See Murray Polner, *Branch Rickey: A Biography* (New York: Atheneum, 1982), 212.

45. Lowenfish, *Branch Rickey*, 141.

46. Monteleone, *Branch Rickey's Little Blue Book*, 122.

47. Polner, *Branch Rickey*, rev. ed., 136.

48. Lowenfish, *Branch Rickey*, 375.

49. Ibid., 376.

50. Neil Lanctot, *Negro League Baseball: The Rise and Ruin of a Black Institution* (Philadelphia: University of Pennsylvania Press, 2004), 14–15.

51. Arthur Mann, *Branch Rickey: American in Action* (Boston: Houghton Mifflin, 1957), 239–40. This was one example of Rickey's negative relationships with sportswriters even though he was good copy.

52. Chalberg, *Rickey and Robinson*, 63.

53. Monteleone, *Branch Rickey's Little Blue Book*, 156, 152.

54. Edna Bonacich, "Class Approaches to Ethnicity and Race," in *Majority and Minority: The Dynamics of Race and Ethnicity in American Life*, ed. Norman R. Yetman (Boston: Allyn and Bacon, 1991), 64.

55. Ibid., 65.

56. Monteleone, *Branch Rickey's Little Blue Book*, 157.

57. Robert J. Young, *Postcolonialism: An Historical Introduction* (Malden, MA: Blackwell, 2001), 47.

58. Allen Guttmann, *Games and Empires: Modern Sports and Cultural Imperialism* (New York: Columbia University Press, 1994), 172–78.

59. Young, *Postcolonialism*, 47.

60. Edward Said, *Culture and Imperialism* (New York: Vintage, 1994), 291.

61. Lowenfish, *Branch Rickey*, 216.

62. Mann, *Branch Rickey*, 135.

63. Light, *Cultural Encyclopedia*, 311.

64. Polner, *Branch Rickey*, rev. ed., 82.

65. Monteleone, *Branch Rickey's Little Blue Book*, 87.

66. Light, *Cultural Encyclopedia*, 312.

67. Lowenfish, *Branch Rickey*, 260.

68. Polner, *Branch Rickey*, rev. ed., 77–82.

69. Robert Obojski, *Bush League: A History of Minor League Baseball* (New York: Macmillan, 1975), 42.

70. Mann, *Branch Rickey*, 226.

71. David Petruska, *Judge and Jury: The Life and Times of Judge Kenesaw Mountain Landis* (South Bend, IN: Diamond, 1998), 3; Lowenfish, *Branch Rickey*, 280.

72. Lowenfish, *Branch Rickey*, 130.

73. Ibid., 280–83.

74. Light, *Cultural Encyclopedia*, 312.

75. Lowenfish, *Branch Rickey*, 260.

76. Light, *Cultural Encyclopedia*, 311.

77. Ibid., 311.

78. Lowenfish, *Branch Rickey*, 354.

79. Monteleone, *Branch Rickey's Little Blue Book*, 81.

80. Ibid., 94–101.

81. Ibid., 29.

82. Lowenfish, *Branch Rickey*, 444.

83. Ibid., 464–67.

84. Ibid., 74.

85. Monteleone, *Little Blue Book*, 162.

86. Light, *Cultural Encyclopedia*, 312.

87. Monteleone, *Branch Rickey's Little Blue Book*, 83–84.

88. Ibid., 37.

89. Jules Tygiel, *Baseball's Great Experiment: Jackie Robinson and His Legacy*, expanded ed. (New York: Oxford University Press, 1997), 50.

90. Jules Tygiel, *Past Time: Baseball as History* (New York: Oxford University Press, 2000), 95.

91. Lowenfish, *Branch Rickey*, 298.

92. Rickey, *American Diamond*, 166.

93. Polner, *Branch Rickey*, rev. ed., 114.

94. Lowenfish, *Branch Rickey*, 324.

95. Polner, *Branch Rickey*, rev. ed., 133.

96. Simon, *Jackie Robinson*, 82.

97. Lowenfish, *Branch Rickey*, 351.

98. Chalberg, *Rickey and Robinson*, 24–25.

99. Mann, *Branch Rickey*, 214–15.

100. Polner, *Branch Rickey*, rev. ed., 134.

101. Lowenfish, *Branch Rickey*, 380.

102. Ibid., 365–68.

103. Lanctot, *Negro League Baseball*, 279.

104. Lowenfish, *Branch Rickey*, 433.

105. Lanctot, *Negro League Baseball*, 274–77.

106. Polner, *Branch Rickey*, rev. ed., 174–75.

107. Ibid., 175–77.

108. Anthony R. Pratranis and Marlene E. Turner, "Nine Principles of Successful Affirmative Action: Branch Rickey, Jackie Robinson, and the Integration of Baseball," in *The Cooperstown Symposium on Baseball and American Culture 1997*, ed. Alvin Hall (Jefferson, NC: McFarland, 2000), 152.

109. Tom Verducci, "Blackout: The African American Baseball Player Is Vanishing: Does He Have a Future?" *Sports Illustrated*, July 7, 2003, 58.

110. Chalberg, *Rickey and Robinson*, 150.

111. Polner, *Branch Rickey*, rev. ed., 194–97.

112. Lowenfish, *Branch Rickey*, 488–500.

113. Ibid., 519.

114. Polner, *Branch Rickey*, rev. ed., 207; Chalberg, *Rickey and Robinson*, 170–71.

115. Light, *Cultural Encyclopedia*, 525.

116. Peter C. Bjarkman, *Baseball with a Latin Beat: A History of the Latin American Game* (Jefferson, NC: McFarland, 1994), 124.

117. Burk, *Much More Than a Game*, 300.

118. Lowenfish, *Branch Rickey*, 547, 564, 573–74.

119. Ibid., 582–92.

120. Rickey with Riger, *American Diamond*; Chalberg, *Rickey and Robinson*, 216.

121. Monteleone, *Little Blue Book*, 163.

INEXTRICABLY LINKED
Joe Louis and Max Schmeling Revisited
—C. OREN RENICK AND JOEL NATHAN ROSEN

INTRODUCTION

Substantive reflection concerning the lives of Joe Louis and Max Schmeling calls for a bit of wordplay, with the first word being *respect*. Joe Louis and Max Schmeling were used, but they were not respected. They were feted but not respected. They were national and racial symbols of achievement during their collective primes in interwar America and Germany, respectively, but true respect did not follow. The tragedy as well as the triumph of their lives can be seen in the absence of respect for what they accomplished and how they conducted themselves at a time when their worlds were being turned upside down through no fault of their own. And yet, genuine respect, while it came belatedly (and at least partially) to Schmeling, came too late for Joe Louis.

Another relevant word for them is *racism*, which deeply affected both Schmeling and Louis but in decidedly different ways. Schmeling had the personal integrity to eschew active engagement with Hitler's Nazi Party while doing battle with the American public for personal and professional legitimacy. Louis had the strength of character not to reject outright the same American state that at once reviled him while it championed him (at least partially) when doing so best suited the country's aims. What allied these two towering figures, men of decidedly different worlds in what often appears to be a most peculiar pairing, however, is a dual narrative born of happenstance in an age of extraordinary political and social upheaval when each would be cast as the embodiment of the culture that he was thought to represent. How indicative each man was of his culture, and how each particular world used him, ultimately links these legendary figures well beyond the boxing ring and the celebrity they engendered, and it is in this regard that their stories—individually and together—provide a cautionary tale regarding the nature of celebrity and the price of aspiration.

JOE LOUIS BARROW

Born on May 13, 1914, in the cotton country near Lafayette, Alabama, Joe Louis Barrow, the man who would become simply Joe Louis, was an African

American of mixed ancestry.[1] The area around Lafayette, located in east-central Alabama in Chambers County by Buckaloo Mountain, was about as rural as the South could offer. La Grange, Georgia, and Auburn, Alabama, were the only cities of consequence within a radius of twenty miles.[2]

Louis's father, Munroe Barrow, was a hardworking sharecropper who was committed to a state mental hospital by the time young Joe was two years old and died when he was four. Joe's mother, Lillie, took in washing to support the family and then married Patrick Brooks when Louis was seven, merging two families of eight children each.[3]

In the summer of 1926, the family became part of the Great Migration, moving north to Detroit, which offered opportunity in the ever-increasing automobile plants. The large Brooks family squeezed into an eight-room house on Macomb Street in the city's Black Bottom district, and Joe attended first Duffield School and then a vocational school, Bronson, until he was seventeen.[4] The boy learned cabinetmaking, took violin lessons, and eventually took up boxing at the suggestion of a classmate.[5]

The transition from cabinetmaking and violin lessons to boxing is likely related to before- and after-school jobs that helped Joe develop his trademark musculature. He worked at the Eastern Market and for a local ice company, where carrying fifty-pound blocks of ice did wonders for his physical development.[6] And, as the story goes, the sixteen-year-old boy took the money his mother gave him for his music lessons to pay for a locker at the Brewster Recreation Center, a popular hangout and training site for amateur boxers, a sport that was all the rage in the 1930s.[7]

As Louis's training led to amateur fights, there is the matter of his rather sudden name change, which often brings out a bevy of subtle disagreements. The easy answer is that he changed his name so that his mother would not find out where her violin money was really going; this explanation is akin to the stories of Jewish fighters forced to go underground by cultural conventions, but it seems less likely in Louis's case.[8] The more plausible explanation is that when he initially filled out a form for an early amateur fight, he did not have enough room on the line for all three of his names. Thus, he fought as Joe Louis and continued to do so from that point forward.[9] Either story works, but the latter rings more authentic while serving as indicator to Louis's approach to life, which seems to trend toward the most direct line possible.

As his amateur boxing career began, Louis worked briefly at the Ford Motor Company but quit as he gained further boxing success. Veterans Alter Ellis and Holman Williams trained Lewis at the Brewster and advised him to get further training help from George Slayton, who managed the respected

Detroit Athletic Club. His amateur career subsequently took off: he reached the Golden Gloves finals in Boston in 1933 before losing a decision to Max Marek, a renowned Notre Dame football player. Fighting as a light heavy-weight, Louis won the AAU national championship in St. Louis before turn-ing pro three months later. As an amateur, he showed tremendous promise, winning fifty of fifty-four bouts, including forty-three by knockout. Perhaps even more telling, all of his four losses were by decision.[10]

Louis's amateur success won him the notice of John Roxborough, a Detroit racketeer.[11] Roxborough, himself a former basketball player, had got-ten wealthy through a number of ventures, legal and otherwise, including his many ties to the illegal gambling circuits and his more legitimate interests supported by a brother who was a state senator and a nephew who worked for the U.S. State Department.[12] Roxborough and Julian Black, a speakeasy owner who also had a hand in the numbers, convinced Louis to turn pro.[13] Not surprisingly, they also led his management team, which was committed to ensuring that Louis's career would not be derailed by the same elements that had done in the first truly great black boxer, Jack Johnson.

Louis was relocated to Chicago, where he was trained by former fighter Jack "Chappy" Blackburn, but this move constituted only the opening salvo by his well-oiled management team. To further shape Louis's image with white America and as a major part of Louis's training regimen, Roxborough reiterated several Johnson-inspired commandments, which included never be photographed with a white woman; never gloat over a fallen opponent; never participate in a fixed fight; fight clean; and live clean. These mandates were put in place to help Louis shake free of most of the expected backlash that had followed every other previous black fighter and especially Johnson.[14] Photographed more than any other black man of his era, Johnson was often seen in the company of white women, the ultimate taboo in Jim Crow Amer-ica. Although these images further underscored Johnson's scandalous repu-tation in the mainstream press—and, by extension, the reputation of black men in general—members of the African American community saw him as a heroic figure in the manner of "bad men" such as Stack-o-Lee and Jesse James, whose exploits struck fear into the white mainstream.[15] Indeed, Johnson was both admired and demonized, but his presence also helped to demythologize salient elements of the prevailing anti-African bias—what W. E. B. Du Bois dubbed "unforgivable blackness."[16] Johnson's athletic prowess dispelled the myth of black cowardice both outside and inside the ring.[17] Moreover, John-son loved the attention—positive and negative—and reveled in his celebrity status; rather than shying away from the spotlight, he sought it out and laid claim to it, wearing his color and his tastes glaringly on his custom-tailored sleeves until he ran headlong into a state that simply could no longer tolerate his bravado.[18]

In July 1934, Louis, barely twenty, officially turned pro, knocking out Jack Kracken in the first round of a scheduled six-round fight in Chicago. Louis earned fifty dollars.[19] By the end of 1934, Louis had won twelve professional fights, including ten by knockout.[20] Already known as the Brown Bomber of Detroit, he was said to have "risen like a star across the fistic heavens,"[21] a romanticized if accurate epithet indicative of the sports reporting of the day.

Louis won his first twenty-seven fights, twenty-three by knockout, between July 1934 and January 1936.[22] Among his more impressive wins was his fourth-round knockout of the enigmatic Max Baer on Louis's wedding day, and a stirring technical knockout of Paulino Uzcudun, a Basque heavyweight who had never before been knocked down or out. Many observers, however, point to Louis's 1935 technical knockout of Italian strongman Primo Carnera as the moment Louis's career began to show the more significant sociopolitical undercurrents that later emerged more emphatically in his matchups with Schmeling. In the eyes of many Americans, Carnera represented the coming conflict with fascism, making a victory over the Italian fighter a victory over Benito Mussolini's emergent regime. Black intellectuals in particular saw in Louis an emblem of racial pride in the face of colonial oppression at home and abroad. Indeed, the popularity of Joe Louis–themed music began with his victory over Carnera.[23]

MAXIMILLIAN ADOLPH OTTO SIEGFRIED SCHMELING

Schmeling enjoyed a more worldly upbringing than did Joe Louis. Schmeling was born on September 28, 1905, in rural northwestern Germany, likely near Brandenburg, where locals virtually ignored boxing. Schmeling's father had watched boxing matches during his travels as a ship's navigator, which, in turn, afforded his son entry into the sport that captivated him from an early age.

By the time he was a teenager, Max Schmeling had seen ample film footage of boxing—typically American boxers, including the heavyweight championship fight between the storied Jack Dempsey and Georges Carpentier, who had been regarded as Europe's best answer to American boxing supremacy. Enthralled by the film and the romance of boxing, Schmeling left for western Germany, where boxing was popular.[24] That Schmeling strongly resembled Dempsey cannot be overlooked; this resemblance, coupled with film's impact on the young man, may well have helped propel Schmeling forward in his quest to become a professional fighter with much broader international aspirations.[25]

Finding success in amateur tournaments, Schmeling gained the notice of Arthur Bülow, who edited Germany's *Boxsport* magazine. Bülow became a significant financial supporter, manager, and mentor to Schmeling during the formative years of his boxing career, at least until Schmeling decided to enter the American boxing scene.

Schmeling turned professional in 1924 and moved to Berlin, where his relationship with Bülow flourished. Also in Berlin, Schmeling soon joined forces with trainer Max Machon, who continued to work with the fighter throughout his career. Within three years, Schmeling had become the European light heavyweight champion, the first German to claim the title. By 1927, his powerful right hand brought him his first title and an introduction to Berlin's elite, who watched as he continued to rise through the European heavyweight ranks with an eye toward his American debut.[26]

Although he was riding on an extraordinarily fast track, Schmeling appears to have handled his nascent celebrity well, shedding vestiges of his rural upbringing while donning a more refined air. He soon exhausted the last of his European competitive options and headed to the United States to compete against a more challenging array of talent on a much grander stage.

Coming to America compelled Schmeling to reinvent his corner. He replaced Bülow with Joe Jacobs, a Jew who aggressively promoted Schmeling and got him the fights he needed to reach the top of the boxing world. Replacing Bülow with Jacobs ultimately paid off for Schmeling, though the decision haunted him from a personal and even a nationalist perspective, given how the Nazi forces eventually turned on him while they reconsidered his role within the nascent German state.[27]

With undefeated champion Gene Tunney retiring in 1928, the heavyweight class was wide open, and Schmeling became part of an elimination tournament to crown a new champion. Referred to rather exotically as the Black Uhlan (a member of the Prussian light cavalry) of the Rhine, Schmeling defeated two leading heavyweights, Johnny Risko and Uzcudun, and in June 1930 faced the heavily favored Jack Sharkey for the title at Yankee Stadium in what was Schmeling's first truly significant match.[28]

Often overlooked in an age of memorable heavyweight bouts, the fight against Sharkey turned out to be Schmeling's notice to the American boxing world in spite of its regrettable ending. Sharkey started fast while Schmeling, a classic counterpuncher, paced himself and fought defensively. Sensing that Sharkey was starting to tire, however, Schmeling began to take the fight to him in the fourth round, but a vicious low blow by Sharkey, the victim of a similar blow in a title shot against Dempsey in 1927, ultimately disqualified the American fighter. In that instant, the virtually unknown Schmeling emerged as the new heavyweight champion of the world, the first European to hold the title. And though his title was certainly tainted by Sharkey's disqualification, as Schmeling regretted, it remained both a legitimate win and a most auspicious debut for the German.[29]

Schmeling successfully defended his title in 1931 with a fifteenth-round technical knockout of Young Stribling, a victory that further validated his championship in the minds of critics though not necessarily in his own mind. He married a blond and beautiful movie star, Anny Ondra, a Czech national, creating a celebrity couple, on par with Americans Marilyn Monroe and Joe DiMaggio and Dick "Night Train" Lane and Dinah Washington.[30]

In 1932, Schmeling squared off against Sharkey in a fifteen-round rematch. The early rounds again were slow, but Schmeling dominated the last five rounds. Sharkey was declared the winner on points, reclaiming his crown in a controversial decision, the first of the many controversies that plagued Schmeling's prime as the relationship between the United States and Germany soured. The referee, a close friend of Sharkey, scored the fight in his favor. Former champ Tunney and the American press were unanimous in condemning the verdict, but nothing changed.[31] Jacobs protested, coining a phrase that has since become famous if not ubiquitous in American culture: "We wuz robbed."[32]

Later that year, Schmeling reaffirmed his preeminence as a heavyweight by pummeling Mickey Welker in an eight-round knockout, but in June 1933, Schmeling suffered a technical knockout at the hands of future champion Max Baer.[33] The loss tarnished Schmeling in American boxing circles, though the decline in his esteem resulted more from national sentiment than from any deficiencies in his talents.[34]

Schmeling's next significant fight took place in 1936 and propelled him into history. He entered the ring as a sacrificial lamb, a 10–1 underdog against the heretofore invincible Joe Louis, but the course that put these two men together ultimately transcended the boxing ring in particular and sport in general.[35]

A CLASH OF CELEBRITY FIGHTERS

A number of similarities existed between Louis's and Schmeling's technique and approach in the ring. Both men were right-handed and fought from rather conventional postures. Both stood right around six feet, one inch tall and weighed just under two hundred pounds, though Schmeling was some eight years Louis's senior.[36]

Schmeling was considered a very good defensive fighter who had a stiff right-hand punch that was effective if for no other reason than because he was not part of the American boxing culture. He remained something of a mystery to many American fighters and their corners. He was also considered one of the more studious fighters of his generation and had a knack for figuring out his opponent's weaknesses through personal observation and film study.[37] Indeed, as his 1936 fight with Louis approached, Schmeling thought he had noticed a flaw in the rising American challenger's approach: after watching Louis beat Uzcudun, Schmeling noted, "I saw something."[38] He later watched film and confirmed that Louis had a tendency to drop his right hand after throwing his jab, offering Schmeling an opening, though no one else had been able to exploit it.[39]

Louis was more of an intuitive fighter—a stalker, relentless, hunting down his opponents rather than merely studying them.[40] He had a powerful left jab to go along with a devastating right hand, and he could unleash his two-fisted attack at short range while demonstrating a killer instinct against a wounded adversary.

That Louis was stronger than most fighters and hence struck fear into his opponents should not discount his studious qualities, however. Prior to his first Schmeling fight, Louis had little need to look for an opponent's flaws: he could simply punch his way out of any jam.[41] His cornermen referred to Louis, with his enormous reach and disproportionately large hands, as a "manufactured killer" rather than the more omnipresent "natural born killer," with its glaring racial connotations emblematic of the age.[42]

Both Schmeling and Louis were regarded as rising if not established stars in their home countries, though the term had not yet entered the lexicon. However, the two men handled the mantle of celebrity differently, as much as a consequence of the political climate of the era as of their differing personalities. While Schmeling's public acclaim developed over time, affording him the opportunity to gain some reasonable footing for the many responsibilities fame brought, Louis's celebrity came swiftly—even unexpectedly, given the political circumstances at home and abroad—while often proving to be somewhat problematic for a younger man caught in between the vagaries of Jim Crow and the rise of Nazi Germany.

Louis's most glaring weakness seems to have been his inability to balance his open, trusting, and affable nature with decisions that were not in his best interest. For most of his adult life, he seemed consistently to lose outside the ring in an often futile search for mutually favorable relationships. Women especially sought him out, and these relationships typically ended badly for him, as indicated by his four rather tempestuous marriages as well as his countless dalliances with both white and black luminaries, among them Lena Horne, Sonja Henie, and Lana Turner.[43]

Hanging out with famous black entertainers (including Bill "Bojangles" Robinson, Duke Ellington, and Cab Calloway) and other black athletes, including stars from baseball's Negro Leagues, also gave credence to Louis's rising celebrity.[44] But his place in the limelight also seemed to distract him from boxing, and he evidenced a decided lack of focus in preparing for the fight with Schmeling. Indeed, Louis's New Jersey camp was beset with crowds of admirers and friends, and he seemed to grow complacent, disregarding the advice of his handlers and succumbing to a range of distractions that included regular rounds of golf. He certainly enjoyed the adulation, but the disruptions were evident during the fight.[45]

THE FIRST BOUT AND ITS AFTERMATH

Louis and Schmeling's first meeting was underscored by a flurry of prefight complications. Attendance for the fight, held at spacious Yankee Stadium, was half what promoters had expected. The widespread assumption that Louis would win easily seemed to dampen enthusiasm. Furthermore, Jews and their supporters of all ethnicities threatened to boycott to bring attention to Hitler's Germany. In addition, a rainstorm caused a one-day delay, and forty dollars for a ringside seat was beyond the reach of many fans still reeling from the Great Depression.[46]

Nevertheless, Schmeling, obviously the hungrier fighter, was undeterred. From the outset, he took the fight directly to Louis, pelting him with a total of ninety-one right-hand leads. Beginning in the fourth round, when Schmeling knocked Louis down, the German remained handily in control, shocking some observers and dismaying others.[47]

Scheduled to go fifteen rounds, the fight lasted only until 2:29 of the twelfth round.[48] Louis was indeed dropping his right hand after throwing his jab, and Schmeling effectively countered, finishing the affair with a straight right that sent Louis to the canvas, knocked out for his first professional loss. Schmeling's victory shocked the sporting public and further increased the anti-German political climate.[49]

The black community was distraught over the loss. Louis had become a beacon to those marginalized by segregation. Rioting broke out in Harlem, where a local man who had bet on Schmeling was hospitalized with stab wounds and a possible skull fracture.[50] Moreover, Middle America gradually realized that the fight had political and cultural subtexts beyond the more conspicuous issue of race.

In Germany, however, the victorious Schmeling reached the pinnacle of his prewar fame. With the rise of Adolf Hitler and the Nazi Party, Schmeling had become a useful pawn in the powerful Nazi propaganda machine.[51] Schmeling had also become a favorite of Hitler, who saw the boxer doing for the Nazi cause what track and field athletes had been unable to do at the 1936 Olympics. Indeed, before the fight, Hitler warned Schmeling, "When you go to the United States, you're going to obviously be interviewed by people who are thinking that very bad things are going on in Germany at this moment. And I hope you'll be able to tell them that the situation is not as bleak as they think it is."[52]

Nazi propaganda minister Joseph Goebbels subsequently held lengthy conversations with Max and Anny Schmeling, who were invited to listen to a rebroadcast of the fight at Goebbels's home. Yet while these points are interesting on their face, if only for their prurience alone, they only tell a fraction of the Schmeling story, which is far more complicated. Schmeling's embrace by the Nazis is typically assumed to be evidence that he was an active member of the party.[53] The Nazis unquestionably saw Schmeling's victory as a national triumph and a vindication of their political views. Goebbels recorded in his diary, "Stayed up all night. . . . At 3 a.m. the fight begins. In round 12 Schmeling knocks out the Negro. Wonderful. . . . The white man defeats the black man, and the white man was a German."[54] Schmeling was the darling of Nazi Germany, returning home onboard the new airship *Hindenburg*. However, the rest of Schmeling's life took a radically different course.

Schmeling remained focused on his boxing career, figuring that his victory over Louis would result in a title shot against "Cinderella Man" James Braddock.[55] But the rising tide of anti-Nazi sentiment in New York made a Schmeling-Braddock fight unacceptable to an American public. Following much closed-door negotiation and even an unsuccessful legal battle, Louis, not Schmeling, was granted the match with Braddock.[56] In a most unanticipated turn of events, national resentment toward Nazi Germany had actually trumped centuries of racial inequity at home, giving a black man a title shot over a white man who by every conceivable standard of the sport had clearly won the right to fight for the championship. The situation hinted at a turning in the racial tide.

A SIGN OF THE TIMES

The extent to which the decision to give Louis the title shot over Schmeling marks a new direction in American life is often underplayed. Paradoxically, Americans used Germany's racial climate as a means both to circumvent competitive standards and to elevate, if only temporarily, a black man to a more loftier place. Louis's handlers were quite aware of and stoked this phenomenon, carefully managing his relationship with a thawing white public.

Joe Louis in every conceivable public way was no Jack Johnson. Whereas Johnson was Stack-o-Lee, Louis was John Henry. But Louis had nevertheless remained in Johnson's shadow. The opportunity to fight Braddock finally and formally brought Louis into the sunshine, making the specter of a black champion palatable if not acceptable to the American sporting public. The political strange bedfellows that had wrought this change were most unexpected and in hindsight appear fraught with numerous questions. Cast in the role of Hitler's nemesis, Louis stood heads above the Aryan interloper, and this image came to dominate this American narrative for decades to come.

Schmeling and his corner were understandably furious over the snub but could do little to counteract it. Louis subsequently knocked out Sharkey, who had previously defeated Schmeling, but that triumph certainly did not negate Schmeling's victory over Louis.[57]

Despite the New York State Athletic Commission's ruling that Schmeling had won the right to fight for the title, Louis was the champ's next opponent. Both Madison Square Garden and Schmeling were denied injunctions to prevent the bout, held in Chicago, and Louis wrested the title from Braddock in the eighth round, paving the way for a Louis-Schmeling rematch. It would be the fight of the century.[58]

THE REMATCH

On June 22, 1938, one year to the day after the Braddock fight, Louis and Schmeling squared off again at Yankee Stadium. The prelude to this fight had been unlike any other in the history of American sport. The country seemed awestruck by the idea of a black man fighting as the American hope against the representative of Nazi Germany's master race. Louis, who mere days earlier would likely have been regarded as at best an interloper and at least an untenable image of Americana, now had come to represent the Horatio Alger ideal of the poor boy rising from abject beginnings, and he would be attempting to redeem himself and the country against Schmeling, who was perceived as practically an enemy agent.[59]

Amid such high hopes, Louis retreated to his boxing camp in Upstate New York, this time training in earnest. But signs continued to indicate that the fight was more than sport. President Franklin D. Roosevelt summoned Louis to the White House, telling him, "Joe, we need muscles like yours to beat Germany."[60] Louis later wrote, "I knew I had to get Schmeling good. I had my own personal reasons and the whole damned country was depending on me."[61] Thus, when Schmeling came to New York accompanied by a Nazi Party publicist who stated that a black man could not beat Schmeling, the rumor mill ran amok while anti-Nazi protesters picketed Schmeling's hotel.[62]

A crowd of 70,043 packed Yankee Stadium on the evening of the fight, with millions more listening on the radio to announcers calling the action in English, German, Spanish, and Portuguese. Driven by a potent mix of rage and revenge and with the nation's gaze firmly on him, Louis went after Schmeling in a way rarely before seen in a championship bout. From the outset, Louis attacked furiously with two powerful left hooks. Louis trapped Schmeling against the ropes, blasting him with a devastating body blow that Schmeling's corner later claimed was an illegal kidney punch. (In hindsight, at least, all of Louis's punches appeared to be legal.) By the time referee Arthur Donovan, who had also refereed the first bout, stopped the fight 2:04 into the first round, Schmeling had gone down three times; he unleashed only two punches before his corner threw in the towel.[63] Schmeling suffered an array of injuries, including cracked ribs and extensive damage to his neck, and was hospitalized for nearly two months. However, the political ramifications dominated the postfight discussions both at the time and subsequently.[64]

REEXAMINING THE SCHMELING-AS-NAZI CLAIM

To most, the moral of this story will always be that Schmeling was a Nazi and, as such, got what he deserved. But although Schmeling was German, that was apparently his sole transgression: no substantive evidence supports the claim that he was anything more than a pragmatic piece in the propaganda war with the Allies. His devastating and quite public thrashing in the rematch made for a very public retreat from the growing notion that Schmeling could represent the Aryan ideal of the *Übermensch* well beyond the abstract, as is demonstrated by the Nazis' dismissal of the news that Schmeling had reclaimed the German heavyweight title a year later.[65] Moreover, following the loss to Louis, Schmeling seems to have dropped out of sight after nearly two years of high-profile acclaim from Nazi high command, which had previously seemed to fawn over him and even his "alien" (and, hence, suspect) wife.

Scholars have noted that the Nazis explained away Jesse Owens's triumphant showing in the 1936 Olympics by harnessing traditional racist claims regarding his African heritage and his physical attributes accordingly, but there is little to suggest that the state made the effort to explain away Schmeling's defeat at the hands of an American Negro as anything more than Schmeling's personal failing. Once a propaganda coup for the Nazi state, Schmeling had become a liability if not an outright embarrassment, and as such, he was swiftly removed from the public eye and drafted into the German Luftwaffe, where he served in the elite Fallschirmjager.[66]

The Nazis had been suspicious of Schmeling based on his conduct before he rose to fame, though the reasons for these suspicions did not come to public light until after his death in 2005. Schmeling's associations with Jews and other racial minorities show him to be much less the Nazi than has typically been believed. In addition to hiring Jacobs, an action that brought him a great deal of heat from his German handlers, he hid two Jewish teenagers during Kristallnacht, a November 1938 anti-Jewish pogrom in Germany and Austria, an action that exposed him to great personal risk. Schmeling made no mention of this incident in his autobiography, but it is part of a pattern of behavior that negates the accusations that he was a Nazi.[67] Schmeling consistently refused to join the Nazi Party, continued to associate with German Jews, and ignored orders to fire Jacobs, confounding Hitler and Goebbels. Schmeling's breaches of etiquette, combined with his humiliating defeat at the hands of Louis, an obvious racial inferior, caused Hitler personally to order Schmeling sent on dangerous—even life-threatening —missions.[68] Finally, although the British briefly interned Schmeling, primarily as a consequence of his erstwhile celebrity, they cleared him of any Nazi crimes and released him.[69] In 1975, Schmeling reflected, "I'm almost happy I lost the fight. Just imagine if I would have come back to Germany with a victory. I had nothing to do with the Nazis, but they would have given me a medal. After the war, I might have been considered a war criminal."[70]

A POST-REMATCH LOUIS

Louis's boxing career was also halted by the war, but where Schmeling would be left for dead, Louis became a most valuable tool in the American war effort. Louis successfully defended his title ten times between December 1940 and March 1942, when he entered the U.S. Army as a private, earning twenty-one dollars a month. Although he won the bouts convincingly, his opponents were known, rather unfairly, as the Bums of the Month. His toughest fight during this run was against Billy Conn, the sort of agile and dangerously deceptive fighter who typically challenged larger men. The first time he faced Louis, Conn led convincingly after twelve rounds but disregarded his corner's instructions to fight cautiously in the thirteenth round. Conn unwisely gave Louis an opening and was knocked out with two seconds left in the round.[71]

Louis continued to abide by his handlers' strictures, remaining cool, courteous, and quietly dignified.[72] Some years later, when Conn asked Louis to lend him the heavyweight crown for a year so that he could make some money, Louis smiled and replied, "I lent it to you for twelve rounds and you didn't know what to do with it."[73]

Louis spent nearly four years in U.S. Army Special Services during World War II. He donated the purses from his final two prewar fights (against Buddy Baer and Abe Simon) to the Army and Naval Relief Funds, netting the funds more than $111,000 and causing former New York mayor Jimmy Walker to exclaim that Louis had "laid a rose on Abraham Lincoln's grave."[74] Louis also staged exhibition fights and participated in other morale-boosting and fundraising events.

Louis reached the rank of sergeant before being discharged and received the Legion of Merit decoration. He also provided leadership for other African Americans in the segregated armed forces, including getting Jackie Robinson and other blacks admitted to officer candidate school. Louis's statements also became slogans for songs and posters that inspired the wartime public, a remarkable achievement for a black man in Jim Crow America.[75] But he was also heading for a quite unenviable fall, exacerbated in part by his charitable contributions and his growing reputation for civic good works.

TRIBULATION

With the war over, Louis returned to championship fighting in 1946, again defeating Conn (telling reporters beforehand, "He can run, but he can't hide"),[76] but his skills had obviously diminished. Louis fought three more times, including two tough fights with Jersey Joe Walcott, and then retired, relinquishing the heavyweight title in 1949. He had amassed a remarkable record of fifty-six wins (forty-eight by knockout), and only a single loss—to Schmeling.[77]

The remaining years of his life were not easy, however. He developed huge financial problems as a consequence of a combination of poor financial counsel and problems with the Internal Revenue Service, which likely began with the fight purses donated to the military relief funds. Just prior to World War II, Louis's accountant reported that the fighter owed eighty-one thousand dollars in back taxes, to which he was said to have casually responded, "Pay it."[78] However, a larger pattern of debt emerged, haunting the champion throughout his later life and ushering in lapses into substance abuse and mental illness.[79]

By 1950, with a divorce settlement looming, Louis had no way to earn his way out of his mounting debt and decided to return to the ring. The decision tarnished his once-stellar reputation. He lost a unanimous decision to Ezzard Charles in a title fight in 1950, won eight consecutive fights from lesser opponents, and was knocked out by Rocky Marciano, who considered Louis his boxing hero, in the eighth round of a ten-round bout on October 26, 1951. He retired permanently from boxing the following December, though he did try his hand at professional golf for a short while.[80] Although Louis won nearly five million dollars from his fights, poor financial advice, ex-wives, and the federal government forced him to become a sideshow attraction to stay afloat financially, a fate similar to that of Jesse Owens. Thus, in addition to quiz and variety shows, where his appearances were openly touted as prompted by his need to pay the government, he suffered through the humiliation of pro wrestling.[81] In 1956, he was introduced on the television show "High Finance" as "the ex-heavyweight champion whose dream is to pay off a debt to the IRS."[82] IRS representatives often claimed Louis's pay even before it reached his hands.

In hindsight, Louis's naïveté contributed to his financial plight. He was a genuinely generous person who gave money to the poor, to friends from his past, and to hangers-on. He bought uniforms and a bus for his softball team in Detroit, the Brown Bombers, and when his stepfather was hurt in an automobile accident and received $250 in welfare checks, Louis's sense of civic obligation caused him to repay the City of Detroit.[83]

In the 1960s, Louis's final wife, Martha Jefferson, the first black woman to practice law in California, ultimately persuaded the IRS to reduce its claims against the fighter, but the damage had already been done. While he was now free of his enormous tax burden, Louis had a reputation as a high-profile panhandler that eclipsed his renown as a fighter. He worked as a greeter at Caesar's Palace in Las Vegas, a position typically reserved for also-rans and empty celebrity shirts.[84]

A BRIEF WAR BETWEEN AFRICAN AMERICAN ICONS

Louis was generous to other boxers, a trait that hastened his public fall both financially and in other ways. He worked with Sonny Liston, the reputedly mob-connected heavyweight champion whose two defeats at the hands of Muhammad Ali helped launch Ali to prominence. But Louis refused to call

Ali by his Muslim name, leading to a rift between the two men, probably a result more of differing worldviews than of genuine dislike. In fact, Ali claimed that Louis had been a boyhood idol, but even those feelings could not check the growing ill will. On one occasion, Louis proclaimed, "Clay has a million dollars' worth of confidence and a dime's worth of courage. . . . I would have whipped him. . . . [T]here would be tears burning his eyes." Stung by the criticism from a man he had long admired, Ali replied, "Slow-moving, shuffling Joe Louis beat me? . . . Joe Louis had a thing called the bum-of-the-month club. . . . If I fought them today . . . they'd boo them out of the ring. . . . How would Joe Louis have knocked me out?"[85]

The "Louisville Lip" routine that Ali adopted early on in his professional career probably exasperated Louis, who throughout his career maintained the quiet, unassuming air advised by his handlers. In an era of pan-Africanism and Black Power, Louis's demeanor could easily be construed as debasing and kowtowing to the white hegemony. The Louis-Ali feud may also have been fueled by their very different responses to a nation at war—Louis the World War II patriot versus the vociferously anti–Vietnam War Ali. In any case, it was now Ali's world. With so much of Louis's fall public knowledge and a younger generation for whom Ali's importance continued to grow, Louis was a relic with suspect politics and priorities in an increasingly tumultuous age.[86]

A QUIETLY ENGAGING FRIENDSHIP

In postwar Germany, the Schmelings were just getting by as farmers. Max Schmeling tried fighting a few times, but his days as a professional boxer were over. He briefly worked as a boxing referee before a former New York boxing commissioner who had become a Coca-Cola executive remembered Schmeling as a non-Nazi German hero and offered him the Coke franchise in Germany. The opportunity enabled Schmeling to become a hugely successful businessman and philanthropist.[87]

During a 1954 trip to the United States, where he visited Jacobs's grave, Schmeling drove to Chicago, and renewed his acquaintance with Louis. The two men became friends, visiting together at least twelve more times before Louis's death in 1981. Schmeling helped pay off some of Louis's debt and may even have paid a portion of Louis's funeral expenses.[88]

Although he was despised as a symbol of Nazi hubris, Schmeling ultimately became revered for his humility, discipline, and character. That this quiet albeit tainted figure would devote substantial time and energy to help the man who had nearly beaten him to death demonstrates the extent to which the general public never knew Schmeling beyond supposition and propaganda.

RECONCILIATION AS DENOUEMENT

How do we reconcile the lives of Joe Louis and Max Schmeling? They do not fit into a neat collection of biographies of celebrity lives. They were significant players on the world stage during one of its most tumultuous times. They were part of what is now popularly referred to as the Greatest Generation. They faced an intractable issue, racism, in its most virulent form. They were its pawns, they rode its wave, but they were not its victims. It did not defeat either of them in the ring or in life or rob them of their humanity. What should we remember, and what should we learn from them?

In many ways, Schmeling overcame his obstacles and was largely rehabilitated in the eyes of his critics. He dreamed of becoming the world heavyweight champion and accomplished that goal. He married a beautiful woman and had a long and happy marriage, and even with the taint of his association with the Nazis and the privations in Germany after the war, he succeeded professionally and personally.

Schmeling repaid his good fortune in obtaining the Coca-Cola franchise by becoming a noted philanthropist. He was a respected, model citizen at the end of his life and was a credit to boxing, to his family, to Germany, and to humankind as a whole. Always studious, introspective, and reflective, he considered his life full and without want. It was not a boast. Rather, it was a simple, direct, and humble statement. In effect, he was satisfied and at peace with his life.

Louis's life, however, is much more complicated. In many ways, he, too, overcame his barriers, but he, too, was a fractured hero. Whereas Schmeling embodies the notion of one who overcomes, Louis's life was one always marked by the struggle to overcome. Whereas Schmeling's life ended with an exclamation point, Louis's life ended with a question mark.

To have emerged from abject poverty and the often faceless tide that marked the Great Migration to become the heavyweight champion of the world at twenty-three is a remarkable tale, but it tells only a portion of what Louis has come to represent. By every accounting, he is the first truly transcendent racial figure in American popular lore, but he is also one of its most tragic. Gifted enough as an athlete to be placed alongside the likes of Jim Thorpe and Paul Robeson (in addition to his stint as a professional golfer, Louis was an accomplished horseman who rode competitively), he and they were victimized by a racial climate that was likely to hold a black man down once he had fallen.

Louis's legacy has, however, received a bit of posthumous rehabilitation. Many public figures attended his Las Vegas funeral. Sammy Davis Jr. sang "For the Winners," and an emotional Frank Sinatra described Louis as a "champion of champions who introduced dignity to the sports square."[89] The Reverend Jesse Louis Jackson, named for Jesse Owens and Joe Louis, delivered the eulogy. Referring both to the Great Depression and racism, Jackson called Louis "a giant who saved us in time of trouble." In fights with Schmeling, "what was at stake was the confidence of a nation with a battered ego and in search of resurrection, and the esteem of a race of people." Jackson went on to reject any talk of "poor Joe." Louis's life had meant much to all Americans as he advanced the cause of black people. He was a generous champion, Jackson closed, noting, "He was in the slum, but the slum was not in him. Ghetto boy to man . . . Alabama sharecropper to champion."[90]

Louis's life, however, is much more than symbolism; rather, it is the story of American racial patterns. His handlers followed a time-honored strategy to help him move across the unforgiving if not outright vitriolic color line. It is easy to look back and criticize the role Louis consequently played, though he never truly played the Uncle Tom figure or openly recoiled before white supremacy. He was the deadpan tough guy with unmatched pugilistic skill who challenged the status quo for himself and others caught between American racial policy and politesse. He broke barriers and established a precedent that allowed black athletes to compete in virtually all American sports. As their champion in the ring, he encouraged others to confront the limits of segregation and discrimination, though today he is often compared less to Ali and more to the rehabilitated image of Johnson, a comparison that places Louis's legacy on rather uneven footing.[91]

Together, Louis and Schmeling transcended the ring. Their struggles were surrounded by cavernous political and social divides in an era of extraordinary racial, national, and international tension. Their fights were international spectacles, spotlighting the substance of both American and German nationalism and bringing it to center stage in American political and cultural life; their second fight has been described as a metaphor for America's World War II effort.

Eventually, the Louis-Schmeling relationship was transformed to put away past hatred and bitterness, just as German-American relations were restored to amity. But the racial transformation of the United States continues. As Georgetown professor Eric Michael Dyson has noted, when the dust had settled from the fights and the war, "Joe Louis died broke, and Max Schmeling died rich."[92] And to some observers, that enormous picture remains far from being reframed.

NOTES

1. Larry Schwartz, "'Brown Bomber' Was a Hero to All," ESPN.com, April 7, 2006, http://sports.espn.go.com/espn/classic/bio/news/story?page=Louis_Joe (March 1, 2010).

2. *State Farm Road Atlas* (Skokie, IL: Rand McNally, 1997), 14–15.

3. Jenny Nolan, "The Brown Bomber—The Man behind the Fist," *Detroit News*, January 24, 1996, http://apps.detnews.com/apps/history/index.php?id=52 (March 1, 2010). It is likely that Munroe Barrow was still alive when Lillie married Brooks, but in the Jim Crow South, official records regarding black citizens often were not kept, and those that are extant can be of questionable accuracy.

4. Ibid.

5. Schwartz, "'Brown Bomber.'"

6. Nolan, "Brown Bomber."

7. Ibid.

8. Schwartz, "'Brown Bomber.'"

9. Nolan, "Brown Bomber."

10. Ibid.

11. Schwartz, "'Brown Bomber.'"

12. Nolan, "Brown Bomber."

13. Schwartz, "'Brown Bomber.'"

14. Jack Johnson, *My Life and Battles*, ed. and trans. Christopher Rivers (Westport, CT: Praeger, 2007), vi.

15. See William Barlow, *Looking Up at Down: The Emergence of Blues Culture* (Philadelphia: Temple University Press, 1989).

16. The most recent references to Du Bois's claim can be found in *Unforgivable Blackness: The Rise and Fall of Jack Johnson* (DVD) (PBS Paramount, 2005); Geoffrey C. Ward, *Unforgivable Blackness: The Rise and Fall of Jack Johnson* (New York: Vintage, 2006).

17. Johnson, *My Life*.

18. "Pardon Is Urged for Boxer in Racially Tinged 1913 Case," *San Antonio Express News*, September 27, 2008, 2A.

19. David Margolick, *Beyond Glory* (New York: Knopf, 2005), 66.

20. Patrick Myler, *Ring of Hate* (New York: Arcade, 2005), 228.

21. Nolan, "Brown Bomber."

22. Myler, *Ring of Hate*, 228–29.

23. Mike Rugel, "Joe Louis Is the Man," *Uncensored History of the Blues*, June 12, 2006, http://www.purplebeech.com/blues/2006/06/show-18-joe-louis-is-man.html (February 7, 2009).

24. "The Fight," *American Experience*, 2004,http://www.pbs.org/wgbh/amex/fight/ (March 1, 2010).

25. Margolick, *Beyond Glory*, 16.

26. "The Fight."

27. Ibid.

28. "Max Schmeling," International Boxing Hall of Fame Web site, n.d., http://www.ibhof.com/pages/about/inductees/modern/schmeling.html (March 1, 2010).

29. Ibid.

30. Ibid.

31. Ibid.

32. Margolick, *Beyond Glory*, 15.

33. Baer was the child of a Jewish father and a Catholic mother and identified himself as a Jew. Still, that he defeated a German national at a time of growing international antagonism held enormous sway for the match, à la Louis versus Carnera.

34. Myler, *Ring of Hate*, 33, 49, 52.

35. Louis Bülow, "Max Schmeling: The Story of a Hero," 2007, http://www.auschwitz.dk/schmeling.htm (March 14, 2008).

36. "Louis Destroys Schmeling in Rematch," International Boxing Hall of Fame Web site, n.d., http://www.ibhof.com/ibhfhv5.htm (March 14, 2008).

37. "Max Schmeling," Cyber Boxing Zone, September 13, 2006, http://cyberboxingzone.com/boxing/max-ger.htm (March 14, 2008).

38. "The Fight."

39. Ibid.

40. "HBO Begins Work on Joe Louis Boxing Bio," December 13, 2007, http://www.saddoboxing.com/6542-joe-louis-boxing-bio.html (March 21, 2008).

41. Schwartz, "'Brown Bomber.'"

42. Joyce Carol Oates, "'Beyond Glory': The Good Fight," *New York Times*, October 2, 2005, http://www.nytimes.com/2005/10/02/books/review/02oates.html (January 30, 2009).

43. Schwartz, "'Brown Bomber.'"

44. Nolan, "Brown Bomber."

45. Ibid.

46. Ibid.

47. Ibid.

48. Myler, *Ring of Hate*, 80–84.

49. Lewis A. Erenberg, *The Greatest Fight of Our Generation* (New York: Oxford University Press, 2006), 90.

50. Nolan, "Brown Bomber."

51. Bülow, "Max Schmeling."

52. "The Fight."

53. Bülow, "Max Schmeling."

54. "The Fight."

55. Ibid.

56. Ibid.

57. Margolick, *Beyond Glory*, 200–201.

58. "Max Schmeling," Cyber Boxing Zone.

59. Nolan, "Brown Bomber."

60. Ibid.

61. Ibid.

62. Ibid.

63. Ibid.

64. Myler, *Ring of Hate*, 135–36.

65. Erenberg, *Greatest Fight*, 170.

66. Ibid., 170–72.

67. "The Fight." The older of the two boys, Henri Levin, later became a Las Vegas hotel owner and verified that Schmeling had saved the lives of the two Levin boys.

68. Bülow, "Max Schmeling."

69. "The Fight."

70. Bülow, "Max Schmeling."

71. Schwartz, "'Brown Bomber.'"

72. Bert Randolph Sugar, *Bert Sugar on Boxing* (Guilford, CT: Lyons, 2003), 106.

73. Ibid., 123.

74. Margolick, *Beyond Glory*, 333–34.

75. Nolan, "Brown Bomber."

76. Schwartz, "'Brown Bomber.'"

77. Myler, *Ring of Hate*, 228–30.

78. Sugar, *Boxing*, 124.

79. Barry Horn, "Hot Air: HBO's Joe Louis Documentary Is a Knockout," *Dallas News*, February 22, 2008,http://www.dallasnews.com/sharedcontent/dws/spt/columnists/bhorn/stories/DN-2chorn-column_23spo.State.Edition1.2fca1b6.html (March 1, 2010). See also Nolan, "Brown Bomber."

80. Nolan, "Brown Bomber." See also Horn, "Hot Air."

81. Schwartz, "'Brown Bomber.'"

82. Horn, "Hot Air."

83. Nolan, "Brown Bomber."

84. Ibid.

85. Myler, *Ring of Hate*, 216–17.

86. Michael Ezra offers a brilliant accounting of this transformation in *Muhammad Ali: The Making of an Icon* (Philadelphia: Temple University Press, 2009), 93–134.

87. "The Fight."

88. See Erenberg, *Greatest Fight*, 231; Margolick, *Beyond Glory*, 349.

89. Erenberg, *Greatest Fight*, 223.

90. Ibid., 223–24.

91. Ibid., 225–26.

92. Ibid.

MORTGAGING MICHAEL JORDAN'S REPUTATION

—JEFFREY LANE

I don't want to be the greatest minority golfer ever; I want to be the greatest golfer ever.
I want to be the Michael Jordan of golf.
—TIGER WOODS

A lion on the court, he was a lamb when his community needed him.
—WILLIAM RHODEN ON MICHAEL JORDAN

INTRODUCTION

Sociologist Pierre Bourdieu understands the consecration of artists as the "magical division" created to distinguish the "sacred" from the "profane."[1] The legitimacy of this magic, however, depends on popular, professional, and critical recognition.[2] Michael Jordan's consecration in basketball culture undoubtedly can be legitimatized popularly (e.g., his team sold out every home game from November 17, 1987, through April 14, 2003), professionally (five MVP awards, six Finals MVPs, and so forth), and critically (the most appearances on the cover of *Sports Illustrated*, ESPN's greatest North American athlete of the twentieth century, among others). But more interestingly, professional basketball is understood through the consecrated figure of Michael Jordan. In a random sample of blog posts and reader comments on the popular basketball blog hoopsaddict.com from January 2006 through April 2008, 54 percent of the 120 references to Jordan are analogical.[3] In other words, Jordan is mentioned as a way of conceptualizing another player (e.g., "the next Jordan," "heir to the Jordan throne"), or a Jordan moment is invoked to understand a second moment in NBA history. Jordan's legacy has become a cognitive map of recent basketball culture, with events organized around the Jordan dynasty, the post-Jordan era, the Jordanless Eastern Conference, the NBA pre-Michael, MJ's Chicago Bulls, and so on. When Kobe Bryant struggled in a title-deciding Game 6 blowout loss to the Boston Celtics in the 2008 NBA Finals, Boston fans chanted, "You're . . . not . . . Jordan!" Bryant's inability to lead the Los Angeles Lakers to the championship was, according to sportswriters, further confirmation that "Bryant is no Jordan"[4] and "a valuable lesson" for "all the people who have been busy comparing" the two.[5]

Consequently, I experienced some dissonance when I was asked to write on Jordan as an illustration of the black athlete whose reputation has declined over time. This is not to say that Jordan has never received negative publicity, either as a player or since retiring: heavy gambling, allegations of adultery (Jordan and his wife divorced in December 2006), perceived maltreatment of teammates and team management, and knocks against Jordan's ability as a team executive—but never as a businessman—have all been part of the Jordan dialogue.[6] But as Henry Louis Gates Jr. points out, "An indiscretion is truly damaging only if it's discordant with your perceived character."[7] So Jordan's gambling, infidelity, bullying, and overaggressiveness become affirmations of his alpha male status and extensions of the same fiercely competitive nature that made him a superstar on the court. An often-repeated quote by Jordan's father, James Jordan, exemplifies this sort of streamlining: "My son doesn't have a gambling problem. He has a competition problem."[8] So while some postretirement drop-off is inevitable for any celebrated athlete, let alone a player once asked (seriously) by a journalist how it feels to be a god, Jordan, who exited the game for the third and final time in 2003, remains a beloved figure—only 6 percent of the Jordan references in the blog sample were critical—and a commercial powerhouse.[9] Two out of every three pairs of basketball sneakers purchased in the United States are made by Jordan Brand, a Nike subsidiary run by Jordan since 1997.[10]

However, since the 1990s, a school of criticism has begun a deeper critique of Jordan's legacy, moving beyond surface-level gripes and gossip-style reproach to consider Jordan's cultural, social, and economic meaning. These criticisms diverge from popular conceptions and instead construct Jordan's reputation and race from a particular sociopolitical vantage point. This work usually comes from one of two places: scholarly writing (critical race theory, sociology of sport, cultural studies, or the like) or a niche of sportswriting that treats sport as reflective of and influencing society rather than a diversion from it. In this genre of criticism, Jordan is constructed as a neoimperialist[11] or, going the other way, a prosaic blank billboard for corporations to fill,[12] a shirker of moral responsibility and indifferent to political and social causes about which he should care,[13] and disloyal to the black community.[14]

While these representations of Jordan are in a sense analytic creations belonging most clearly to these critics and discordant with the empirical reality of Jordan's lionization, they are insightful because they reveal popular lines of thinking about race, community, capitalism, and morality that surpass Jordan. Sociologist Gary Fine provides a useful framework for thinking of these claims: "Reputations are not only made, they are *used* for purposes beyond characterizing the figure to address the circumstances or community in which he acted."[15] I have consolidated the criticism into four dominant issues critics take with Jordan, and I analyze how his critics, who function as custodians of Jordan's reputation, resolve those issues. Each resolution is a decision about Jordan's moral relationships to the larger literal or symbolic constituencies of which he is considered a vital part—the NBA, corporate America, the black community, and so on—and about which parties are ultimately responsible for the problem. The choice of problems to associate with Jordan and how these problems are worked out analytically show how Jordan's race and reputation are constructed anew even as they are deconstructed. As it relates to public icons, reputation may be understood in terms of the issues critics deem relevant to a public figure's legacy, how these critics choose to resolve such issues, and the resonance of these critical narratives with the audience.

MICHAEL JORDAN AS SUBSTANCE/SYMBOL

Jordan debuted in the NBA, signature Nike sneakers on his feet, in 1984, the same year the visionary David Stern took over as league commissioner and a cross-coastal rivalry between Magic Johnson's Los Angeles Lakers and Larry Bird's Boston Celtics stood tied at two titles apiece. Jordan quickly distinguished himself as the league's most talented and exciting individual player and attached his name and image to a multitude of products (including foam furniture, ring binders, and aprons) as well as to America's most visible brands (Coca-Cola, McDonald's, Gatorade).[16] With Stern's new marketing initiatives, better television technology, and perhaps its greatest assemblage of talent yet, the NBA, previously on the verge of bankruptcy and sadly underexposed (the 1980 NBA Finals aired on tape-delay), grew steadily in revenue and popularity through the 1980s. Over the following decade, Jordan and the Chicago Bulls became, according to basketball writer Harvey Araton, a "television monolith" and "global phenomenon," with Jordan establishing himself as arguably the greatest basketball player of all time, leading the Bulls to six championships and earning Finals MVP honors each time, along with a host of other accolades and elite achievements—ten scoring titles, ten-time All-NBA first team selection, and nine-time NBA All-Defensive first team selection, among other honors.[17] He notched these achievements despite a quick departure from the league between "three-peats"—as the Bulls' championship runs in

1991–93 and 1996–98 came to be known—to play Minor League baseball. The 1998 Bulls–Utah Jazz Finals, Jordan's final go-round in Chicago, scored an overall 18.7 Nielsen rating, the highest in league history and an unmistakable indicator of the sporting world and popular culture significance of the NBA and of Jordan, its main attraction.[18]

On January 13, 1999, during an NBA lockout, Jordan retired for a second time. Roughly one year later, Jordan became president of basketball operations and part owner of the Washington Wizards, a post he held for twenty-one months before his third comeback (at age thirty-eight) to play the 2001–2 and 2002–3 seasons on injury-riddled knees. Although his Wizards finished with 37–45 records in both years and missed the playoffs, the team sold out all eighty-two home games. And even though he was in his twilight, Jordan was sometimes capable of tremendous play, scoring fifty-one and forty-five points, respectively, in back-to-back Wizards wins against the Hornets and Nets. Largely because of Jordan's presence, the world tuned in to the NBA: Games were broadcast in 212 countries and territories in Jordan's final playing season.

In accordance with NBA rules, Jordan relinquished his front office position and slice of ownership to come back as a player, and did not return to the organization upon his final retirement; Abe Pollin, the Wizards principal owner, fired Jordan on May 7, 2003. Approximately three years later, Jordan became the managing member of basketball operations and a part owner of the Charlotte Bobcats. In February 2010, he became the team's majority owner.

In 2001, Michael Eric Dyson remarked that Michael Jordan's unprecedented notoriety had "blurred the line" previously separating "substance and symbol."[19] Jordan's performance on the basketball court—the most meaningful substance of his legacy—was often commodified simultaneously: his games aired live, he played in Air Jordan sneakers and apparel on sale at the same moment, and he produced a steady output of highlight material replayed during and after games on sports shows and later consolidated into NBA Entertainment programs, videos, and eventually Web content. The symbols of Jordan's legacy have paid better than the substance: Jordan earned approximately $94 million in salary as a player and nearly five times that amount (approximately $454 million) in endorsements during the same period.[20] These deals continue to serve Jordan: a 2005 *60 Minutes* interview estimated his annual earnings at $35 million.[21]

Jordan's most famous symbol—other than perhaps his uniform number, 23—is the Nike-created Jumpman logo, a silhouette of Jordan midflight, with legs spread, which first appeared on the Air Jordan III in 1988. Often driving

Jordan's commodification and blurring the substance/symbol line was Nike, which experienced, through its collaboration with Jordan, a cultural and financial ascendance that resembled and nearly coincided with that of the NBA. Nike, a publicly traded company starting in 1980, signed Jordan to a shoe contract before his rookie season and soon reaped the benefits. With well-designed products such as the Air Jordan high-top and Air Max running sneaker, Nike buffered the images of its products with innovative marketing that incorporated life philosophy taglines (e.g., Just Do It), popular music (e.g., pairing Bo Diddley with Bo Jackson, Beatles songs), and other sides of popular culture. Spike Lee's Mars Blackmon character, a nerdy but stylish Brooklynite infatuated with basketball in Lee's film *She's Gotta Have It*, became Jordan's foil in television advertisements. Nike became the clear leader of the athletic footwear industry by the end of the 1980s.

The Nike expansion continued rapidly, and today the brand annually produces fifty thousand different products in seven hundred factories in fifty-two countries, selling goods around the world; Nike finished its 2007 fiscal year with gross profits of about $16.3 billion.[22] The brand's most successful sneaker genre, however, has long been basketball sneakers—in particular, high-end basketball shoes (those over one hundred dollars) headlined by the Air Jordan; a Forbes report recently put Nike's domestic share of this elite market at more than 95 percent.[23] Reflecting his status on the basketball court, Jordan and his sneaker are Nike's luxury class.

Against this backdrop, I now consider the four interrelated criticisms of Jordan's legacy that guide the scholarly and progressive sportswriting literature: Jordan's commercial viability is predicated on political sterility; this political neutrality corresponds to race neutrality; Jordan has abandoned the black community; and Jordan behaves as a ruthless capitalist. Close examination of these critiques demonstrates how race oscillates between fiction and realism in even liberalistic discourse and how critics leverage a public figure's reputation and race to make political claims beyond the individual in question.

CRITICAL ISSUE: POLITICAL NEUTRALITY AS PRECONDITION OF FAME

Michael Leahy, a *Washington Post* writer who chronicled Jordan's tenure with the Wizards in *When Nothing Else Matters: Michael Jordan's Last Comeback*, remarks on an ending with the organization that saw Jordan fired less than a month after completing his final playing season and in spite of his intention to resume his front-office position: "A sporting god enjoys supreme power only as long as he plays, earns, and fills seats. The moment he ceases to be a team's principal revenue stream is the moment his dominion ends. One day Jordan enjoyed nearly all of the sway in his relationship with Wizards officials; the next day, none."[24] Though he starts the conversation, the argument Leahy ultimately makes is not that athletes, no matter how famous or well compensated, are only as valuable as their fast-expiring physical selves. Rather, Jordan, in Leahy's account, was fired from a position he would have had back had he not clashed miserably with Pollin; the owner's top aide, Susan O'Malley; and players/teammates, whom he notoriously called his "mules" in a postgame interview. Jordan, after all, had likely been denied a team executive position and ownership stake in Chicago because of his strained relationships with vice president and general manager Jerry Krause and to a lesser extent with owner Jerry Reinsdorf.[25] As Leahy explains, the seeds of a doomed existence in Washington were planted the moment Pollin, burdened with an unpopular, money-losing team and competing with the Charlotte Hornets for Jordan's name and services, acquiesced to Jordan's impractical terms of hire. In addition to partial ownership, Jordan "demanded the freedom to work merely part-time in Washington," rejected any scouting obligations, and agreed to "attend only a handful of Wizards games . . . and accept only minimal marketing and promotional responsibilities."[26]

In contrast to Leahy's framing of Jordan's firing as a blatant mismatch of personalities and interests with an obvious outcome, William C. Rhoden, sports columnist for the *New York Times* and author of *Forty Million Dollar Slaves: The Rise, Fall, and Redemption of the Black Athlete*, returns the discussion to Jordan's body. Rhoden estimates that Jordan produced a net income of seventy million dollars for the Wizards in his two playing seasons, facilitating a turnaround for an organization that had been forty million dollars in the red the preceding year. But his return to the court reiterated that Jordan's sole value lay in his physical output, and Pollin no longer felt morally obligated to teach Jordan the business, as he had allegedly hoped. So the legendary Jordan, in Rhoden's conception, became "just another black athlete . . . put in his place."[27] Although he disregards Jordan's tenuous relationship to the franchise (as detailed thoroughly by Leahy), Rhoden is not wrong: at the end of 2003–4 season, when Jordan intended to resume his presidency and reclaim his minority stake in the franchise, all twenty-nine of the league's owners, twenty-five general managers, and twenty-four head coaches were white, while roughly 80 percent of the players were black. The "place" of blacks in the NBA was in shorts, not slacks.

Rhoden and Leahy come together on the charge that Jordan failed to use his time in the spotlight to cultivate a single platform—a political cause, moral calling, an interest, anything—to stabilize his life and legacy after his playing days were over. According to Leahy, Jordan had "made himself a blank slate in all matters outside of basketball."[28] Rhoden is more pointed in his critique: Jordan's failure to align himself with the black community in general and fellow black athletes in particular in the tradition of his politically active predecessors (e.g., Muhammad Ali) came back to bite Jordan in middle age, when his physical gifts were spent and he wanted to be taken seriously as a team executive and owner.

Here we have the beginnings of critics' first issue with Jordan: the commodification of his body is contingent on his political and moral silence. Jordan's commercial potency resides entirely in the body. In this trope, his mouth and mind are impotent and remained so to propel Jordan to the highest echelons of popularity and commercial success. No critic comes precisely to this conclusion—and some, including Gates, directly dispute the notion[29]—but their arguments are articulated in this framework, and different resolutions emerge from it.

Progressive sportswriter Dave Zirin reproves Jordan in his 2005 *What's My Name, Fool? Sports and Resistance in the United States*, which features a close-up of Ali's face on the cover. According to Zirin, "While Ali was driven by a keen social conscience, Jordan seems to get his motivation from a drive for profit."[30] Zirin highlights Jordan's aversion to fighting injustice in his own backyard, citing his decision not to push Nike to reform exploitative labor practices in shoe plants across Asia, charges well documented by numerous labor groups and a national media story by the mid-1990s, as well as Jordan's failure publicly to support black U.S. Senate candidate Harvey Gantt in Jordan's home state, where Jordan starred for the University of North Carolina Tar Heels in the early 1980s. Gantt twice ran unsuccessfully against incumbent Jesse Helms, an Old South segregationist long dominant in local politics. Said Jordan of his decision not to back Gantt, "Republicans buy sneakers, too."[31] For Zirin, Jordan's corporate arrangements and marketability hinge on political and moral indifference—a purely moneymaking orientation that separates Jordan from black athlete-activists such as Jim Brown and Arthur Ashe, who used their fame to expose social ills.

Fine's conception of the leveraging of reputation can inform our thinking regarding Zirin's approach to Jordan's legacy. In Fine's model, a reputational entrepreneur uses the reputation of a public figure to "characterize a historical period or community."[32] This characterization contains a moral lesson to be learned and hence an implicit call to action (what to do to learn the lesson, to learn from the past). Zirin designates Jordan the representative of a community of profit-centered contemporary athletes severed from its lineage as athlete-activists. Zirin is, after all, unabashedly a sportswriter on a mission to cultivate a (rainbow-colored) team of athletes, sportswriters, and fans that will change sports back to a meaningful vehicle for social change.

But Zirin later pulls back his criticism: "We need to revise our expectations of Jordan. . . . Why should we expect him to have a social conscience in the first place? It is simply not in his interest to embarrass the Nike brass."[33] Zirin wants a movement but knows that it is both unfair and futile to expect Jordan to lead it. The self-reflexive Zirin knows that a white author who laments that black athletes have lost their way is engaging in patriarchic behavior that undermines Zirin's intentions. To assign the task of reviving athlete activism to Jordan because he is black treats social justice as a black cause rather than universal imperative. Zirin resolves the issue of Jordan's political apathy by acknowledging that the politics he desires for Jordan belong to Zirin and like-minded others. On final reflection, Jordan's inaction constitutes a missed opportunity—the potential enormity of what Jordan could have done—rather than moral delinquency.

In June 1998, Henry Louis Gates Jr., a professor of African and African American studies, wrote a *New Yorker* piece on Jordan's legacy, responding to the charge that Jordan's commercial vibrancy hangs on political anemia.[34] In the feature, published a day after the 1998 NBA Finals matchup had been determined and Jordan's stature had arguably reached its highest point to date, Gates regards Jordan's body as a canvas for select brands. Jordan understands that product endorsement offers reciprocal benefits. Brand status transfers back and forth as the favorable qualities Jordan describes of the products he endorses slide onto the messenger and vice versa in the minds of those receiving his message (an effect known as trait transference in social psychology). At a certain point, Jordan became a product unto himself—something like America or the American Dream embodied—and his endorsements simply became scaffolding for this megabeing. Gates claims that selling one's body need not be self-undermining and that quite the opposite holds true for Jordan.

Gates resolves the issue that Jordan has compromised his political potential for economic viability in part by shifting focus onto the sincerity of Jordan's commercial self. Just as we speak of a "natural" in sports, Jordan is a "natural" of commercialism. This exposition functions as the article's dominant frame, set up by an anecdote from Jordan's agent, David Falk. On one occasion, when Jordan was in his early twenties, a reporter at a press conference asked Jordan whether he preferred the recently released "New Coke" or regular Coke. Jordan, the anti-deer-in-headlights, immediately replied, "Coke is Coke. They both taste great."[35]

Jordan's ability to equivocate in the name of commercialism is held up again when Gates moves the conversation to Jordan's exemplary "nimbleness in sidestepping political controversy." According to Gates, "It must have been discomfiting when subsequent controversies arose over Nike's use of low-paid overseas labor. But Jordan has handled the situations with considerable skill, chastising neither the company nor its critics."[36] In this construction, it is not that Jordan knows the right thing to do and then holds back but that Jordan is inherently phlegmatic. "Michael is definitely apolitical," Falk explains; rather than allowing himself to be pushed into a disingenuous position, he deftly gets away.[37]

Both Gates and the Reverend Jesse Jackson praise Jordan's political agnosticism in a second context. Jackson, who announced an Operation PUSH (People United to Serve Humanity) boycott of Nike in 1990, imputing that the company was not adequately protecting the black community from which it was profiting, takes issue with Nike but not with Jordan. Jackson believes that an athlete is not equipped "to be an astute sociopolitical analyst." That is Jackson's job. Fortunately, Jordan "has not succumbed to that temptation."[38] Jackson calls this restraint "a great contribution," before explaining why Jordan specifically should not be implicated in Nike's labor practices. "The issue of trading with Indonesia without regard to human rights or child labor is fundamentally a matter that United States trade policy must address. It isn't right to shift the burden to [Jordan] because he's a high-profile salesman."[39]

In Jackson's understanding, Jordan serves society by staying silent on political matters and thus keeping the pressure off uninformed athletes and putting it on the capitalist structures—that is, Nike and the U.S. government—that precipitate exploitation. According to Fine, the success of a constructed reputation depends on, among other factors, the "narrative resonance of the reputation."[40] Jackson seems to know that Jordan is untouchable—widely perceived as a sports miracle to behold—and to construct Jordan as a social leader. To construct Jordan as someone who has failed to speak out on behalf of the community would, particularly in 1998, when Jordan was perhaps the most beloved black man in the world, serve Jackson poorly. Jackson upholds the notion of Jordan as immune to moral criticism and casts himself as Jordan's advocate and therefore the people's advocate.

Gates does not challenge Jackson's claims but attempts (unconvincingly) to challenge the notion of Jordan as politically incurious, an assumption with which Gates concurs elsewhere. Gates procured unusually intimate access to the highly guarded celebrity and his camp. He interviewed Jordan, his (now former) wife, key friends, and Falk, and Jordan related to Gates, revealing more personal information than he usually offers interviewers. Gates presents as proof of mildly partisan allegiances Jordan's support for Colin Powell and cites Jordan's description of the alleged dominance of blacks in sports marketed at the expense of images of blacks excelling in other occupations as a "curse" and as evidence of "a strong social conscience."[41] With little supporting evidence—and contradicting his earlier construction of Jordan as a commercial natural—Gates comes to an ill-fitting conclusion regarding Jordan's identity: "In one magical package, Michael Jordan is both Muhammad Ali and Mister Clean, Willie Mays and the Marlboro Man."[42] We can think of Jordan as commodified symbol in the vein of the invented Mister Clean (both with piratical gold hoop and shiny head) or the Marlboro Man (both icons stylize addiction, be it nicotine or gambling), but why pick Ali and Mays over other great black athletes? Both were often despised during their playing days for their perceived radicalism—Ali for converting to Islam, refusing to serve during Vietnam, and declaring his black pride, and Mays for his central part in integrating baseball.

Historian Walter LaFeber disputes the idea that a social consciousness is somehow married to Jordan's commercial persona: "When commerce clashed with social need [for Jordan], commerce too often won."[43] Douglas Kellner, a media scholar and philosopher, goes a step further, arguing that Jordan and Nike have collaborated to make political apathy cool. Kellner believes that Jordan "has abrogated his basic political and social responsibilities in favor of expensive clothes, commodities, and a mega-stock portfolio. Nike has played a key role in promoting these values and is thus a major cultural force, a socializer and arbitrator of cultural and social values, as well as a shoe company."[44] But Gates pushes back against the charge of social negligence and the belief that Jordan's mainstream success is predicated on political dullness. Gates resolves the issue by simultaneously disputing Jordan's alleged apathy, depicting Jordan as a natural of the corporate game, and aligning Jordan's commercial persona with the figures of Ali and Mays.

CRITICAL ISSUE: POLITICAL NEUTRALITY AS POSTULATE OF RACELESSNESS

Implicit in the criticism of Jordan as either politically insouciant or repressing his beliefs for greater commercial prowess is the notion that Jordan has downplayed his blackness and attachment to the African American community. Jordan's alleged refusal to support Gantt over Helms, a notoriously antiblack politician wielding significant power, to avoid marginalizing potential sneaker consumers pits political apathy against blackness. By refusing to speak out against someone like Helms, Jordan projects the image of a public figure who is both politically neutral and race neutral. The equation of the two—Jordan as apolitical and raceless and apolitical because he is raceless (and vice versa)—appears across considerations of Jordan's image.

For Rhoden, the two notions are part and parcel of Jordan's celebrity: "The condition for Jordan's global appeal was his racial and political neutrality."[45] Norman Denzin, a sociologist of media and culture, argues that given the predominance of blacks in many areas of sports and entertainment, there is a sense that to be a superstar is to become colorless.[46] In this mode of thinking, a certain degree of fame renders a superstar's race irrelevant (though we are implicitly talking about people of color becoming colorless rather than whites losing their whiteness). So if a fan adores a celebrity enough, the fan becomes temporarily color-blind. Falk makes the point in interviews with both Gates and Rhoden that "Celebrities aren't black. People don't look at Michael as being black."[47] Another white businessman who has managed and profited from Jordan's image, Bulls owner Jerry Reinsdorf, says the same thing: "Michael has no color."[48]

David L. Andrews, a sport and cultural studies scholar, remarks that Jordan's "identity has been shrewdly severed from any vestiges of African American culture."[49] Andrews's comment and the widespread belief that Jordan is not seen as black leads the question of what it means to be black in this context. Based on these accounts, Jordan transcends blackness by doing nothing other than looking extremely good on the basketball court or in commercials for products from top American companies. Any deviation from this purely physical self that speaks only of basketball or the excellence of brands threatens this transcendence into the nonracial. Following this line of thinking, to speak out is to be black. Ethnic studies professor David J. Leonard adds another conception of blackness as it relates to black ballplayers in his exploration of Kobe Bryant. According to Leonard, Bryant lost his Jordan-like status as colorless when he was charged with rape in 2003.[50]

Blackness, as understood here, denotes either political or criminal deviance. These two conceptions have fused together at numerous moments in history and certainly in the days of civil rights and Black Power—Malcolm X's *by any means necessary*, sit-ins, Angela Davis's appearance on the FBI's list of most wanted fugitives, and so forth. Criminalized political resistance on the part of black athletes such as Ali, who refused induction in the U.S. armed forces in 1967, and Ashe, arrested in 1985 during an apartheid protest in Washington, D.C., stands as another representation of the black athlete, a representation invoked by Zirin and Rhoden. Authors Michael Omi and Howard Winant[51] and Steven Gregory[51] highlight the politicization of racial identity during the 1960s, when identifying as either black or an activist, white or black, meant—by virtue of common sense—espousing certain core political imperatives.

But in contemporary basketball, these meanings of blackness rarely intertwine: the image of the black basketball player as criminal usually mixes not with resistance but with its opposite, indulgence—the debauched hedonism paraded in commercial rap videos—to form the hip-hop athlete.[53] Hip-hop icon and former NBA star Allen Iverson is not political in the sense of championing issues such as human rights or rallying the black community around core issues, but no one would say he is not black enough. Iverson, like the famous rappers murdered during his 1996–97 rookie NBA season, Tupac Shakur and the Notorious BIG, can be thought of as hip in the way that *New York Times* culture critic John Leland interprets the concept: Hip "likes a revolutionary pose [but] is ill equipped to organize for a cause."[54] Not surprisingly, the depoliticization of racial identity is a fundamental feature of post-civil-rights America whereby the significance of race is minimized or denied or race is denounced as destructive.[55]

Andrews expands his point that Jordan has separated himself from African American culture to make a general statement about what black athletes and entertainers must do to thrive in the mainstream:

> If you're black you are not expected to harp on it. . . . African Americans are tolerated, and even valued, if they abdicate their race and are seen to successfully assimilate into the practices, value system, and hence identity, of white America. Moreover, African American membership in this exclusive club requires constant affirmative renewal. Any fall from grace (ranging from the judicial severity of a criminal misdemeanor, to the tabloidic scandal of sexual impropriety, to even the supposed democratic right of asserting one's racial identity) cancels membership, and recasts the hitherto American person as a criminally deviant, sexually promiscuous, or simply threatening racial Other, exiled to the margins of American society with the bulk of the minority population.[56]

In this view, figures such as Jordan must play down their blackness to be liked by white fans. But the action of muting one's racial identity is not carried out by the athlete; rather, "Nike's promotional strategy systematically downplayed Jordan's blackness." Andrews cites Nike's pairing of Jordan with risky, more "urban" foils such as Spike Lee's Mars Blackmon character and outspoken NBA star Charles Barkley.[57] Andrews resolves the issue of Jordan's racelessness buffering his commercial appeal by pointing out that Nike has appropriated control of Jordan's image. Of course, Andrews's understanding of Jordan's popular image contradicts Gates, who commends Jordan for smartly directing his own representation. Meanwhile, Rhoden recognizes that the white-controlled sports industry dictates the marketing of black athletes but holds Jordan personally responsible for his whitewashing. Rhoden's resolution implicates both Jordan and the corporate bodies handling him.

That Andrews is a white writer and Rhoden a black one may be relevant in the assigning of agency around Jordan's representation. Andrews would not raise Rhoden's suggestion that Jordan is a sellout to his race. But in considering the meaning of white and black in the popular imagination, Andrews falls into a common trap when writers (including me) explore race as social construction. While scholars of race know that race is a fictitious social creation made real only in its consequences, at a certain moment in the analysis, black and white become a real opposition with some stable meaning for each. In Andrews's view, being charged with a misdemeanor, appearing in a tabloid sex scandal, or asserting one's racial self are three actions that, when involving a person of color, are exaggerated by an American society that treats these events as confirming evidence of one's blackness. They signal an extreme—a fall from grace—that marginalizes the formerly esteemed figure. But as these three events are cast in opposition to the unidentified "practices," "value system," and "identity" of a white America that would find them offensive, these three behaviors become black behaviors. We can say that both whites and blacks assert their racial identity but that only black assertions offend whites; however, why would a misdemeanor charge or "tabloidic sex scandal" not be equally offensive to blacks and whites? That a misdemeanor charge or alleged sexual impropriety would be differently perceived and have less severe implications for a white person compared to a person of color is different from saying that a misdemeanor and sex scandal are deviant only to white America.

By criticizing Jordan as a black celebrity rather than simply a celebrity who remains idle, the focus shifts away from that which endows a celebrity to "make a difference"—high levels of exposure as well as social, cultural, and financial capital—and toward Jordan's blackness. If these charges concern blacks' failure to do something about societal maladies, then these neglected problems constitute the responsibility of black persons rather than all people. In a sense, nonblacks are off the hook. This view can be seen as another effect of white hegemony: making problems "black problems" to remove accountability from nonblacks.

Echoing Rhoden, writer and activist bell hooks believes that athletes like Jordan have compromised the "subversive potential" of the black male body.[58] The white-owned companies steering the market set the agenda of political sterility, but the black athlete submits his body to be objectified in whatever way will make him money. Two elements of hooks's critique are relevant to this discussion. First, the black athlete is implicated in his exploitation; second, the black body contains an essence, the capacity to subvert. We can think here in terms of social construction. The black body signals subversion in collective American consciousness. But hooks argues that these black men give up their true self to be whatever marketers want. Here, blackness means subversive power and obliges its owner to exercise this power.

Culture scholar Michael Eric Dyson argues that the commodification of the black athletic body in general and Jordan's in particular needs not signal complicity in exploitation, depoliticization, or the segregation of blacks to the physical. Jordan represents "both consent and opposition in exploitation" in his mastery of the "new athletic entrepreneur who understands that American sport is ensconced in the cultural practices associated with business."[59] At one moment, Jordan promotes expensive sneakers as worthy of youth's concentration and money. At the next he represents "possibility" exemplified in his taking a sport "denigrated as a black's man's game and hence deemed unworthy" of broad interest and making it the center of the sporting world's attention.[60] His likeness then, as Gates notes, is not an empty billboard for American brands but an active carrier of the dream to amaze, dominate, be genius. Dyson resolves the issue of Jordan as politically sterile as an oversimplification unresponsive to the complexity of the modern world's sports-industrial complex.

As in arguments by Andrews and hooks, race becomes real in Dyson's treatment of Jordan. Contextualizing Jordan's impact on basketball within the wider picture of black athletes' reconfiguration of the sports world from which they were previously excluded, Dyson remarks that whites have been motivated to segregate sports by a fear of black physical superiority. During the segregated era in American sports, "the potentially superior physical prowess of black men . . . helped reinforce racist arguments about the racial regimentation of social space"; in the integrated era, however, "the physical prowess of the black body would be acknowledged and exploited as a supremely fertile zone of profit."[61] Dyson does not dispute the idea that blacks are physically superior, and this potentiality resides in the background as Dyson shifts the discussion to Jordan's game, a marriage of elite ability and brilliant style. According to Dyson, at least three elements of African American culture inform Jordan's style of play. Jordan embraces "spontaneity," "stylization of the performed self," and "edifying deception" (the acrobatics and creativity that trick us into believing that his hang time really defies human limits).[62] The infusion of black cultural style makes his game alluring and uniquely suited for commodification and consumption. While these three stylistic parts of Jordan's game reflect black cultural traditions—a claim with which Jordan may or may not agree—Jordan's black body possesses a superior physical endowment.

Sociologist Earl Smith provides useful criticism of three of Dyson's assumptions. First, that a unique and definable African American culture exists is up for debate. Second, biological advantage (a level of innate ability so high that it distinguishes a tiny proportion of individuals from the rest of the population) is not interchangeable with racial advantage (the notion that people of a certain racial group naturally possess elite degrees of talent). Smith grounds this important distinction in the argument that race is a social creation rather than a biological category and thus that a racial advantage cannot be a biological one. Racial groups are not pure in any sense as a result of nonbiological forces such as migration, colonization, and slavery, and scientists believe that genetic variation within racial groups exceeds differentiation between groups.[63] Finally, as W. I. Thomas and later Robert Merton assert, the self-fulfilling prophecy makes real what is based on false premise. The historical claim that blacks are naturally physically superior facilitates the concentrated participation and veneration of black athletes in sport.[64]

How does one reconcile these meanings of blackness—politically subversive, deviant, uniquely performance-oriented, and athletically superior—with what we know about race? Race has always been a fluid, socially constructed category, signaling different things at different historical moments and in different contexts. It meshes with class, gender, nationality, sexuality, and other markers of difference to form identity and hierarchy.[65] Biological knowledge verifies that differences within racial groups outnumber differences between racial groups. These critics' racial meanings are constructions, but they too are treated as realism at certain moments. Race may cease to be spoken of as construction in its leveraging for political purposes. Such is how things are done in a world in which race has functioned as social scaffolding since at least the 1400s.[66] In its politicization, race comes to contain expectations for its "members," certain truths at its core. The entrepreneurs characterizing

Jordan's reputation sometimes rely on realist interpretations of Jordan's race to legitimize political purposes.

CRITICAL ISSUE: JORDAN AS DISLOYAL TO HIS BLACK COMMUNITY

Rhoden's criticism of Jordan functions as an impassioned call from a black elder to younger blacks to rally around issues directly relevant to their welfare and to highlight their blackness in an era of color-blind rhetoric and political lethargy. Rhoden starts with a flat admonition: "Black athletes like Jordan have abdicated their responsibility to the community with an apathy that borders on treason."[67] Rhoden then poses and responds to the question that often goes unasked and unanswered in this dialogue: What exactly should Jordan be doing? Rhoden criticizes Jordan's refusal to support Gantt, inaction at Nike, and aversion to involvement with the creation of a black cultural center at the University of North Carolina in the early 1990s because he believed that such a center was exclusionary (even though his mother was already involved). The center's creation took off after members of the school's football team became interested. Because scholarships may be put at risk, Rhoden maintains, activism on the part of athletes at top sports schools is rare, and such courage should be supported so that it mushrooms across campuses. Athletes should speak out as much as the rest of the student body.

Thus, in Rhoden's view, Jordan has dismissed every chance to do the right thing, even when that opportunity has been handed to him on a silver platter. Rhoden grounds his critique in his own coming into black consciousness in the 1960s, when blacks joined together to fight for civil rights gains that Jordan's detached generation now enjoys. Rhoden proclaims that Jordan's "right to remain silent is what we won."[68] Rhoden is only thirteen years older than Jordan but maintains that a mountain of change happened so quickly that a cultural gulf divides them. In 1963, the year Jordan was born, Medgar Evers and John F. Kennedy were killed, Martin Luther King Jr. gave his "I Have a Dream" speech, and protesting was epidemic. While Jordan may have missed this formative era in black history, he is close enough to it, in Rhoden's estimation, that his politics should reflect these critical moments at least as much as they resemble the orientation of today's hip-hop athletes born in the late 1970s and 1980s. For Rhoden, a "historical mission" still unites and obligates black athletes, since work remains to be done.[69] But Jordan "does not relate to the [black] struggle."[70]

There is irony in castigating Jordan for living out King's wish that a man be judged by the content of his character—or, more apt here, his ability (which Rhoden acknowledges)—and for failing to lead a movement to which he does not relate (which Rhoden does not mention). If Jordan does not feel part of a symbolic black community, then why would he see himself as part of any community other than the literal one of his family, friends, and colleagues? Rhoden does not address this tension but instead changes course to reveal that deep down, he believes, Jordan feels "the struggle" but consciously disengages from it. According to Rhoden, during a 1997 interview, he and Jordan shared a moment between "Brothers" in which Jordan brought up how much worse temporarily disgraced white NBA announcer Marv Albert would have been treated had he been black.[71] For Rhoden, Jordan is disloyal because he understands the black dilemma but knowingly serves as part of the problem rather than the solution, a treacherous listlessness that came back around when Pollin disposed of Jordan after he could no longer perform on the hardwood.

Rhoden's singling out and criticism of Jordan is really about the alleged absence of a contemporary coherent black political movement that resonates with black athletes. To Rhoden, as reputational entrepreneur, Jordan embodies an entire class of post-civil-rights blacks who have shunned a mission and consciousness. In the end, Rhoden settles for the conclusion that Jordan's inaction constitutes not treason but, just as Zirin ultimately sees it, a missed opportunity to parlay his fame and resources into constructive social change—a what could have been. Rhoden's reprove is also a rhetorical push to empower black athletes: "At a time when they could actually *own* the boat—rather than just rock it—the level of apathy is greater than before."[72]

David Halberstam, the Pulitzer Prize–winning writer, in his 1999 *Playing for Keeps: Michael Jordan and the World He Made*, similarly remarks that Jordan shied away from political endorsements for "fear that he might taint his value as a commercial spokesman" and represents "a different generation of young blacks in America, for whom many doors once closed, not only educationally but commercially and socially, were now opened."[73] But like Gates and Dyson, Halberstam considers Jordan's athletic excellence, poise under pressure, and business acumen as public deeds on behalf of black America. Jordan's success has "helped open" doors.[74]

Halberstam brings in class and family history to understand Jordan's political neutrality. As Halberstam tells it, Jordan's parents were eager to be part of a more modern integrated South. The Wilmington, North Carolina, couple was "catapulted forward in no small part by that great conduit of blacks into the middle class, the United States military": James Jordan, a U.S. Air Force veteran who went on to work at General Electric, and Deloris Jordan, a bank teller, combined two incomes and a military pension to support five children and a solidly middle-class lifestyle.[75] Jordan's parents, "beneficiaries . . . of profound legal and social change," instructed their children that the "less they themselves factored in race as a determinant" of their success, then "the less it would be factored in against them."[76] Jordan's unprecedented athletic and commercial successes thus confirmed American society as color-blind meritocracy. Halberstam, weighing in on the apathy charge, decides that judging Jordan by his commitment to political causes is "unfair," since "accomplished white athletes" are "not put to any comparable test of their speaking out on broader social issues."[77] In this construction of Jordan's reputation, not only is his race-neutrality authentic and an extension of familial values, but the case is made for color blindness not as rhetorical mask for enduring inequalities but as an equalizing force and legitimate rather than dishonorable enabler of mainstream achievement.

CRITICAL ISSUE: JORDAN AS BRUTAL CAPITALIST

The denunciation of Jordan's apolitical nature as a prerequisite for advancement implies that Jordan has compromised his moral worth for net worth. The last principal critical issue taken with Jordan is that his legacy—in and through its interdependence with Nike—signals corporate greed and hyper-capitalism, profits over people.

According to media scholar Carol A. Stabile, one of Nike's first "high-profile" controversies was "an association that emerged between sneakers and the media's representations of inner-city violence." Beginning in 1989, "a spate of publicity . . . suggest[ing] that children were killing each other over athletic shoes" signaled a sneaker crime wave.[78] A 1990 *Sports Illustrated* article detailed the lethal implications of wearing Air Jordans and helped make the Air Jordan the prime symbol of sneaker violence even while sympathetically framing Jordan as deeply disturbed by this unforeseen outcome.[79] In response to the purported sneaker crime wave and Jackson's PUSH boycott alleging Nike's failure to invest in black communities, Nike launched a public relations campaign headlined by PLAY (Participate in the Lives of America's Youth), an effort that Jordan helped promote to provide clean and safe recreational facilities and opportunities for young people. While the sneaker crime wave dissipated, Nike kept the Air Jordan price point high, maintaining its status as luxury item, and the violence around the sneaker may have added to its mystique in sneaker culture. Chris Vidal of Flight Club, a sneaker consignment shop and online marketplace based in New York, explains the dangerous fascination with Jordans he experienced while growing up in New York City in the 1980s: "I remember when everybody used to get robbed for their Jordans. People used to walk up next to you and put their foot next to you … and they're just measuring up their foot to see if that size is near their size. … If you had a pair of Jordans and you were able to go out every day and you came home with them, it was like, 'You the man.'"[80]

In the mid-1990s, another media dialogue formed around Nike and violence, this time on the production rather than consumption end. Nike, which outsourced its sneaker production to Japan in the 1960s and has since chased the cheapest labor around Asia (China, Vietnam, Indonesia, and Thailand now produce the bulk of Nike footwear), was effectively outed for its use of sweatshop labor by a reform movement that included the National Labor Committee; journalists, including Bob Herbert; and the Pittsburgh Labor Action Network for the Americas. Nike has long farmed out social responsibility by contracting overseas labor with the lowest possible standards for minimum wage, workplace safety, waste management, and so on. In response, Jordan said he would visit the Asian factories (though he never did) and then quickly removed himself from the conversation.

As LaFeber's account makes explicit, the issue here is Jordan's alleged complicity in Nike's corporate practices as the public face of the brand. That rebuke hinges, symbolically if not logically, on Nike's business structure: Nike is only a face, an image. Author Gary Gereffi explains the recent global shift from a supplier-driven to a buyer-driven world economy in which a transnational brand such as Nike designs the products it wants, names its price, and contracts production.[81] Nike produces nothing tangible and instead conceives of shoes, cultivates markets, brokers the distribution of sales, and coordinates "a complex logistical enterprise that weaves together material and non-material inputs [into footwear and apparel] across national boundaries."[82] This is how a brand, retailer, or even manufacturer based in the deindustrialized United States can thrive in the global economy while an industrialized nation may suffer.

Nike spectacularly exemplifies the hollowed corporation of the modern buyer-driven economy.[83] Nike creates images, taglines, symbols, and pop philosophies, all of which Jordan represents: a television commercial showing a Jordan drive that stops time as the world watches and a running sink in the bathroom overflows, the Jumpman logo, a black-and-white poster six feet across of Jordan's outstretched arms with the word "Wings" and a William Blake quotation, the contradiction that an athlete can *Just Do It* but that *It's Gotta Be the Shoes.*

Does Jordan represent, as the title of one of LaFeber's chapters asks, "'The Greatest Endorser of the Twentieth Century' or 'An Insidious Form of Imperialism'?"[84] LaFeber treats Jordan as metaphor for capitalism; thus, how we feel about Jordan reflects our feelings about capitalism. Even as we waver in our stance, we are always implicated—buying sneakers, an evening gown, or a DVD player likely relies on sweatshop labor.

CONCLUSION

In 2008, top-selling rapper Nelly released a single about how good he looks wearing and how good he feels buying Air Jordans. Although retired from the basketball court, Jordan is as meaningful as ever, which probably has something to do with our collective memory of Jordan, the player—the Jordan years of the NBA—rather than Jordan, middle-aged retiree. In the blog sample, 109 of the 120 mentions of Jordan refer to Jordan the player (only 9 references are to Jordan as team executive and 2 references are to Jordan as businessman). *60 Minutes* interviewer Ed Bradley could find only "one stain on Jordan's otherwise clean image": "the allegation that he had a compulsive gambling problem," a charge chalked up to his competitive drive.[85] The scholarly and progressive sportswriting criticisms are essentially disconnected from Jordan's public existence.

But this deeper-level criticism is instructive, collectively revealing the constructionism of reputation. According to Fine, reputational entrepreneurs may draw on different "historical material" to create "several distinct reputations."[86] Jordan's critics have produced and deployed multiple constructions of his reputation. Jordan has come to embody much that goes far beyond him, including color-blind rhetoric and the commodification of black celebrities; the purported political apathy and lost consciousness of contemporary black athletes and post-civil-rights African Americans; American hegemony in global capitalism; the hollowed-out global brand that makes nothing but imagery and rhetoric. That there is an unknowable quality to Jordan, the product of revealing little of himself in most public appearances and shrewdly manipulating reporters, makes the questions of who he is and what he stands for all the more open to interpretation.

With the exception of Gates, the consensus in the literature is that Jordan's image and body are either washed clean or naturally void of politics and then inscribed with quasi-patriotic messages of major American brands—being the best, color blindness, the meritocracy and empowerment of *Just Do It*. Some writers implicate Jordan in this process by articulating that he has suppressed his true self to cultivate a more viable apolitical, race-neutral persona. For Rhoden and hooks, Jordan compromised the subversive potential of the black body. He has, in their model, sold himself at the expense of his race and a black community that needs him to do more. Rhoden understands Jordan as an entire generation of African Americans free-riding off the hard work of their elders. Here, blackness contains a real and stable meaning, an imperative for its owners—subversion.

At one moment, these critics leverage both reputation and race, treating these constructions as objective and real. But at the next moment, these same critics hedge their claims on Jordan as neoimperialist or turncoat to his race to implicate the corporate entities sculpting and profiting from his image, capitalism in general, and generational differences, among other factors. In the end, the critic grapples with being political and being ethical (i.e., producing a thorough and fair treatment of Jordan) and with reputation and race as stable and real or flexible and created.

NOTES

1. Pierre Bourdieu, *Distinction* (Cambridge: Harvard University Press, 1984), 6. See also Vaughn Schmutz, "Retrospective Cultural Consecration in Popular Music," *American Behavioral Scientist* 48 (2005): 1511.

2. Pierre Bourdieu, *The Field of Cultural Production* (New York: Columbia University Press, 1993). See also Michael Patrick Allen and Anne E. Lincoln, "Critical Discourse and the Cultural Consecration of American Films," *Social Forces* 82 (2004): 871–94; Schmutz, "Retrospective Cultural Consecration."

3. Hoopsaddict.com features original content and reposts of basketball news from around the Web. I included in my random sample only posts that appear as text on hoopsaddict.com. I did not include posts stored on other sites to which hoopsaddict.com directs visitors. I omitted references to Jordan as object (i.e. Jordan rookie card or Jordan Brand) and references to his various aliases (e.g., MJ, His Airness).

4. Harvey Araton, "Celtics Show Bryant Is No Jordan," *New York Times*, June 18, 2008, D3.

5. Mitch Lawrence, "Kobe Bryant's No Air Apparent," *New York Daily News*, June 18, 2008, http://www.nydailynews.com/sports/basketball/2008/06/17/2008-06-17_kobe_bryants_no_air_apparent.html (June 18, 2008).

6. Such dialogue was the focus of two Jordan exposés: Michael Leahy, *When Nothing Else Matters: Michael Jordan's Last Comeback* (New York: Simon and Schuster, 2004); Sam Smith, *The Jordan Rules* (New York: Simon and Schuster, 1992).

7. Henry Louis Gates Jr., "Net Worth," *New Yorker*, June 1, 1998, 57.

8. James Jordan as quoted by Ira Berkow, "Jordan's Haunting Words," *New York Times*, August 14, 1993, A25.

9. William C. Rhoden, *Forty Million Dollar Slaves: The Rise, Fall, and Redemption of the Black Athlete* (New York: Three Rivers, 2006), 202. For a discussion of his deification in the media, see Edward G. Armstrong, "Michael Jordan and His Uniform Number," in *Michael Jordan, Inc.: Corporate Sport, Media Culture, and Late Modern America*, ed. David L. Andrews (Albany: State University of New York Press, 2001), 15–33.

10. Darren Rovell, "Sports Biz with Darren Rovell: No Shoe Windfall for NBA Draft Picks," *CNBC*, June 23, 2008, http://www.cnbc.com/id/25330766 (June 23, 2008).

11. Walter LaFeber, *Michael Jordan and the New Global Capitalism* (New York: Norton, 1999).

12. Leahy, *When Nothing Else Matters*. See also Charles P. Pierce, "Bull Market Cipher: Michael Jordan," *National Post*, January 14, 2005, S2.

13. Jack E. White, "Stepping Up to the Plate," *Time*, March 31, 1997, 90. See also Todd Boyd, "Hoopology 101: Professor Todd Boyd Deconstructs the Game," *LA Weekly*, May 23, 1997, 49; Douglas Kellner, "The Sports Spectacle, Michael Jordan, and Nike: Unholy Alliance?" in *Michael Jordan, Inc.*, ed. Andrews, 37–63; Ben Carrington, David L. Andrews, Stephen J. Jackson, and Zbigniew Mazur, "The Global Jordanscape," in *Michael Jordan, Inc.*, ed. Andrews, 177–216; Harvey Araton, "Jordan's Same Old Song Is Turning into Sad One," *New York Times*, October 25, 2005, D1; Dave Zirin, *What's My Name, Fool? Sports and Resistance in the United States* (Chicago: Haymarket, 2005); Rhoden, *Forty Million Dollar Slaves*.

14. Rhoden, *Forty Million Dollar Slaves*.

15. Gary A. Fine, "Reputational Entrepreneurs and the Memory of Incompetence: Melting Supporters, Partisan Warriors, and Images of President Harding," *American Journal of Sociology* 101 (1996): 1175–76.

16. For a list of other items endorsed by Jordan, see Gates, "Net Worth."

17. Harvey Araton, *Crashing the Borders: How Basketball Won the World and Lost Its Soul at Home* (New York: Free Press, 2005), 112.

18. Ibid.

19. Michael Eric Dyson, "Be Like Mike? Michael Jordan and the Pedagogy of Desire," in *Michael Jordan, Inc.*, ed. Andrews, 259.

20. "Players: Michael Jordan," Basketball-Reference.com, n.d., http://www.basketball reference.com/players/j/jordami01.html (June 23, 2008); see also Leahy, *When Nothing Else Matters*, 363.

21. *60 Minutes*, CBS, October 23, 2005.

22. Nike, "Corporate Responsibility Report," 2005–6, http://www.nikebiz.com/responsibility/cr_governance.html (June 15, 2008).

23. Matt Woolsey, "Market Scan: Nike's Game Plan: Growth in China, India," *Forbes*, February 7, 2007, http://www.forbes.com/markets/2007/02/07/nike-earnings-china-markets-equity-cx_mw_0207markets09.html?partner=links (June 15, 2008).

24. Leahy, *When Nothing Else Matters*, 6.

25. For further discussion, see Smith, *Jordan Rules*.

26. Leahy, *When Nothing Else Matters*, 7

27. Rhoden, *Forty Million Dollar Slaves*, 206.

28. Leahy, *When Nothing Else Matters*, 37.

29. Gates, "Net Worth," 57.

30. Zirin, *What's My Name, Fool?* 247.

31. Chicago sportswriter Sam Smith claims to have overheard the comment, which Jordan has never publicly disputed. Jordan later said that at the time of the campaign, he was not aware of Gantt's political history (Gantt was the first African American to enroll at South Carolina's Clemson University) and later donated money to Gantt's campaign. See Mark Vancil, "Playboy Interview: Michael Jordan," *Playboy*, May 1992, 51–164.

32. Fine, "Reputational Entrepreneurs," 1186.

33. Zirin, *What's My Name, Fool?* 248.

34. Gates, "Net Worth."

35. Ibid., 48.

36. Ibid., 57.

37. Ibid.

38. Ibid., 58.

39. Ibid.

40. Fine, "Reputational Entrepreneurs," 1186.

41. Gates, "Net Worth," 58.

42. Ibid., 61.

43. LaFeber, *Michael Jordan*, 96.

44. Kellner, "Sports Spectacle," 53.

45. Rhoden, *Forty Million Dollar Slaves*, 215.

46. Norman Denzin, "Representing Michael," in *Michael Jordan, Inc.*, ed. Andrews, 3–13.

47. Gates, "Net Worth," 54.

48. Jesse Kornbluth, "Here Comes Mr. Jordan," *TV Guide*, April 22, 1995, 22–26.

49. David L. Andrews, "The Fact(s) of Michael Jordan's Blackness: Excavating the Racial Signifier" in *Michael Jordan, Inc.*, ed. Andrews, 107–52.

509. David Leonard, "The Next M. J. or the Next O. J.? Kobe Bryant, Race, and the Absurdity of Colorblind Rhetoric," *Journal of Sport and Social Issues* 28 (2004): 284–313.

51. Michael Omi and Howard Winant, *Racial Formation in the United States* (New York: Routledge, 1986).

52. Steven Gregory, "We've Been Down This Road Already," in *Race*, ed. Steven Gregory and Roger Sanjek (New Brunswick: Rutgers University Press, 1994), 18–38.

53. For a discussion on hip-hop in the NBA, see Larry Platt, *Keepin' It Real: A Turbulent Season at the Crossroads with the NBA* (New York: Morrow, 1999); Larry Platt, *New Jack Jocks: Rebels, Race, and the American Athlete* (Philadelphia: Temple University Press, 2002); Todd Boyd, *Young, Black, Rich, and Famous: The Rise of the NBA, the Hip Hop Invasion, and the Transformation of American Culture* (New York: Doubleday, 2003); Jeffrey Lane, *Under the Boards: The Cultural Revolution in Basketball* (Lincoln: University of Nebraska Press, 2007).

54. John Leland, *Hip: The History* (New York: Ecco, 2004), 97.

55. Ruth Frankenberg and Lata Mani, "Crosscurrents, Crosstalk: Race, 'Post-Coloniality' and the Politics of Location," *Cultural Studies* 7 (1993): 292–310. See also Dana Takagi, *The Retreat from Race* (New Brunswick: Rutgers University Press, 1993); Gregory, "We've Been Down This Road"; Eduardo Bonilla-Silva, *Racism without Racists: Color-Blind Racism and the Persistence of Racial Inequality in the United States* (Lanham, MD: Rowman and Littlefield, 2003); Leonard, "The Next M. J. or the Next O. J.?"

56. Andrews, "Fact(s)," 128.

57. Ibid., 128–29.

58. bell hooks, "Feminism Inside: Toward a Black Body Politic," in *Black Male: Representations of Masculinity in Contemporary American Art*, ed. Thelma Golden (New York: Whitney Museum of American Art, 1994), 127–40.

59. Dyson, "Be Like Mike?" 264–65.

60. Ibid., 267.

61. Ibid., 261.

62. Ibid., 263.

63. Earl Smith, *Race, Sport and the American Dream* (Durham: Carolina Academic Press, 2007), 63.

64. Robert Merton, "The Self-Fulfilling Prophecy," in *Social Theory and Social Structure* (Glencoe, IL: Free Press, 1957), 421–36; W. I. Thomas and Dorothy Swaine Thomas, *The Child in America* (New York: Knopf, 1928), 572.

65. Gregory, "We've Been Down This Road," 28.

66. Roger Sanjek, "The Enduring Inequalities of Race," in *Race*, ed. Gregory and Sanjek, 1–17.

67. Rhoden, *Forty Million Dollar Slaves*, 200.

68. Ibid., 199.

69. Ibid., 200.

70. Ibid., 214.

71. Ibid., 210.

72. Ibid., 217.

73. David Halberstam, *Playing for Keeps: Michael Jordan and the World He Made* (New York: Random House, 1999), 359.

74. Ibid.

75. Ibid., 17.

76. Ibid., 18.

77. Ibid., 359.

78. Carol A. Stabile, "Nike, Social Responsibility, and the Hidden Abode of Production," in *Gender, Race, and Class in Media: A Text Reader*, ed. Gail Dines and Jean M. Humez (Thousand Oaks, CA: Sage, 2003), 197. See also C. L. Cole, "Nike's America/America's Michael Jordan," in *Michael Jordan, Inc.*, ed. Andrews, 65–103.

79. Cole, "Nike's America"; Rick Telander, "Senseless," *Sports Illustrated*, May 14, 1990.

80. Chris Vidal, interview by author, New York, January 3, 2008.

81. Gary Gereffi, "International Trade and Industrial Upgrading in the Apparel Commodity Chain," *Journal of International Economics* 48 (1999): 37–70.

82. Robert Goldman and Stephen Papson, *Nike Culture: The Sign of the Swoosh* (London: Sage, 1998), 6; Gereffi, "International Trade."

83. Ibid., 4.

84. LaFeber, *Michael Jordan*, 130–64.

85. *60 Minutes*, CBS, October 23, 2005.

86. Fine, "Reputational Entrepreneurs," 1187.

A PRECARIOUS PERCH

Wilt Chamberlain, Basketball Stardom, and Racial Politics

—GREGORY J. KALISS

INTRODUCTION

When Wilt Chamberlain announced in May 1955 that he would attend the University of Kansas at Lawrence (KU) on a basketball scholarship, KU fans and the local media celebrated. Standing more than seven feet tall and moving with a grace and agility uncommon to many big men, Chamberlain, a Philadelphia resident, was easily the most sought-after high school player in college basketball history. Nearly every major college and university had attempted to recruit him, so his selection of KU marked a major accomplishment for the team's prestigious basketball program. Fans envisioned the big man leading KU to multiple conference and national championships. The media deluged readers with front-page stories, photographs, and countless insider accounts detailing the successful campaign to recruit the prized basketball player. That he was a black man and the region still segregated did not appear to dampen many local residents' reactions. Chamberlain's celebrity and astonishing skills appeared to trump any misgivings observers may have had regarding his race.

Topeka Capital sports editor Dick Snider was one of the newsmen who joined in the celebration. He predicted that the "stable, well-mannered youngster" would lead KU to the top of the Big Six conference and make the team a national powerhouse.[1] Countless area writers echoed those assessments of Chamberlain's character and potential. Three years later, however, Snider offered a different perspective on Chamberlain. When the big man announced his decision to leave school one year early to play professionally for the Harlem Globetrotters, Snider wrote that although Chamberlain had always "been praised by those close to him as a model boy," he had not lived up to that reputation. According to Snider, "There were stories being circulated, indicating that Wilt was beginning to consider himself bigger than the institution he represented."[2] Others joined Snider in offering more critical assessments of Chamberlain at that point, suggesting that Chamberlain had been a prima donna and that he had betrayed those close to him by leaving school early. What had changed? How had Chamberlain gone from a nearly universally admired celebrity to a figure who represented a distasteful side of amateur athletics?

White fans' and media figures' enigmatic responses to Chamberlain during his college basketball career at KU augured the mixed reception he would receive later in his career and life. Initially starstruck by Chamberlain's dominating presence on and off the court, some capricious fans and writers soured as his career wound on, frustrated by his "failures" on the court and his decision to leave school early. Racial politics underlay many of these frustrations. In the glaring media spotlight, Chamberlain faced extraordinary pressure, as demeaning stereotypes of black masculinity haunted whites' reception of his great achievements. Conflicting assessments of Chamberlain's role as a leader on and off the court, frustrations with his flirtations with a professional career, and his legacy after his days at KU—including his infamous boast to have slept with twenty thousand different women—reveal how racial politics clouded public perception of a man who began his career as an outsized and beloved celebrity.

CHOOSING KU

The controversies that dogged Chamberlain, many implicitly about racial politics, spoke to the enormous publicity that followed him throughout (and after) his career. Indeed, even before he arrived in Lawrence, Chamberlain was quite possibly the most publicized high school basketball player in the history of the game. Born in 1936 into a large family in Philadelphia, Chamberlain possessed great height, remarkable coordination, and a competitive spirit that combined to make him an excellent basketball player. By the time he was a senior at Overbrook High, he had become a national sensation, with magazines such as *Life* publishing feature stories about him.[3] Playing in one of the country's most competitive high school basketball conferences, Chamberlain led his team to three all-public school championships and two all-city championships, setting numerous records in the process. Professional success, however, would have to wait: since the National Basketball Association (NBA) prohibited players from joining its professional league until after their class had graduated from college, Chamberlain had to continue his career at the collegiate level or with a traveling team such as the Harlem Globetrotters. Given Chamberlain's on-court prowess, the competition for his services was intense: more than 120 schools offered him scholarships (and other inducements that violated the rules set forth by the National Collegiate Athletic Association [NCAA]). Surprising many, Chamberlain selected KU in May 1955.[4]

KU offered an attractive option for Chamberlain because it was located away from the prying East Coast media and because its head coach, Forrest "Phog" Allen, was generally considered one of the best. KU's history with black athletes, however, was relatively limited. In fact, as the school's athletic director during the 1920s, Allen had been a leading proponent of segregation. Chamberlain was only the school's third black player, and the only other black player during Chamberlain's time at the school was Kansas City native Maurice King, a senior starter when Chamberlain made his varsity debut in the fall of 1956.[5] The two athletes were part of a small but growing community of black students on campus, with the school averaging 149 black students out of a total enrollment of close to 10,000 during Chamberlain's time there.[6]

Black students often faced discrimination in a number of forms at the school and in Lawrence. Although the town prided itself on its progressive stance toward African Americans (the town had been strongly pro-abolition prior to the Civil War), most public accommodations, including hotels, restaurants, and hospitals, remained segregated, as did local neighborhoods. Segregation extended to the campus as well, where white fraternities and sororities refused to admit black students. The Negro Student Association (NSA) was formed in 1950 largely to arrange social events since blacks were denied access to many campus events.[7] Even nearby Kansas City, which had a sizable black population, continued to have segregated eating places, although black leaders had integrated hotels, theaters, and municipal parks.[8]

Despite the unequal nature of race relations in the area, when Chamberlain announced his decision to attend KU on May 14, 1955, nearly anything seemed possible to the local media, which celebrated gleefully. And although area newspapers primarily emphasized Chamberlain's impact on the basketball court, they also discussed the importance of race in his decision. The local black newspaper, the *Kansas City Call*; mainstream newspapers such as the *Kansas City Star*, the *Lawrence Daily Journal-World* and the *Topeka Daily Capital*; and the university's *Daily Kansan* announced Chamberlain's decision in bold headlines as the lead story on the sports pages or even the front page. Nearly all of these newspapers also emphasized the importance that black alumni and area residents played in Chamberlain's decision. The *Call*, no doubt inspired by the active role of black KU alum Dowdal Davis, the paper's managing editor and a prominent community leader who had helped recruit Chamberlain, celebrated local African Americans' involvement in bringing the star out west. Chamberlain told the newspaper that "the Negro people interested in Kansas had an awful lot to do with" his decision, specifically citing Davis, black concert singer (and KU alum) Etta Moten, and black Lawrence businessman Lloyd Kerfords.[9] The widely circulated Associated Press story regarding Chamberlain's decision featured Allen's praise of the "outstanding alumni of the Negro Race" who helped bring Chamberlain to KU.[10] Allen said that Davis, Moten, and Kerfords had done "an especially fine job in advancing Kansas' strong points which carried great weight with Chamberlain."[11] The importance of race to Chamberlain's decision was unavoidable in newspaper coverage, an apparent recognition of the ongoing struggles with Jim Crow segregation in the region.

A closer look at the discourse surrounding Chamberlain's announcement, however, suggests that black and white observers were often talking past one another as they discussed the importance of race. Black leaders hoped that Chamberlain, as a nationally known athletic superstar, would inspire area whites to integrate their communities (including, of course, Lawrence). Davis and others were eager to see Chamberlain use his status as an icon to push through integration in the town and surrounding area. By dominating interracial, on-court competition, Chamberlain could show whites the fallacy of a color system that rested on assumptions of black inferiority.

While black leaders wanted Chamberlain to serve as a role model to whites, convincing them that segregation was morally and ethically wrong through his feats of athletic excellence on an integrated team, many white Kansans hoped Chamberlain would be a "good" role model for African Americans and would showcase the university's and region's liberal racial attitudes. The *Journal-World*'s Bill Mayer, for example, emphasized Chamberlain as a sign of progress and a role model for the black community at large: "In past interviews, Chamberlain has said one of his primary goals in going to college is the furtherance of the Negro race. He has deep convictions here and states emphatically he hopes his future actions will reflect great credit on his people." Mayer believed that "the Negroes couldn't have a finer emissary in this area" because Chamberlain was "a first-class gentleman in every respect, possessed with great social poise, a sharp sense of humor and high intelligence in addition to his athletic ability." From Mayer's viewpoint, Chamberlain would be a model of humbleness and virtue and would prove that blacks could be responsible citizens. Indeed, Mayer praised Kerfords and his wife for their role in the process, describing them as "outstanding citizens of their community for many years." Mayer guessed that Chamberlain "saw how much this family had done for its race and was inspired by the fact he might be able to do likewise out West."[12] From Mayer's perspective, Chamberlain could improve race relations not by revealing the injustices of the color line but rather by living responsibly, working hard, and setting a good example for other African Americans.

Mayer either missed or purposefully reinterpreted African American leaders' hopes for Chamberlain. From the perspective of black leaders, after all, whites needed changing and inspiration, not African Americans. Like Coach Allen, who thought that Chamberlain was persuaded to attend the school because of its "fine points" for African Americans, Mayer focused on what the university and town could provide Chamberlain and on Chamberlain's potential as a role model for blacks, not on what Chamberlain could do to influence area whites.[13] These differing expectations reflected varying perspectives on who was responsible for bringing about racial integration in the region—whites or African Americans—and on whose terms. These writings represented some of the earliest conflicting responses to Chamberlain's career and reveal the extent to which race affected his reception.

THE CENTER OF ATTENTION

By the time Chamberlain arrived in Lawrence for the start of his freshman year in September 1955, narratives regarding Chamberlain as a race leader had largely disappeared from media stories. And yet race would continue to color people's responses to Chamberlain's college career. During the 1956–57 basketball season, Chamberlain's first with the KU varsity, the numerous responses to the black star player and celebrity were highlighted. The season contained triumphant moments and gut-wrenching disappointments for KU fans and members of the team alike. As Chamberlain led the team to the Big Seven conference championship and a runner-up finish in the NCAA national championship tournament, he generated an enormous amount of media attention from both the black and white press. As writers and readers celebrated the KU season, they inevitably focused on Chamberlain, without question the team's best player and the person most responsible for its success. The varied readings of his performances illuminated contradictory assessments of black male leadership and character.

Responses to Chamberlain's varsity debut on December 3, 1956, illustrated local enthusiasm. In an 87–69 victory over Northwestern University, Chamberlain poured in a record-setting 52 points and dazzled fans and opponents alike with his agility and strength. On the whole, the local newspapers delighted in celebrating Chamberlain's accomplishments. The *Call*'s banner headline in the sports section announced "Bill Russell Is Gone, but the Stilt Has Arrived." The accompanying story proclaimed Chamberlain the new

Chamberlain's jaw-dropping slam dunks inspired many youthful admirers—white and black—during his time at KU. However, those dunks also proved alarming to whites who resented the sight of a black man dominating white opponents. Photos courtesy of University Archives, Spencer Research Library, University of Kansas Libraries.

"king" of college basketball in the wake of Russell's graduation from the University of San Francisco.[14] If the other newspapers did not crown Chamberlain, they nonetheless marveled at his feats. The editors of the *Star* believed that Chamberlain had lived up to the hype: "Wilt 52, It's All True," a headline declared.[15] The fans apparently agreed with that assessment, as "the crowd of 15,000 was more preoccupied by what Chamberlain was doing than with the progress of the game."[16] Analyzing Chamberlain's first performance, writers celebrated more than his physical skills. Mayer, for example, praised Chamberlain's ability "to adapt and adjust quickly to a given situation" as well as his "tremendous stamina."[17] For a fan base eager for another national championship after two consecutive years of mediocrity, and with newsmen excited to have a sensation who would sell more newspapers, Chamberlain's stunning debut delivered the goods.[18]

Chamberlain's dazzling display of strength and athleticism undoubtedly disquieted some observers even as it excited others. Local papers ran numerous photographs of him dunking, for example, physically dominating white opponents in ways that could have been visually inspiring or disturbing to observers. One photo in the *Journal-World*, for example, displayed Chamberlain forcefully dunking, his mouth open as though letting out a primal scream, while three players watched, one Marquette athlete unmistakably cowering at Chamberlain's power and size.[19] This photograph was potent enough to destabilize long-standing racial hierarchies. Jim Crow segregation rested on fundamental assumptions of black inferiority that were often tied to stereotypes of black male shiftlessness and inadequacy. Images of Chamberlain dominating white competition clearly undermined these stereotypes.

Or did they? Another stereotype of black men revolved around the image of the "brutal black buck," which film historian Donald Bogle describes as "big, baadddd niggers, over-sexed and savage, violent and frenzied as they lust for white flesh."[20] For these viewers, Chamberlain's on-court dominance might well have "proven" bestial physical prowess and little more. Some Kansas sports followers certainly were eager to discount Chamberlain's greatness. Mayer later felt the need to defend the big man against some "capricious fans" who believed that Chamberlain was "washed up and probably never ... really great at all" after he only scored twelve points in a one-point win over Iowa State in the Big Seven tournament. After praising Chamberlain's defense, rebounding, and teamwork, Mayer also had a few choice words for those who criticized Chamberlain "for missing several key free throws—five in the second half." Had those fans noticed that Gary Thompson, the "celebrated" (and white) star guard for Iowa State "noted for his coolness under fire" also missed four free throws "in a crucial game."[21] Chamberlain's excellence only went so far in convincing skeptical observers of the inaccuracy of certain stereotypes, even when he dominated the competition night in and night out. Chamberlain might be the star, but "scrappy" white players might be more "clutch" or "cool" under pressure.

Chamberlain continued to garner a great deal of media attention, nearly all of it complementary of him on and off the court. As the universally acknowledged best player on the successful KU team, Chamberlain earned acclaim for "leading" the team to victory after victory, although some subtle differences in the coverage provided by the local newspapers reflect some alternate approaches to Chamberlain's status as a team leader. While the *Call* unequivocally praised Chamberlain as KU's team leader and considered his accomplishments in the context of the successes of other black athletes and black coaches, other newspapers focused on Chamberlain's leadership in various statistical categories: scoring, rebounds, and blocked shots. Even as these papers acknowledged Chamberlain's centrality to KU's success, they shied away from praising him as the inspirational leader of his integrated team.

The writers and editors of the *Call* placed Chamberlain at the center of their coverage of KU, arguing that whatever successes the team enjoyed resulted primarily from Chamberlain's presence. In sports editor John I. Johnson's wrap-up for 1956, for example, the final athlete mentioned was Chamberlain, "who has done a big part in pacing the team to a string of early victories and who may, barring misfortune, lead the squad to high national honors."[22] From Johnson's perspective, Chamberlain set the pace for his teammates, leading them almost single-handedly to their successes. Similarly, the *Call*'s story about the Jayhawks' second meeting with Colorado indicated that Chamberlain "turned in another leadership job" in his team's 68–57 victory, which guaranteed the squad at least a tie for the conference title.[23] The emphasis on Chamberlain as a leader fit into the newspaper's broader pattern of coverage. When Tennessee State became the first black school to win the National Association of Intercollegiate Athletics basketball tournament, which featured the best teams from some of the nation's smaller schools, on March 16, 1957, Johnson enthusiastically praised the school's head coach, Johnny B. McLendon, for being "a great coach, period." Johnson was heartened by the success of a black male head coach, which continued to prove that "given an equal opportunity," African Americans could succeed in "almost any field of activity."[24] Johnson saw both Chamberlain and McLendon as embodying successful black male leaders who had proved their worth competing against whites, a powerful message for the newspaper's editors and writers.

This commentary framed Chamberlain as a figure not only of remarkable physical prowess and ability but of broader talents and character.

Mainstream publications, however, deemphasized Chamberlain's leadership skills. Although all the major publications in the Lawrence area lauded Chamberlain's accomplishments on the court, his role as a leader of an integrated team was rarely mentioned. Newspapers certainly praised Chamberlain's scoring prowess and his defense and rebounding. And after both of the team's regular-season losses, the newspapers went out of their way to absolve Chamberlain of any blame, noting that tight defense had prevented him from taking over the contests. However, these articles also shied away from depicting Chamberlain as inspiring his teammates. The *Daily Kansan* referred to Chamberlain as the "hero" of certain games, and Mayer mentioned Chamberlain's "loose" nature in the locker room before big games, but even these newspapers did not suggest that Chamberlain was the leader of the team.[25] Nor did they assign this label to King. In fact, the team's cocaptains were white senior starters John Parker and Gene Elstun. These two players may have been selected for reasons other than race, but the decision fit into a broader pattern in integrated athletic competition where team leadership positions were occupied by whites. Finally, before the Big Seven preseason tournament, which KU would eventually win behind Chamberlain's record-setting ninety-three points over its three wins, the *Daily Capital* printed a cartoon of white Iowa State player Gary Thompson captioned, "A Real Leader."[26] No similar cartoon appeared for Chamberlain throughout his two-year career.

Although Chamberlain's role as a racial leader had been largely forgotten in the coverage of his debut, Mayer returned to that topic three weeks after the season's start. Mayer's effusive praise continued to see Chamberlain as a leader for black people rather than for whites:

> Wilt, by the way, deserves some orchids for something he's been doing in addition to playing great basketball. When the towering Negro came west from Philadelphia, he did so with the idea that by being a great performer on the court and a good citizen—a gentleman—off the maples, he might be able to contribute toward the advancement of his people. So far everything he has done has reflected tremendous credit to his race, and Negroes everywhere have every right to be proud of him.
>
> Despite the constant pestering by newsmen and photographers, he's remained calm and polite and usually smiling and jovial, always ready with a quip. Though battered and booed on the court, he's never lost his poise and composure. Never has he given any displays of temper. Those

who have been skeptical have ended up admiring him for his ability AND his gentlemanly ways.[27]

Mayer certainly seemed genuine in lauding Chamberlain's character, encouraging readers to be proud of him, and undoubtedly saw Chamberlain as an important figure in area race relations. However, Mayer declined to identify who needed to be led by Chamberlain, whose behavior needed to be changed. Mayer remained vague about how Chamberlain could "contribute toward the advancement of his people." Implying that the onus of racial change lay on blacks, that they needed to follow Chamberlain's model of persevering, remaining composed, and avoiding public pronouncements on controversial issues, Mayer outlined a narrow view of African American advancement that asked little of whites. He continued to heed stereotypes that limited black men to subsidiary roles in political, social, and economic life.

TRIUMPH AND TRIBULATION

Kansas concluded the 1957 regular season in impressive fashion, with a 21–2 record and an 11–1 mark in the Big Seven. Chamberlain finished the year averaging 29.52 points per game, easily the best in team history, and set a variety of other team records. He was also named to first-team all-America squads by every major news and sporting publication, including the prestigious Associated Press. KU's team was ranked second in the nation, behind only the undefeated squad from the University of North Carolina, and many observers picked Kansas to win the national championship tournament.[28]

To play for the title, however, the team had to survive two western regional games in Dallas, including an opening-round game against hometown Southern Methodist University. Racism marred the entire experience, no doubt accentuated by Chamberlain's starring role on the KU team. The squad's living accommodations were the first sign of trouble. Instead of staying in downtown Dallas with the other three teams, the Jayhawks booked rooms in Grand Prairie, a suburb nearly thirty miles away, because no Dallas hotels would permit Chamberlain to stay with the rest of the team. Chamberlain wrote in his autobiography that he and his teammates believed Allen's understudy and first-year head coach Dick Harp's explanation that he wanted to keep the team "together in a quiet spot, away from the big city" until "someone burned a cross in the vacant lot across from our motel."[29] Teammate John Parker later lamented that "no restaurant would serve" the team, so the players "took all [their] meals together in a private room."[30] Although the integrated

Kansas squad would be permitted to play, these and other signs indicated how unwelcome and symbolically threatening some Texans found the team.

Their reception was even worse on the court. The team first struggled before a hostile crowd in an overtime win over Southern Methodist (SMU). According to Parker, the KU players "were spat upon, pelted with debris, and subjected to the vilest racial epithets imaginable."[31] Chamberlain wrote that the "hostile" fans "booed and jeered" and used a variety of derogatory terms, including: "'nigger' and 'jigaboo' and 'spook' and a lot of other things that weren't nearly that nice."[32] Pleased to escape with the win, the players assumed that the worst was over since the hometown SMU team had been eliminated. They were wrong. In fact, the team's second game against Oklahoma City University (OCU) involved even worse crowd behavior. Dallas fans, outraged that an integrated team had defeated their school, switched allegiance to OCU and continued to taunt and harass the KU squad. To make matters worse, OCU coach Abe Lemons and several of his players participated in the unruly behavior. Before the game, Lemons warned referee Al Lightner that there would be problems "if that big nigger piles onto any of my kids."[33] As the game proceeded, the scene verged on bedlam as OCU players deliberately attempted to injure Chamberlain and King by tripping them.[34] As Chamberlain recalled, "One of the Oklahoma players kept calling me 'nigger' and a 'black son-of-a-bitch,' and he jabbed me and tried to trip me every time he went by."[35] At one point, according to the *Call*, Lemons "charged one of the officials and said: 'If you don't call some fouls on that big n——r we will get him.'"[36]

As Kansas pulled away to a convincing victory in the second half, the chaos became even more intense. Not even pleading from the SMU athletic director and other public officials could calm outraged fans, who threw a variety of objects, including coins, paper airplanes, seat cushions, and food, onto the court. According to longtime KU radio broadcaster Max Falkenstein, the atmosphere was so "dangerous" that "armed police officers escorted the team off the court and all the way back to the airport."[37] This hostile reaction showed the dark underside to Chamberlain's role as a celebrity. Although success gave Chamberlain a freedom and esteem uncommon to many black men in Lawrence and its surroundings, his on-court dominance also distressed whites who did not support his team. The big man appeared single-handedly to undermine notions of black inferiority, an unacceptable development in the segregated South.

Even among his fans in Kansas, Chamberlain occasioned ambiguous responses. A few days after the games in Dallas, the *Star* published a curious newspaper advertisement. A simple black-and-white cartoon featured Chamberlain in his Kansas uniform dunking the basketball. Two columns wide and the entire height of the page, the image was explained by an accompanying poem:

> There was a young man named The Stilt
> Who for basketball playing was bilt.
> When he dunked one to score
> There went up a roar
> Of "Bravo!" or "He ought to be kilt."

Beneath the poem was another line of text: "It takes a *man* to do a *man's* job. In basketball, Wilt (The Stilt) Chamberlain—In selling goods, the Kansas City Star."[38] The advertisement expresses admiration for Chamberlain on some level and explicitly identifies Chamberlain as a manly man who gets the job done, a remarkable development given Chamberlain's race and the weight of long-held stereotypes about black men. But it also suggests the intense negative reaction to his achievements, in the poem's "joking" final line. Chamberlain occupied a tenuous position as a star black athlete, surrounded by pressures and animosities white athletes did not have to face.

After the turmoil in Dallas, KU players, coaches, and fans eagerly looked forward to the national semifinals and final, to be played in Kansas City's Municipal Auditorium. But although KU easily defeated the defending champion University of San Francisco in the semifinal, the Jayhawks lost 54–53 in three overtimes to the all-white University of North Carolina Tar Heels. As with their coverage of KU's earlier defeats, sportswriters largely exonerated Chamberlain from blame, despite the fact that he missed a key free throw that could have won the game in the second overtime. The *Journal-World's* Earl Morey, for example, believed that Chamberlain "probably should be awarded some sort of a sportsmanship honor this season for his splendid actions on the court," emphasizing that Chamberlain had led both KU and North Carolina in scoring and rebounding.[39]

However, other aspects of the mainstream press coverage of the game spoke to the ways in which Chamberlain's performance and that of his team in general could be denigrated because of racial politics. While the black press celebrated the significant presence and high-level performance of black players during the championship weekend, the area's white newspapers consistently praised the Tar Heels' "poise." Mayer noted the trend and responded with exasperation: "You hear so cotton-pickin' much about the 'tremendous poise' demonstrated by" North Carolina in the national championship game. But, Mayer pointed out, Kansas had surely played with "poise" as well. Although "Kansas made errors, blew free throws and was guilty of bad passes in the clutch," the North Carolina players made the same mistakes: "There certainly was no fantastic 'poise differential' as far as we could see."[40] Although Mayer did not make the case that these alternate interpretations were based on race, racial stereotypes of coolly rational whites and overly emotional blacks likely influenced the discourse surrounding the game.

After the disappointing conclusion to a remarkable season, Chamberlain pondered his future in Lawrence. Although he still had two more years of school remaining, rumors began to swirl that he would end his education early and join the Harlem Globetrotters, a popular traveling troupe of black basketball players who dazzled crowds with comedic routines. Chamberlain considered the possibility, privately complaining to some KU alumni about the pressures he faced as the star athlete at the school: "It's a job . . . and as long as it's a job, I might as well be paid. . . . Here at Kansas the pressure is on me—we have to win."[41] Those pressures unquestionably were heightened by his race. As he weighed his options, the press closely followed the story.

Publications such as the *Call* had a vested interest in having Chamberlain stay in school and finish his degree. Chamberlain could only serve as a "race man," as a leader in bringing about integration, if he played by the rules. Leaving school early would not only remove him from the area spotlight but would mark him as a dropout, a quitter. Jerry Dawson, writing in the *University Daily Kansan* about Chamberlain's impending decision, indicated that some worried "that if Wilt leaves, integration in Lawrence will suffer a 25-year setback."[42] The editors of the *Call*, almost certainly led by Davis, were so anxious to see Chamberlain stay that they devoted an editorial to the matter despite the fact that the newspaper almost never discussed sports on its editorial page. "Don't Do It, Wilt!" expressed "hope that Wilt the Stilt will not let the lure of big money take him away from college basketball." The editorial board urged Chamberlain to "turn down all offers to enter the professional ranks until after he graduates," arguing that Wilt would be "a bigger man" if he finished his education.[43]

Others ignored the racial implications of Chamberlain's pending decision and emphasized its business implications. Bill Brower, writing for the American Negro Press newswire, defended Chamberlain's right to play professionally if he chose to do so, unworried over any damage to the race at large. Brower pointed out that "no great hue and cry" arose when Major League Baseball's "bonus babies," left college to cash in "on their athletic potential" and wondered why Chamberlain's case should be different. Brower believed that Chamberlain should "make hay while the sun shines," taking the fifteen thousand dollar annual salary offered by the Globetrotters.[44] Mayer, meanwhile, painted Chamberlain's ruminations in a positive light: "Many persons admire the youngster for even considering the situation, for they contend that the average person would leap at the chance to make" such a considerable sum of money.[45]

Chamberlain's potential decision to leave school, however, bothered many observers mostly because it reflected the state of (supposedly) amateur college athletics. Snider thought it was "a sad commentary" on college sports that Chamberlain was thinking of leaving and cynically pondered whether Chamberlain had actually asked KU alumni for "advice, or a raise."[46] With Chamberlain on the verge of leaving KU, sportswriters felt no obligation to maintain his image as a well-meaning celebrity, instead depicting him as a hired gun who had come to Lawrence not to excel in school or make a difference in race relations but rather to cash in on alumni gifts. *Kansan* writer George Anthan found Chamberlain's consideration of a professional offer distasteful and worried that college basketball was "becoming tainted, ever so slightly, by this aura of professionalism."[47]

As Chamberlain mulled his decision, he was barraged by reporters looking for a scoop. Frustrated by the constant telephone calls, he hung up on the *Star*'s Lawrence correspondent and then on sports editor Bob Busby. Busby did not take kindly to the slight: "Chamberlain has become quite sensitive in talking about the matter, but as long as he leaves his answers on a hazy leaving-the-door open basis, he will continue to be queried by sportswriters and broadcasters and getting huffy about it and hanging up the telephone won't do him any good with public relations. . . . He is a public figure and what he does is of public interest and his advisers should certainly remind him of that fact."[48] Although the newspapers had generally praised Chamberlain's character, this one act of defiance was enough to generate chiding. From Busby's perspective, Chamberlain had stepped out of line and needed to be reminded of his "proper" place.

With all of these competing forces pushing on him, Chamberlain finally issued a press release announcing that he would return to school. Nearly everyone breathed a sigh of relief. The local white newspapers heaped praise on Chamberlain for making the right decision.[49] Although these authors emphasized the benefits of education and Chamberlain's potential as a role model, they were surely equally excited to have Chamberlain's celebrity presence for at least one more year. For Harp, of course, Chamberlain's return would only aid his team's fortunes on the court. He could now plan for the coming season, secure that Chamberlain would be at the center of the team's campaign. Chamberlain would also continue to remain at the center of a host of conflicting interests and watchful eyes. The pressures that had caused him to ponder leaving school early would remain unabated.

LEAVING KANSAS

Although many fans and journalists predicted a return to the NCAA championship for the KU squad in the 1957–58 season, it was not to be. The team started off well, winning the preseason Big Seven tournament for the second consecutive year, but Chamberlain was injured in an early season contest and missed two games, both of which KU lost. Chamberlain's injury provided another example of the contradictory readings fans could assign to nearly every aspect of the big man's life. Accidentally kneed in the groin during the preseason tournament, Chamberlain's testicles became infected, and he was bedridden in the hospital for nearly a week. Given standards of propriety at the time, the school referred to Chamberlain's illness as a "glandular infection," and most newspapers used the same phrase. By and large, the public coverage of Chamberlain's illness was positive, and the newspapers expressed hope that he would recover quickly from the illness. The *Star*, for example, printed an Associated Press story in which Chamberlain lamented that the team would "be short without" him.[50] However, another unpublished story lingered under the surface of this pleasant dialogue. Although the university never specifically identified Chamberlain's condition, rumors soon began to spread, and according to Chamberlain's recollection, "It seemed like everyone on campus knew the precise anatomical location of my problem . . . and the rumor that I had the clap swept the campus. Kids started snickering and referring to me as 'The Big Dripper.'"[51] Although the gossip was most likely not malicious, it nonetheless fit into the stereotype of the sex-crazed black male, and its circulation suggests the permeation of that image.

Stereotypes infected other representations of Chamberlain as well. In anticipation of KU's first regular-season game against the Kansas State Wildcats, the *Kansan* published a front-page cartoon of Chamberlain shaking two wildcats, one in each hand, with the caption, "Wilton the Wildcat Killer."[52] The cartoon exaggerated not only Chamberlain's long legs but also his lips and teeth. The drawing's minstrel qualities show how pervasive stereotypes could creep into representations of Chamberlain and other black men, even in cases when the intent was to express admiration.

Although the press still covered the team closely throughout the season, the newspapers' flood of articles and photographs subsided as fans acclimated to the big man's presence. When starting guard Bob Billings missed three late-season games with a back injury, the team's hopes for a return to the NCAA tournament were quashed by two straight losses. Chamberlain, worn out from the physical abuse he received on the court, tired of the nonstop media attention, and bored by the slowdown tactics employed by opponents, decided to leave school after finishing his junior-year exams. As he departed to spend a year with the Globetrotters before joining the NBA, Chamberlain faced hostility in the white press.

Busby broke the news by observing that Chamberlain "has washed his hands of collegiate basketball and headed his $5,500 fire-red convertible back home to Philadelphia." Busby was particularly irked and felt betrayed that Chamberlain had "issued [a] strong denial" when news of his decision had been leaked a few months earlier.[53] By failing to show proper deference to the local news media, Chamberlain earned their scorn. Snider suggested that Chamberlain "let down some people … who think he should have stayed and completed his education. Some will think he owed it to KU to remain for his final year of eligibility, and some will say he represents an investment on which the school deserves three years of service." The media's perception of Chamberlain had shifted from that of an esteemed celebrity to an ungrateful child. Snider also took shots at Chamberlain's character, accusing him of "most disappointing … those who had the most faith in him." According to Snider, although Chamberlain had always "been praised by those close to him as a model boy," he had not always lived up to that reputation: stories had "circulated" that showed that "Wilt was beginning to consider himself bigger than the institution he represented." Chamberlain allegedly sometimes made "his own travel arrangements, arriving for a game a full day behind the rest of the team."[54] No longer a surefire draw for reader interest, Chamberlain became the target of accumulated resentment.

As Chamberlain headed back to Philadelphia, he left behind fans and foes, some who lamented his loss and others who criticized his decision. Had he "promoted interracial good will," as he had hoped?[55] The contradictory reactions to his career at KU indicated that no easy answer to that question existed.

CHAMBERLAIN'S LATER CAREER AND LIFE

The years following Chamberlain's departure from KU highlighted similar themes. In the fall of 1959, after a fun-filled and lucrative year with the

Harlem Globetrotters, Chamberlain entered the NBA with the Philadelphia Warriors. Over the course of his fourteen years in the league, Chamberlain would smash countless league records, claim two championships, and dazzle fans across the country with his skills. But he remained an enigmatic figure who inspired both adulation and derision, and racial politics continued to influence people's reception of him.

Chamberlain's debut in the NBA occasioned the same sense of anticipation that preceded his arrival in Lawrence. Sportswriters, coaches, and players pondered the big man's impact on the game, as there had seemingly never before been a player like him.[56] Although Russell had been an instant success with the Boston Celtics, he lacked Chamberlain's offensive repertoire, and some observers wondered if Chamberlain could be stopped. Nevertheless, the enigmatic response characteristic of Chamberlain's later years in Lawrence continued. Although fans turned out in droves to watch him play and sportswriters ratcheted up the superlatives to describe his achievements, he alienated many by "retiring" after one year to rejoin the Globetrotters. According to sports historian John Taylor, when Chamberlain returned to the Warriors after spending only the summer with the Globetrotters, "his original decision to quit [seemed] empty and disingenuous." As a result, many people "simply dismissed him as a petulant attention-seeker who couldn't be taken at his word."[57] Although national sportswriters selected Chamberlain the league's Rookie of the Year, he also offended people with an article in *Look* magazine at the conclusion of the season in which he complained about the on-court abuse he had taken.[58] Some veteran players thus came to consider the big man "a lazy, immature, stubborn, pampered cry-baby."[59] And while some fans marveled at his offensive exploits, others complained about Chamberlain's scoring binges, especially his frequent dunks. They were quick to assume that he was selfish, a reputation that dogged him in comparison with Russell.[60]

Russell played a central role in another key aspect of fans' and sportswriters' assessment of Chamberlain as a loser who could not win the most important games. This criticism proved particularly vexing to Chamberlain, who expressed his disgust with the label in his first memoir, *Wilt: Just Like Any Other 7-Foot Black Millionaire Who Lives Next Door*: "For most of my career, of course—right up until the Lakers won the NBA championship in 1972, in fact—I'd been called a 'loser.' ... For damn near half my life, I'd lived with that 'loser' label stuck on me like some big, ugly scar from an operation I'd never had."[61] Although Chamberlain maintained that "all that loser crap really got started" during his career at Kansas, when he failed to lead the school to a national championship, his rivalry with Russell undoubtedly exacerbated this image. Russell, three years older than Chamberlain, had led the University of San Francisco to back-to-back NCAA championships in 1955 and 1956 before leading the Boston Celtics to eleven NBA championships in thirteen years. Russell's team also defeated Chamberlain's squad in seven of their eight post-season contests. Thus, Russell became known as an unselfish winner, while Chamberlain was often depicted as an egotist who could not lead his team to victory.

Chamberlain's race almost certainly colored these responses. Russell deservedly earned praise for his performance on the court, but he was, in some ways, less threatening than Chamberlain. Russell always emphasized defense, a vital but less glamorous role than that occupied by Chamberlain. Indeed, Russell never led his team in scoring over the course of a season. But Chamberlain occupied center stage. As a prolific scorer who often made white opponents look bad, Chamberlain proved more distressing to white fans who did not want to see the sport dominated by a black man.

Those responses continued in ensuing years. Although some white fans and sportswriters certainly marveled at Chamberlain's stunning dunks and record-setting performances, he was always a controversial figure. During his early years in the NBA, stories circulated that his teammates were told to pass to him or sit the bench; other accounts had him yelling at a team-mate who took a wide-open layup instead of passing to Chamberlain. The big man's dunks and assault on the league's scoring records made him a villain to many. Even teammates and coaches had some difficulty getting used to Chamberlain's presence and thus did not defend him against some of the charges levied against him in the press. Although Chamberlain got along reasonably well with his teammates, he was also, according to historian Gary Pomerantz, distant from his white peers, who felt inadequate in his presence. He disappeared after games to his separate life—his nightclub in Harlem and his women and all the rest—and they did not get to know him well.[62]

In addition, as the 1960s wore on, some black activists expressed frustration with Chamberlain's low-key approach to civil rights issues. Early in his NBA career, Chamberlain distanced himself from overt activism, telling reporters, "I'm not crusading for anyone. . . . I'm no Jackie Robinson. Some persons are meant to be that way . . . others aren't."[63] Sociologist Harry Edwards, who led the efforts to have black athletes boycott the 1968 Summer Olympics in Mexico City, believed that Chamberlain was not involved enough in civil rights causes: "Wilt wasn't a guy that existed at a level where you went up and got in his face and got into an argument and discussion with him about his politics. . . . You simply looked at him, saw him for what he was, and moved on."[64] And as Pomerantz would note, when Chamberlain joined Richard Nixon's 1968 presidential campaign, "almost all" of the center's African American friends expressed their surprise and anger. Chamberlain explained that he believed Nixon to be a moderate figure and that Nixon had handled himself well at Martin Luther King Jr.'s funeral (an event Chamberlain attended). But this stance clearly alienated Chamberlain from more left-leaning black activists.[65]

One final event, long after his playing days had ended, indelibly altered people's perceptions of Chamberlain and threatened to make a mockery of his brilliant basketball career. In 1991, more than eighteen years after playing his last NBA game, Chamberlain published his second memoir, *A View from Above*. Written without the help of a ghostwriter, Chamberlain's book is a scattered, wide-ranging treatise that contains Chamberlain's observations on a whole host of subjects, including women's athletics, the opposing players he most admired, the serious problems associated with drug abuse in the ghettos, and his postbasketball volleyball career. One subject, however, generated a considerable amount of media attention and forever altered Chamberlain's image. In the book's last chapter, Chamberlain bragged that he had slept with more than twenty thousand women.[66]

Although Chamberlain qualified the boast to some degree, observing that having sex with "the same woman a thousand times" would be a "greater achievement" than having sex with a thousand different women, that nuance was lost in the media coverage that followed.[67] Instead, commentators alternately tittered and scoffed. In the days immediately following the book's release, journalists slyly giggled at the number, acknowledging its absurdity but enjoying the silly banter. The response of the *Boston Globe*'s Dan Shaughnessy is characteristic of this attitude: "Wow. And to think they called Lou Gehrig the Iron Horse. We thought 100 points in a single game was unbeatable, but this, this is ridiculous."[68] A *Saturday Night Live* skit, "Remembrances of Love," spoofed Chamberlain's claim by supposedly reenacting his encounter with "Cheryl," woman 13,906 in his list of conquests.[69]

Soon, however, commentary turned more serious. Only weeks after Chamberlain's book came out, NBA legend Earvin "Magic" Johnson shocked fans when he announced his retirement from basketball because he had contracted the HIV virus. Chamberlain's claim no longer seemed amusing but instead spoke to the dangers of promiscuity. In a self-written *Sports Illustrated* article, Johnson even referred to Chamberlain's boast: "Before I was married, I truly lived the bachelor's life. I'm no Wilt Chamberlain, but as I traveled around NBA cities, I was never at a loss for female companionship."[70] After

Johnson's announcement, sales of *A View from Above* plummeted.[71] Commentators worried that Chamberlain's boast would have potentially damaging effects on the black community as a whole.

New York Times writer Erik Eckholm wondered whether Johnson's pronouncement would increase funding for AIDS prevention and research, especially among poor, urban African Americans, or whether "the stereotypes of promiscuity and recklessness," seemingly bolstered by Chamberlain's boasts, would continue to hamper efforts.[72] African American tennis legend Arthur Ashe, infected by HIV as a result of a blood transfusion, sternly criticized both Chamberlain and Johnson in his posthumously published memoir, *Days of Grace*, for providing details and numbers regarding their sexual conquests. Such revelations, Ashe feared, would "reinforce" stereotypes of African Americans as "sexual primitives."[73]

In a matter of weeks, then, Chamberlain went from pushing a successful memoir to defending himself against charges that he promoted promiscuity. Several years later, in his little-read third book, *Who's Running the Asylum?*, Chamberlain tried to heal the wounds he had caused. He acknowledged that he might have "overdone it" by exaggerating the number of his conquests, and he grumbled that "every dunce in the world (especially those who found time to read *only* those few lines), took the number quite literally, not realizing it was a figure of speech."[74] He cautioned young people against promiscuity and apologized to his many female partners, insisting that "none" of these women was "ever just a number to me."[75] But the damage had been done. When Chamberlain died of heart failure in 1999, his obituaries emphasized his considerable skills on the court, highlighting that he was the man who had once scored one hundred points in an NBA game, but they also remembered him as the boastful fool who claimed to have had sex with twenty thousand women.[76] Even in the end, he remained an enigmatic and contradictory character.

A FRANKLY INEVITABLE FALL

Wilt Chamberlain could not avoid the spotlight. He quite literally stood out in a crowd. Tall, physically imposing, verbally effusive, and athletically brilliant, Chamberlain garnered significant attention everywhere he went, especially during his lengthy career as a basketball player. The mixed responses to Chamberlain during his time in Lawrence, from celebration of him as a hero and celebrity, to derision of him as a malcontent and prima donna, spoke to the ways in which racial politics left black athletes little room to maneuver.

Always on a short leash from the white-dominated media, black athletes such as Chamberlain could little afford to take any missteps, as whites seemed all too eager to believe in or rely on long-held stereotypes regarding African American lawlessness, sexuality, and inability to lead. That these same attitudes hounded Chamberlain during his brilliant NBA career and in the response to his ill-fated memoir should not be surprising. Although Chamberlain ruled the record books of college and professional basketball in unprecedented ways, his perch at the top of public opinion was always precarious, resting as it did on the publicity provided by mainstream newspapers. His fall from grace was nearly as inevitable as his ascension to stardom. As he once said, "Nobody roots for Goliath,"[77] to which it might have been appropriate to add, "especially if he's black in a racially divided America." White America was not yet ready for a black superstar who rewrote the record books and unabashedly proclaimed his own greatness on and off the court. The question remains: Is it ready even now?

NOTES

1. Dick Snider, "Capitalizing on Sports," *Topeka Daily Capital*, May 15, 1955, C-3.

2. Ibid., May 24, 1958, 16.

3. For more on the hoopla surrounding Chamberlain as a high school player and for an excellent narrative of Chamberlain's career at KU, see Aram Goudsouzian, "'Can Basketball Survive Wilt Chamberlain?': The Kansas Years of Wilt the Stilt," *Kansas History: A Journal of the Central Plains* 28 (Autumn 2005): 150–73, esp. 152.

4. For more on Chamberlain's early years, see Robert Allen Cherry, *Wilt: Larger Than Life* (Chicago: Triumph, 2004), 3–39; Wilt Chamberlain and David Shaw, *Wilt: Just Like Any Other 7-Foot Black Millionaire Who Lives Next Door* (New York: Macmillan, 1973), 6–47.

5. In that era, freshmen were ineligible to play varsity basketball, so Chamberlain did not play for the KU varsity in 1955–56.

6. Amber Reagan-Kendrick, "Ninety Years of Struggle and Success: African American History at the University of Kansas, 1870–1960" (Ph.D. diss., University of Kansas, 2004), 19, 32, 167.

7. Ibid., 6, 167.

8. Dowdal Davis to Roy Wilkins, December 23, 1955, Dorothy Hodge Johnson Papers, Correspondence—General, 1953–56, Spencer Research Library, University of Kansas, Lawrence.

9. "Phenom Cager, Wilt Chamberlain, to Attend K.U.," *Kansas City Call*, May 20, 1955, 10.

10. See, for example, "Star Cager Chooses K.U.," *Kansas City Star*, May 15, 1955, 3-S.

11. "Wilt the Stilt Picks Kansas to End Frantic Talent Chase," *Lawrence Daily Journal-World*, May 14, 1955, 1–2, evening ed. On May 24, 1955, Allen also thanked Davis for "the fine and continuous job that you did in interesting Wilton Chamberlain in the University

of Kansas" (Forrest C. Allen to Dowdal H. Davis, May 24, 1955, Correspondence—DD and KU Athletic Department, May–November 1955, Johnson Papers).

12. Bill Mayer, "Bill Mayer's Sport Talk," *Lawrence Daily Journal-World*, May 16, 1955, 9.

13. The pervasiveness of white writers' pride in KU's supposedly progressive nature could also be seen the following fall when Snider wrote that during Chamberlain's recruitment, "an Oklahoma representative" attempted "to talk Wilt into being the first to crack the color barrier at" the University of Oklahoma. According to Snider, Chamberlain responded, "Tell 'em I'll let the next guy do that for 'em." Snider seemed to delight in the fact that KU led Oklahoma in terms of racial integration, despite the fact that KU had integrated its sports teams only recently and had few black athletes ("Capitalizing on Sports," *Topeka Daily Capital*, September 6, 1955, 14).

14. Herschel Nissenson, "Bill Russell Is Gone, but the Stilt Has Arrived," *Kansas City Call*, December 14, 1956, 10. Russell, another African American center, and Chamberlain were often compared throughout their careers.

15. "Wilt 52, It's All True," *Kansas City Star*, December 4, 1956, 22, morning ed.

16. "The High and Mighty" (photograph), *Kansas City Star*, December 4, 1956, 22, morning ed. The afternoon edition of the newspaper featured a different photograph of Chamberlain about to dunk the ball over two white Northwestern defenders ("That Helpless Feeling" [photograph], *Kansas City Star*, December 4, 1956, 23).

17. Bill Mayer, "Bill Mayer's Sports Talk," *Lawrence Daily Journal-World*, December 5, 1956, 17.

18. Longtime KU broadcaster Max Falkenstein notes that "Kansas basketball had been spinning its wheels" before Chamberlain's arrival, as two "mediocre" seasons had followed the team's national championship in 1952 and runner-up finish in 1953. Fans viewed Chamberlain as "their ticket to another national title." See Max Falkenstein with Doug Vance, *Max and the Jayhawks: 50 Years on and off the Air with KU Sports* (Wichita, KS: Wichita Eagle and Beacon, 1996), 61.

19. Bill Snead, "Look Out Below!" (photograph), *Lawrence Daily Journal-World*, December 10, 1956, 11.

20. Donald Bogle, *Toms, Coons, Mulattoes, Mammies, and Bucks: An Interpretive History of Blacks in American Films* (New York: Continuum International, 2002), 13.

21. Bill Mayer, "Bill Mayer's Sport Talk," *Lawrence Daily Journal-World*, December 28, 1956, 8.

22. John I. Johnson, "Sport Light: 1956 Has Been Memorable for Many," *Kansas City Call*, December 28, 1956, 7.

23. "The Stilt Paces Ku Jayhawks Win over Colorado," *Kansas City Call*, March 8, 1957, 11.

24. John I. Johnson, "Sport Light," *Kansas City Call*, March 22, 1957, 10.

25. "KU Ready for League Play after Tourney Sweep," *University Daily Kansan*, January 3, 1957, 4; Bill Mayer, "Bang on Door Fuels K.U. in Vital Game," *Lawrence Daily Journal-World*, March 7, 1957, 15.

26. Cliff Long Jr., "Iowa State's Gary Thompson" (cartoon), *Topeka Daily Capital*, December 26, 1956, 12.

27. Bill Mayer, "Bill Mayer's Sport Talk," *Lawrence Daily Journal-World*, December 21, 1956, 10.

28. See, for example, "K.U. Is Choice to Win N.C.A.A.," *Kansas City Star*, March 11, 1957, 19, morning ed.

29. Chamberlain and Shaw, *Wilt*, 65. None of the newspapers or later accounts of the situation mention this event. It is possible that it is apocryphal, because Chamberlain was known to exaggerate, and some other facts do not add up. Chamberlain claimed that he was not allowed to go to a drive-in movie in his own car while in town, but he had flown down with the rest of the team, so his car was in Lawrence. Whether or not this specific incident took place, however, it is quite clear that the integrated team was an unwelcome guest in the area at large.

30. Falkenstein, *Max and the Jayhawks*, 66.

31. Ibid., 66.

32. Chamberlain and Shaw, *Wilt*, 65.

33. "A Racial Taint in O.C.U. Game," *Kansas City Star*, March 18, 1957, 17.

34. Falkenstein, *Max and the Jayhawks*, 66.

35. Chamberlain and Shaw, *Wilt*, 66. On the same page, Chamberlain praised Oklahoma City center Hubert Reed, who "came over and apologized to me for [another player] and the fans several times, and that more than offset all the abuse."

36. "Roudiness [*sic*] Mars KU–Okla. City Game in Dallas," *Kansas City Call*, March 22, 1957, 11.

37. Falkenstein, *Max and the Jayhawks*, 66.

38. "There was a young man . . ." (advertisement), *Kansas City Star*, March 22, 1957, 35.

39. Earl Morey, "N.C. Proves Ranking by Edging Jay Quint," *Lawrence Daily Journal-World*, March 25, 1957, 10.

40. Bill Mayer, "Bill Mayer's Sport Talk," *Lawrence Daily Journal-World*, March 27, 1957, 19.

41. Bill Mayer, "Wilt, Loneski State They'll Stay at K.U.," *Lawrence Daily Journal-World*, May 4, 1957, 2.

42. Jerry Dawson, "So What?" *University Daily Kansan*, May 7, 1957, 2.

43. "Don't Do It, Wilt!" (editorial), *Kansas City Call*, May 10, 1957, 18.

44. Bill Brower, "Beating the Gum," *Kansas City Call*, May 24, 1957, 10.

45. Mayer, "Wilt, Loneski State They'll Stay," 2.

46. Dick Snider, "Capitalizing on Sports," *Topeka Daily Capital*, May 5, 1957, C-1.

47. George Anthan, "Along the Jayhawker Trail," *University Daily Kansan*, May 7, 1957, 6.

48. Bob Busby, "On the Level," *Kansas City Star*, May 23, 1957, 25, morning ed.

49. See, for example, "R-o-c-k C-h-a-l-k—Wilt to Stay!" (editorial), *Topeka Daily Capital*, May 27, 1957, 4; "Wilt's Big Decision" (editorial), *Lawrence Daily Journal-World*, May 25, 1957, 4.

50. "One-Man Team? Jayhawks Say No," *Kansas City Star*, January 7, 1958, 14.

51. Chamberlain and Shaw, *Wilt*, 74.

52. Bob Sweet, "Wilton the Wildcat Killer" (cartoon), *University Daily Kansan*, February 3, 1958, 1.

53. Bob Busby, "On the Level," *Kansas City Star*, May 27, 1958, 23, morning ed.

54. Dick Snider, "Capitalizing on Sports," *Topeka Daily Capital*, May 24, 1958, 16.

55. Chamberlain reaffirmed his commitment to improving race relations in his article in *Look* magazine in which he explained his decision to leave KU. See Wilt Chamberlain with Tim Cohane and I. R. McVay, "Why I Am Quitting College," *Look*, June 10, 1958, 94.

56. For a summary of these reactions, see Cherry, *Wilt*, 93–97.

57. John Taylor, *The Rivalry: Bill Russell, Wilt Chamberlain, and the Golden Age of Basketball* (New York: Ballantine, 2005), 141.

58. Wilt Chamberlain with Tim Cohane, "Pro Basketball Has Ganged Up on Me," *Look*, March 1, 1960, 51–55.

59. Taylor, *Rivalry*, 239.

60. Gary M. Pomerantz, *Wilt, 1962: The Night of 100 Points and the Dawn of a New Era* (New York, Crown: 2005), 124–25.

61. Chamberlain and Shaw, *Wilt*, 2.

62. Pomerantz, *Wilt*, 67–68, 84.

63. Ibid., 54.

64. Ibid., 198.

65. Ibid., 202.

66. Wilt Chamberlain, *A View from Above* (New York: Signet, 1992), 258.

67. Ibid., 276.

68. Dan Shaughnessy, "With Wilt, Courtship Reached New Heights," *Boston Globe*, November 6, 1991, 73.

69. The transcript of this skit is available at http://snltranscripts.jt.org/91/91hwilt.phtml (November 7, 2008).

70. See Magic Johnson with Roy S. Johnson, "I'll Deal with It," *Sports Illustrated*, November 28, 1991, 22. Chamberlain's claim to have bedded twenty thousand women was also featured in E. M. Swift, "Dangerous Games," *Sports Illustrated*, November 28, 1991, 40–43, which discusses the dangers associated with widespread promiscuity among athletes.

71. Pomerantz, *Wilt*, 218.

72. Erik Eckholm, "Facts of Life: More Than Inspiration Is Needed to Fight AIDS," *New York Times*, November 17, 1991, E3.

73. Arthur Ashe with Arnold Rampersad, *Days of Grace* (New York: Knopf, 1993), 238.

74. Wilt Chamberlain, *Who's Running the Asylum?* (San Diego: ProMotion, 1997), 91.

75. Ibid., 91–92.

76. For two good summaries of the responses to Chamberlain's death, see Pomerantz, *Wilt*, 6; Taylor, *Rivalry*, 370.

77. This quotation is often attributed to Chamberlain in the popular press and in biographies. It was apparently a favorite expression of his, although its exact origin is unclear.

JIM BROWN
The Rise and Fall (and Rise) of a Cultural Icon
—ROBERTA J. NEWMAN

INTRODUCTION

In his 2002 HBO documentary, *Jim Brown: All American*, director Spike Lee declares his subject to be "the greatest football player ever."[1] While Lee's assessment may be something of a hyperbole, there is no question that James Nathaniel "Jim" Brown is considered to be one of the greatest fullbacks in the history of the sport. According to his Pro Football Hall of Fame page, "Brown was more than just a one-of-a-kind running back. He caught passes, returned kickoffs, and even threw three touchdown passes. His 12,312 rushing yards and 15,459 combined net yards put him in a then-class by himself. Jim was a unanimous first-team All-NFL pick eight times, 1957 through 1961, 1963–1965. He played in nine Pro Bowls in nine years and was the game's outstanding back three times. He closed out his career with a three-touchdown outburst in the 1966 Pro Bowl."[2]

Brown's college record is, if possible, even more impressive. Not only did he excel at his primary sport (rushing for 986 yards, averaging 6.2 yards per carry, and scoring fourteen touchdowns during his senior year at Syracuse University, for example), but he was also a first-team all-American in lacrosse, scoring 43 goals in ten games.[3] He also competed in track events, including a decathlon, and played some college hoops. Indeed, by all standard measures, Brown's star should shine brightly. As a former athlete who also took up acting, he should be ubiquitous, a pop culture idol in his own right. He should, moreover, be that elusive creature for whom parents, educators, and sports commentators search, often in vain. He should be a "role model." His image recently has taken a significant turn for the better, but in the past, Brown's reputation was anything but sterling, slowly sliding from its apex in the midpoint in his professional football career with the Cleveland Browns to its nadir at the end of the twentieth century.

To see the downward trajectory of Brown's public image, it is useful to dip into his 1964 autobiography, *Off My Chest*, coauthored with Myron Cope, where Brown offers his take on the issue of race in America: "The first thing the white man must understand is the depth of our protest. Does he realize that the Black Muslim's basic attitude toward whites is shared by almost 99 percent of the Negro population? I protest prejudice, but I am a prejudiced man. The white man has forced me to be prejudiced against *him*."[4]

Brown emphasizes that he is "not a Black Muslim, but rather, a member of the more rational NAACP [National Association for the Advancement of Colored People]."[5] Nevertheless, with the publication of his book, the outspoken running back's public image took a self-inflicted hit. Brown's legal troubles, which began in 1965 and for the most part stemmed from allegations of violence against women, certainly would do little to improve his public image. Yet from the moment Brown began to get his sentiments regarding race "off his chest," he was no longer just Jimmy Brown, the player who helped elevate the NFL into mainstream American consciousness. Rather, he took the first steps toward becoming Jim Brown, angry black man.

WRITING JIM BROWN

Off My Chest, the first inside-the-locker-room, tell-all book written by an athlete, predated Jim Bouton's landmark memoir, *Ball Four*, by six years and did little to endear Brown to large segments of his fan base. The book alone did not precipitate his public fall from grace. Nor, in fact, were his legal problems entirely responsible for his slide. But if identification with the Black Muslims coupled with a series of criminal allegations, however unproven, were not enough to precipitate a downturn in his public image, what was? To a great extent, Brown's image as an athlete, action hero, and activist, whether high or low, was and remains his own creation. As biographer Mike Freeman notes, "The main cause of Brown's trouble was Brown."[6] Despite Freeman's assertion, however, Brown did not bear sole responsibility for the changing perceptions of his public image. He had help from the press, including the mainstream media as well as traditional black publications. Thus, an examination of the various ways in which Brown was received by and represented, among them his contributions to the body of Brown literature, may shed further light on his downward spiral.

As is so often the case, Brown's early reputation is both a product and a reflection of the point in history in which he came to prominence. Brown first broke onto the national scene in 1955 as a sophomore at Syracuse University, at the same time the struggle for civil rights came to the attention of mainstream America with the Montgomery Bus Boycott and just one year after *Brown v. Board of Education* outlawed de jure segregation. While college football in many parts of the country was already desegregated, Brown was only the second African American to play for the Orangemen. His predecessor, quarterback Avartus Stone, was apparently talented and well liked by his teammates. Unfortunately, however, Stone had a taste for the campus coeds, many of them white.[7] Indeed, football coach Ben Schwarzwalder, whom Brown portrays as overtly racist, warned the young player not to "be like" Stone, "the greatest lover who ever walked the Syracuse campus."[8] Schwarzwalder was apparently concerned that Brown's race would make him irresistible to white women. Although Stone may have provided Schwarzwalder and some other Syracuse coaches with a negative model of the African American football player, their fear of the sexual potency of black men was hardly uncommon at the time. It is instructive to note that 1955 was marked not only by Rosa Parks's well-orchestrated act of defiance but also by the lynching of Emmitt Till for the imagined crime of whistling at a white woman. This is not to say that attitudes toward race in Syracuse, New York, were the same as those in Money, Mississippi. Still, fear that white women would necessarily be drawn to black men—especially athletic, good-looking black men such as Brown—provided a subtext to race relations.

At the same time that Brown's visible presence on the Syracuse gridiron threatened some observers, others saw it as a sign of progress. During his college years, Brown was described by Marion E. Jackson, sports columnist for Atlanta's black newspaper, the *Daily World*, as the "lithe, fleet scatback whose bronze features and broad intelligence have made him the idol of Syracuse."[9] For Jackson's readers, Brown understandably served as a potent source of race pride. Indeed, from the moment he caught the attention of both the mainstream and the black press, Brown and his story were subject to mythmaking, a process that continued during the early years of his professional career in Cleveland. The process not only applied to Brown's role as a star in the NFL but colored the way in which his past was represented.

Brown was born on February 17, 1936, on St. Simons Island, one of Georgia's barrier islands. This is, perhaps, the only biographical fact of his childhood that the media has not subjected to embroidery and amplification. Cleveland's press, covering Brown during the early part of his NFL career, transformed his modest but comfortable childhood home into a "dilapidated cabin,"[10] a description Brown labels "romantic."[11] By overemphasizing his humble beginnings, Cleveland's sportswriters appear to have set about portraying Brown as an exemplar of the American Dream: an impoverished child—an African American, no less—who, by hard work and athletic ability rises from poverty in a ramshackle hut to stardom. Brown provided a shining example not only for his race but for all Clevelanders and by extension for all Americans.

When Brown's heroic star was at its height, Sam Lacy of the *Baltimore Afro-American* also engaged in mythmaking, comparing the player's early history to that of another great African American sports icon and beacon of race pride, Jackie Robinson. Lacy called them "peas in a pod." In a speech at Howard University's all-sports banquet, Lacy noted:

> I had discovered that, aside from being tremendous competitors, Brown and Robinson had early lives which paralleled to a great extent... Both were born in Georgia—Jackie at Cairo and Jim at St. Simons Island, a small patch of land off the south coast of the state. Both were moved early, Robinson's family moving to California and Brown's parents settling in Manhasset, Long island.
>
> Jackie was a ten-letter man at UCLA, so was Jim at Syracuse. . . . Robinson excelled in football, basketball and track in college, then made his biggest mark in baseball, the sport he cared least for. . . . Brown was tops in football, basketball and track, took up lacrosse because the baseball season in upstate New York was too short, became an All-American at it. . . . Either is expert at anything he sets his mind to do, whether it be pinochle or poker (Jackie plays for stakes, Jim doesn't), tennis, billiards, checkers or golf.[12]

With such comparisons, Lacy valorizes Brown, raising him to Robinson's level. Although Lacy claims that the original intent of his speech was to entertain "several hundred youngsters" and the readers of his column, "A to Z," rather than "to preach to this generation on the importance of setting goals," the sportswriter does exactly that and more.[13] He extends what amounts to sainthood, the mantle in which Robinson was cloaked, to Brown. Lacy seems to imply that Brown and Robinson's similar backgrounds were necessary for their respective ascendancies, linking them as icons as well as men. While such may, in fact, be the case, Lacy seems to suggest that because the bare facts of Brown's early life mirror that of Robinson, Brown in effect represents the second coming of Robinson.

One of the coincidences Lacy cites, the implication that had Brown not attended university in Upstate New York, he, like Robinson, would have chosen baseball as his profession, is baseless. Brown certainly played baseball as a child, and he may have even been considered a prospect, though hardly a great one. According to *Off My Chest*, "It was true that the Yankees and Braves had offered to sign me. Casey Stengel had written me. Honey Russell, a Braves scout, had tailed me. But my guess is that they were interested in me only because of my size and speed. . . . Actually, baseball was my weakest sport." Still, Brown was invited to attend spring training with the Cleveland Indians in 1958. Brown implied that despite what Indians general manager Frank Lane suggested, the move was motivated by the money the team would make by wheeling Brown "out into vast Cleveland Stadium for a debut that would pack the house with the curious."[14]

Given the fact that Brown did not play college baseball and by his own admission was encouraged to take up lacrosse by the coach, Roy Simmons, who also served as an assistant to Schwarzwalder,[15] why does Lacy privilege baseball in his Robinson/Brown comparison? In 1961, the year Lacy's column appeared, lacrosse was little known outside bastions of the sport in the Northeast and Canada. It certainly did not receive regular coverage in Lacy's *Afro-American* and its ilk or in the mainstream press. While lacrosse is America's oldest team sport and was invented by Native Americans, its seems fair to say that in Brown's day, the sight of an African American playing the game was far from common. Football, however, was covered fairly extensively by the black press. Still, in 1961, the NFL lacked the hold over the imagination of Lacy's readership that baseball possessed, and among those African American athletes who succeeded at team sports in a formerly segregated arena, none was more iconic than the breaker of the Major League color line. Although Robinson excelled at football in college, Lacy mentions it only as one of a list of sports, placing almost no emphasis on this legitimate point of comparison. Thus, it is possible to suggest that to raise Brown to the reputational level of Robinson, it was preferable, if not necessary, to associate the younger athlete with the older not just by biographical coincidence but by the sport with which Robinson was synonymous to Lacy's readers.

Another aspect of Brown's life prior to Syracuse and the NFL that was subject to mythmaking of a different type was his brief career as a member of a "gang," the Gaylords, which he claims to have joined after moving with his mother to Long Island, New York. Of the Gaylords, their presumed allies, and their rivals, Brown notes, "Our Long Island gangs. . . were not of the zip gun variety known in Brooklyn. Our boys carried switch blade pen knives only to build up their own egos. They liked to stand on corners clicking their knives, but they never used them in fights."[16] Furthermore, "Actually, I guess I never quite fit the mold of a gang warlord. Though I never minded a fight, I never picked one, and I disliked bullies."[17] Freeman characterizes the Gaylords as a "gaggle of kids that could loosely be called a gang" and that contributed little to Manhasset's crime rate. The Gaylords did, however, play a lot of football.[18]

If the Gaylords wreaked any havoc at all, it went equally unnoticed by many of Brown's contemporaries and the local press.[19]

Brown's stature as a gang warlord, however, is amplified in subsequent profiles of the athlete, changing and becoming more central to his myth, depending on the position and purpose of the individual profiler. In the introduction to a 1968 *Playboy* interview with Brown, by then a full-time actor, Alex Haley describes his subject as "always big and strong for his age": "Brown applied his talents more in the streets than in school, and soon fought his way to 'warlord' status in the Gaylords."[20] Here, Haley embroiders the facts, essentially turning Brown from a kid whose gang activity he characterized as "an enactment of the *West Side Story* bit"[21] into a bona fide street fighter who battled his way to the top of an already established violent organization. Again, Haley's depiction of Brown's gang activity is a function of the purpose of the interview—to profile an actor whose on-screen personae were always fighters.

James Toback takes the image of Brown as street fighter even farther in *Jim: The Author's Self-Centered Memoir on the Great Jim Brown*. Following a tennis match between Toback and Brown, the athlete turned actor tells the writer, "I don't rap if I have nothing to say to someone. I just walk away. And if a cat or chick's rappin' to me and don't have nothin' to say, I'll turn them right out." Toback's response to Brown's exegesis on personal interactions is most telling: "It was not impossible that he had said exactly the same words, with the same hard look, following the same laugh, to a candidate for the Gaylords, a formidable gang on the South Shore of Long Island which he ruled as warlord twenty years before."[22] Here, Toback makes Brown into a hardened leader who treats wannabe gang members with nothing but contempt. Unlike Haley, whose image of Brown stems from an interview, Toback's is entirely the writer's creation. In fact, his source for information regarding Brown's role in the Gaylords is *Off My Chest*. Toback's image is a representation of the way the writer chooses to imagine Brown as a teenager.

Toback's motive for imagining Brown as a cold, dispassionate leader of a "formidable gang" is informed by the title and purpose of his book. Reviewing *Jim* for the *New York Times*, Calvin C. Hernton writes, "James Toback reveals as much about himself in this book as he does about his subject. In fact, the book reads like an autobiographical-biographical sensitivity encounter between Toback and Brown and, as the title suggests, Toback makes no bones about his underlying motivations for wanting to interview Brown. It is not merely because Brown is a great athlete and a great man, it is because he is also a black man around whom exists an aura of mammoth sexuality."[23]

Indeed, Toback does more than interview Brown in this book. With his marriage having collapsed and having abandoned a profile of the athlete/actor originally slated to appear in *Esquire*, Toback moved in with Brown, availing himself of the opportunity to bask in Brown's reflected masculinity and sexual magnetism. By portraying Brown as a true gang leader and warlord, with no time to rap with a cat or chick who has nothing of interest to say, Toback, a cat with whom Brown has regularly chosen to rap, elevates himself to the status of one of Brown's gang of imagined warriors. In Toback's mind, he is a Gaylord. Building on Brown's reputation as an action hero, already established by Haley and other writers, Toback's real goal here is to enhance his personal reputation.

A CROSSED STAR

Brown began his NFL career, his reputation still trending upward, as the first-round draft pick of the Cleveland Browns. Although his signing received scant coverage in the mainstream media, the black press duly noted the elevation of the college star into the professional ranks, showering him with accolades. In any era, a football player of Brown's ability would have shone brightly. That Brown was one of the faces of the newly popular NFL made it shine all the brighter. Of the increasing visibility of football and with it the increasing visibility of African Americans such as Brown, David Halberstam writes, "In terms of the coming technology and the coming of gifted black athletes, a dual revolution was sweeping across the country: in the quality of athletic ability of those able to play, and in the number of people now able to watch. Professional football, which in comparison with professional baseball, had been virtually a minor sport before the arrival of television, now flowered under the sympathetic eye of the camera, its importance growing even as the nation was being wired city by city and house by house for television."[24]

Indeed, as Halberstam notes, Brown was nothing if not the telegenic face of the newly popular, newly visible sport.[25] But visibility in a televised world did not come without the price of intensified scrutiny, and as the face of the NFL—an African American face in a country still polarized by race—Brown's public image, which to this point had been constructed by the sporting press, both mainstream and black, was primed for a hit when advance notice and early excerpts of *Off My Chest* appeared in the press in 1964.

Not at all surprisingly, reactions to Brown's "as-told-to" autobiography varied according to the source. For *Los Angeles Times* sports columnist Sid Ziff, *Off My Chest* was certainly controversial, but that controversy was not racial but centered on Brown's assessment of his former coach, Paul Brown, the team's architect and namesake. Though there was no love lost between the Browns' Browns, the specific issue referenced by Ziff was a "cribbing scandal," the result of the coach's inflexibility. According to Jim Brown, Paul Brown "clung to certain rituals that made his training camp famous." Among these were aptitude tests that were virtually impossible to pass. To do so, players, even those who had been with the team for years, carried "gyp sheets" into the test with the tacit knowledge of the coaches who proctored the exam. According to Brown, "The extent of their use in Paul's celebrated examinations made the West Point Cribbing Scandal look like child's play."[26] Brown was scandalized neither by the use of the gyp sheets nor by Paul Brown's irrationality at subjecting players to tests they could not hope to pass without cheating but rather by the fact that Jim Brown had outed his former teammates, who "would vaguely evade the issue [of the tests]. They didn't want to put their ex-teammates who still had to deal with the exams, on the spot." Ziff continues, "The way Jim Brown lashes out at his former coach in that book is absolutely brutal."[27] Brown's exposure of the scandal branded him as a less than exemplary teammate, a crime far worse than cheating on a quiz.

Response to Brown's violation of the sanctity of the clubhouse was nothing in comparison to the negative reaction stirred up by his favorable comments about the Black Muslims. Many white Americans had been introduced to the Black Muslims by means of Alex Haley's interview with Malcolm X, which appeared in *Playboy* in May 1963. Haley prefaces the interview by describing the sect as "a relatively unknown and radical religious Negro religious cult," grown into an impressive movement, with views "spiked with a black-supremacy version of Hitler's Aryan radical theories."[28] Indeed, Brown follows up his statement of support for the movement with a critique of its teachings: "Certainly if a Muslim approaches the average Negro in the street and tells him every white man is a devil and that we Negroes must one day form a separate nation, the Negro in the street will laugh at him."[29] Nevertheless, much of the negative reception of *Off My Chest*, excerpted in *Look* in advance of its publication, focused entirely on Brown's observations regarding the perception of whites by much of African America, without a word about his criticism of the sect's extremism.

In what might be best described as an anti-Brown diatribe written in the form of a letter to the athlete published in the *Los Angeles Times*, Jim Murray reacts to Brown's statement that he is "all for" the Muslims, also referencing Haley's Malcolm X interview.

Now, just a darn minute, Jim. Running with a football doesn't make you General Manager of the world, baby. Do you know what these Muslims are putting down?

Well, I'll tell you, since you and Cassius Clay have brought the subject up.

In the first place, one of the head guys in that outfit recently told his story in print. He was a cuckolder, pimp, hophead, burglar, numbers hustler, jailbird and with a history of insanity in the family. Of course, nobody's perfect. But how'd you like your sister married to him, Jim?[30]

That Murray did not read Brown's words thoroughly is clear enough, but the columnist's lack of accuracy is unimportant. The level of vitriol aimed at Brown is indicative of the shift in Brown's public image. And Murray was not alone in his rage. According to the *Washington Post*, Brown was the subject of at least one bomb threat, received by a producer at Cleveland's KYW television.[31]

As might be expected, the black press's reaction to Brown's statement was considerably more positive than that of Ziff, Murray, and the potential bomber. Bill Nunn Jr., sports editor of the *Pittsburgh Courier*, supported Brown: "A surprising number of people are of the opinion that Cleveland's Jim Brown should have kept his opinions about the Black Muslims to himself. We disagree wholeheartedly with those individuals. We agree with Brown when he says that any group that helps the Negro in his drive for first class citizenship is doing a job, whether we agree with their motives or not."[32]

It is hardly surprising that Nunn would support Brown's stance. After all, if what Brown wrote was accurate, the player was not telling the *Courier*'s readers anything they did not already know. Despite Nunn's support, the damage to Brown's reputation, apparently even among African Americans, was such that he felt compelled to refute any connection to the Black Muslims, at least according to an advertisement for an article in *Ebony* that ran in the *Afro-American* in December 1964. The ad features a crude drawing of an angry-looking, powerful Brown next to a bold headline, "I'm No Black Muslim."[33]

If his vocal support of the Black Muslims, bolstered by personal and business relationships with Cassius Clay and other members of the Nation of Islam, and his partnership in Main Bout, a company that arranged television rights for prizefights, hurt Brown's reputation, his legal troubles, which began in 1965, dealt a series of even harder blows. On June 22, Brown was arraigned and subsequently tried for assault and battery. His accuser, the first woman to publicly claim to have been attacked by Brown, was eighteen-year-old Brenda

Ayres. Surprisingly, his arrest garnered little or no attention in the mainstream press. Trial reportage by the *New York Times*, the *Washington Post*, and the *Chicago Tribune*, for example, was limited to a few column inches buried inside. None of those papers sent writers to report on the proceedings, relying instead on coverage from the Associated Press and United Press International. The relative lack of attention as well as the dispassionate approach to the case would seem to be in keeping with those publications' images as outlets for "serious" news. Although America's obsession with celebrity arguably began in the 1920s, and although the lives of celebrities were certainly more visible in the age of television than prior to it, the intense scrutiny of the private lives of public figures was not deemed material appropriate for coverage by the "papers of record" and their ilk. However, given the column inches devoted more recently to the legal travails of Barry Bonds and Michael Vick, it is perhaps a bit surprising that more attention was not paid to the trial of a player of Brown's magnitude, at least in the papers' sports sections.

The same cannot be said for the black press, which uniformly treated this case in the most sensational terms, featuring headlines such as the *Amsterdam News*'s front-page shocker, "The Jim Brown Case: Too Sexy to Be Printed!"[34] The *Pittsburgh Courier*'s coverage was less lurid but no less attention-grabbing: "'Jim Brown Slapped Me on Three Dates'"[35] First prize for sensationalism might well have gone to *Jet*. The lead paragraph of its coverage of the final verdict, under the headline of "The Spicy Trial of Jim Brown: Grid Star Denies Sex Acts," begins, "In the intimate art of love making, James Nathaniel (Jim) Brown was accused by a Cleveland teen-ager of bringing gridiron tactics into the bedroom. Attractive high-school dropout Brenda Ayres charged that the powerful football hero hit, kicked and made attempts to force her into a repugnant love-making act after having normal sexual intercourse." The article further notes Brown's acquittal in a trial "presided over by a red-haired, attractive woman, Judge Blanche Krupansky." The spectators, according to *Jet*, "heard some juicy testimony during the spicy trial."[36] Here, the opening paragraph reads more like the beginning of a soft-core "rape-romance" novel—a bodice ripper—than journalism. The article's language— its description of what amounts to a violent act of "lovemaking" and its focus on "juicy testimony"—seems anachronistic, to say the least, to contemporary, twenty-first century readers. To a great extent, this may be explained by the source. For all its status as the mouthpiece of urban African America, the black press, dailies and weeklies alike, were first and foremost tabloids. Like all tabloids, these papers tended to sensationalize stories relating to sex and violence—and in this case, both.

The Ayres case and the failed paternity suit that followed initially appear to have done little damage to Brown's reputation at the time. But it and an earlier, barely publicized accusation of rape by a twenty-one-year-old Ohio woman who ultimately chose not to press charges[37] contributed to Brown's failing public image over the next few years.

At the same time, Brown shifted careers, a move that also negatively affected his reputation. In 1966, fast on the heels of the Ayres case and a successful NFL season in which he won his second MVP award, Brown became embroiled in a showdown with Cleveland owner, Art Modell, the result of an unforeseen delay in shooting the player's second feature film, *The Dirty Dozen*. When the shooting schedule prevented Brown from attending training camp, Modell threatened to release him. In response, Brown retired.

A. S. "Doc" Young offered his take on Brown's retirement in the *Chicago Defender*: "This is not said in disrespect of Brown. It may well be true that just as he said, he has quit the gridiron. It may also be true that he honestly beleives [*sic*] he's quit the gridiron. Destiny knows a little secret: He'll be back." Still, suggesting that Cleveland fans go ahead and plan "Jimmy Brown Day," Young notes, "There are some who say Jim Brown's retirement is no more than a coolly calculated publicity stunt for the MGM movie, 'Dirty Dozen.' Others say this is no more than a coolly calculated play to get a raise and make him more highly-paid than Willie Mays and Bill Russell, if not King Pete [*sic*], the Brazilian soccer star."[38]

That Young's prediction proved false is relatively unimportant here. Central to the construction of Brown's public image is the distrust with which the journalist treats Brown's motives for retirement. Young is careful to qualify his statement, noting that he does not intend to suggest that the former player was either engaging in a publicity stunt or using retirement as a negotiating ploy, only that "some" people are making such allegations. Nevertheless, the language of the column displays a certain suspicion as well as a certain realism regarding Brown's reputation that was not present in earlier coverage in the pages of the *Defender* and other black periodicals, not even in regard to the Ayres case. Where did this suspicion and realism come from? The revised take on Brown evidence by Young and the "others" who say things about Brown may have been colored by the mounting evidence that Brown was not in fact the second coming of Robinson but rather, the sort of person who might behave in a manner not befitting the mythologized public image with which he had been bestowed.

As an actor, at least at the outset, Brown had moderate success. He received decent reviews in the mainstream press for *The Dirty Dozen* and *Ice Station*

Zebra as well as several minor action films. Indeed, according to United Press International Hollywood correspondent Vernon Scott, Brown displayed the "qualities of a John Wayne," as audiences could identify with both actors' "rugged individuality, an outer gentleness masking the brute strength of the man."[39] Brown's brute strength and rugged individuality also led feminist journalist Gloria Steinem to write, "It isn't surprising now, at the age of thirty-two, with four movies released and four more finished, that the kind of star he's becoming is a black John Wayne; or maybe John Wayne with just a hint of Malcolm X thrown in."[40] While this assessment may seem like high praise from Steinem,[41] her *New York* magazine article also addresses Brown's tendency toward personal and professional violence. Replying, though perhaps not directly to Vernon Scott, Steinem writes, "The Jim Brown mask, a reputation for rare but deadly violence on the playing field, and an unmatched record for emerging unscathed from bone-chilling attempts to bench him, for the game if not for good: all these things he built up in football, and brings them with him to the screen." Steinem understands, however, that Brown's tendency toward violence is "underlined by news stories from time to time, mostly involving women."[42]

Later in her profile of Brown, Steinem refers directly to his second high-profile arrest for a violent crime, this time involving a girlfriend, Eva Bohn-Chin, a biracial Swiss model. Of Brown's taste for women of Bohn-Chin's "type," Steinem, who also "dated" Brown, according to Freeman,[43] writes, "Being a male chauvinist, he has low standards for women, and always seems to be surrounded by squadrons of manicurists, sales girls, and that international breed of models who don't model and actresses who don't act."[44] On June 10, 1968, police responded to a phone call from a neighbor, reporting what sounded like a bloody brawl, and found Bohn-Chin, a model who did not model, lying unconscious, twenty feet under the balcony of Brown's apartment. Authorities arrested Brown and charged him with having pushed her. Brown was also charged with "felony battery against a peace officer"— that is, shoving a policeman. Charges were dropped after Bohn-Chin refused to name Brown as her assailant.[45]

Although Brown was never officially charged with harming Bohn-Chin, the incident seriously damaged his public image in a way that even his praise of the Muslims and his growing radicalism, the Ayres case, and the circumstances of his retirement from football had not. Taken together, however, Brown's outspokenness regarding race, his decision to quit football at the height of his career, and, most particularly, his occasional outbursts of rage, informed public opinion regarding Bohn-Chin's injury. Indeed, in that court of public opinion, he was tried and convicted.

In regard to the persistent stain on his reputation left by the Bohn-Chin incident, Brown had plenty to say. More than a year after the arrest, Brown was again taken into custody, this time after a traffic accident. The angry Brown dictated a press release to Toback in which the former player offered his response to both cases. He suggested that the Los Angeles County Sheriff's Office was looking for an excuse to incarcerate Brown. According to Brown, Bohn-Chin "fell from the balcony."[46] Not until 1989, when Brown was promoting *Out of Bounds*, his second autobiography (coauthored with Steve Delsohn), did Brown offer a reason for Bohn-Chin's accident, telling Megan Rosenfeld of the *San Francisco Chronicle* that Bohn-Chin jumped. According to Brown, he and Bohn-Chin were arguing about plans for "a playful evening" involving the couple and three of her female friends when the police came to the door. "While Brown was trying to persuade the cops that it was just a minor domestic dispute, Eva Bohn-Chin tried to vamoose over a balcony, but fell and rolled under it."[47] In this version, what straightforward wire-service coverage reported as a "dispute" violent enough to have left blood all over Brown's apartment turned into a planning session for group sex. Here, Brown's reason for rewriting or at least editing history seems quite clear. His career in bad shape, Brown needed to sell books, and nothing sells like sex. As such, Brown attempted to use the event to recast himself in one of his favorite roles, that of the Hollywood swinger.

In 2002, however, Brown told Spike Lee a different story, claiming that Bohn-Chin jumped from the balcony to escape possible deportation. According to Brown, his companion was in the United States on an expired visa and feared arrest. Here, Brown again engages in revisionist history in an attempt to recast his reputation from that of swinger with a flippant attitude toward women, especially young women, to that of full-time social activist, engaged in antigang intervention. After all, for the companion of a socially aware, respected member of the community such as Brown to have run away from the fascistic police, bent on deporting her for no good reason, is certainly understandable. For the girlfriend of a swinger to have gotten into an argument about how many women to invite to an orgy is not.

Even without the benefit of hindsight and Brown's attempts to recast the story, opinions regarding the incident differed widely. Of Brown's culpability and the response of Hollywood and his audience, Steinem writes, "It's the kind of *Rashomon* story that no one, including the principals, will ever be totally clear on. Headlines assume an independent truth (early stories said the girl had a broken neck, and Jim was charged with intent to commit murder), but the public relations men needn't have worried. What audiences don't forgive are acts that belie the images they cherish. . . . If violent Jim Brown is accused of more violence, that's forgivable [because] he is potentially the Bad Black Man, and both Negro and white audiences enjoy it."[48]

As Steinem suggests, Brown's public image as a Bad Black Man was not out of keeping with someone who was always cast as the Bad Black Man. Although earlier in his career, a few roles such as that of Captain Leslie Anders in *Ice Station Zebra* may not have been cast according to racial stereotypes, the characters Brown played became increasingly in keeping with his public image.

In 1969, Brown costarred with Raquel Welch (who played an Indian vixen) in *100 Rifles*, notable because it featured Hollywood's first interracial sex scene. The film was a box-office success. So, too, was . . . *tick* . . . *tick* . . . *tick* (1970). Nevertheless, in the years following the Bohn-Chin incident and the later flap surrounding the car accident, Brown's star, already tarnished, began to fade. He was fully aware that one of the factors that led his acting career to, as he put it, grind "to a halt," was his reputation for violence, especially against women. In an excerpt from *Out of Bounds* published in *Ebony*, Brown notes, "In 1969 [*sic*], I received national headlines for supposedly throwing a woman off a balcony. It didn't happen. I was never even charged, but trial by headline is a powerful force. If I was to be fair about this, and if I was a producer, and an actor got the same headline, I might have been reluctant to hire him myself."[49]

Brown, however, did not blame just his track record regarding violence toward women for the paucity of parts he was offered, remarking instead,

> I think the primary factor (in Hollywood's snub of me) was my activism. I was increasingly perceived as a militant. I had even spent some time with Malcolm X, made no attempt to hide that fact, and Malcolm made many people nervous. Even after Malcolm was killed, many people believed I was a Muslim, despite the fact that I was never a Muslim, though I had Muslim friends, and despite the fact that Malcolm himself had broken from the Muslims before his death. Regardless, when people want to bring things out of your past, pit them against you, they do, and my personal relationships did not endear me to Hollywood. Nor, later on, did my friendship with Louis Farrakhan. I also used my celebrity status to make statements about the oppression of blacks.[50]

Although Brown chooses to represent himself as having been silenced by a film industry threatened by his radicalism and association with the Black

Muslims, just as white and even some African American football fans had been alienated in Cleveland in 1964, a look at Brown's filmography from the first half of the 1970s tells a very different story. Audiences, as Steinem suggests, had no trouble seeing Brown cast as an angry black man, so much so that he became a star of "Blaxploitation" films.

Blaxploitation, a subgenre of action films aimed at African American audiences, was so designated by *New York* magazine in its description of *Superfly* (1972). According to Ed Guerrero, the films, exemplified by Melvin Van Peebles's *Sweet Sweetback's Baadasssss Song*, virtually always involve a "'bad Nigger' who challenges the oppressive white system and wins, thus articulating the main feature of the Blaxploitation formula."[51] Brown's participation in Blaxploitation films *Black Gunn* (1972), *Slaughter* (1972), and *Slaughter's Big Rip-Off* (1973) may have done little to burnish his reputation with mainstream audiences. Nevertheless, it is clear that Brown's assessment of Hollywood's reluctance to employ him in the 1970s is not accurate.

Predictably, the mainstream press—in this case, the decidedly genteel *Christian Science Monitor*—had nothing good to say about Brown's forays into Blaxploitation or about the genre itself, for that matter, accusing Brown in his title performance in *Slaughter's Big Rip-Off* of glorifying "vengeful, dehumanizing violence. Casual, dehumanizing sex. A perverse worship of guns and other weapons. A sly reliance on elements of racial hatred."[52] Precisely these characteristics, however, made the genre popular with its target audience. Indeed, Brown's self-defined radicalism, positing himself as just the sort of "bad nigger" the *Monitor* decried, may very well have helped him secure roles in Blaxploitation films, at least for a while.

THE ANTI-SIMPSON

Contrary to Brown's notion that he was too hot for Hollywood to handle, compounded by his inaccurate assertion that "in the 1970's, if a black actor was fortunate, he went back to playing second honcho to the white hero,"[53] Brown's acting career may have continued to fade because after a while, his films failed to draw. By any standard, 1973 was a banner year for the Blaxploitation genre, owing to the release of *Coffey, Cleopatra Jones, Shaft in Africa,* and *The Mack,* among other films. But *Slaughter's Big Rip-Off* made less money at the box office than its nearest competition in the genre, *Scream, Blacula, Scream.* Brown's reputation for "badness" not withstanding, he ceased to attract audiences. After 1974, Brown's on-screen appearances were limited to a series of spaghetti westerns and to guest spots on television programs on the order of *CHiPs* and *The A Team*. Indeed, by the late 1970s, Brown's public image had gone from that of a fresh-faced college football star, capable of inspiring fans of all races, to that of a brilliant athlete who was arguably the first NFL superstar, albeit with a chip on his shoulder, to a movie star with a history of violence against women, and finally to irrelevance.

On the visibility of black male athletes in sculpting the public image of African Americans in the 1950s, 1960s, and early 1970s in general, Leon E. Wynter writes,

> Even as black male athletes like Bill Russell, Willie Mays, "Sugar Ray" Robinson, and Wilt Chamberlain were bringing acceptance of color into professional sports in the post–Jackie Robinson era, they had to come off as noble warriors, not as renegade, arrogant, or boastful bluesmen. Muhammad Ali and Jim Brown, of course, were far off the scale in this regard, but so were their absolute athletic talents. They survived all that their mouths got them into—Jim Brown even made a few mainstream movies toward the anything-goes end of the 1960s. But neither really became a legitimate commercial pop icon until the 1980s, when rap and hip-hop vindicated all of Ali's arrogance and Brown's combination of nationalism, misogyny, and gangsterism, in general and by name.[54]

As Brown's reception by the press earlier in his career indicates, he entered the public eye as a commercial pop-cultural icon, a noble warrior, as Wynter suggests. But Brown did not really reenter the public eye again until the 1980s. Unlike Ali, who reentered the public consciousness and attained commercial viability as a national hero, Brown played the public role of villain. He may have "survived" the trouble brought on by his mouth, but his image was anything but clean. Black nationalism, misogyny, and gangsterism may have been vindicated by rap and hip-hop, but Jim Brown was not.

Brown's reputational resurrection ultimately may not have been entirely of his own doing or his own press. In 1969, as Brown was making interracial love to Welch on screens across America, the Buffalo Bills selected as the draft's first overall pick a celebrated running back out of the University of Southern California, a Heisman Trophy winner. According to Murray, never a fan of Brown, a Heisman winner such as Orenthal James (O. J.) Simpson was required to be "trustworthy, loyal, helpful, friendly, courteous, kind, obedient, cheerful, thrifty, brave, clean, and reverent. He should make an Eagle Scout look shiftless." Murray continued, "Joe Namath never even came close, Paul Hornung was the only one they almost made give it back. Jim Brown got tackled on the goal line."[55] Murray implies that Simpson's receipt of the award testifies to his good character, while Brown's failure to win the Heisman shows that he was a ne'er-do-well radical who bit the hand that fed him. Simpson was not only a better man than Brown but arguably a better ballplayer. He of the sterling reputation and Heisman also was the first professional fullback to rush for 2003 yards in a single season, breaking Brown's decade-old record of 1,863. Simpson was also a more successful mainstream actor than Brown. In 1974, just one year after *Slaughter's Big Rip-Off* tanked at the box office, Simpson had a hit with *The Towering Inferno*. He also went on to appear in all three wildly popular *Naked Gun* films. Though Brown was no stranger to product endorsements during the height of his popularity, Simpson eclipsed his predecessor there, too, starring in a long-running series of commercials for Hertz Rent-a-Car, among other products. As Wynter notes, Simpson broke new ground for retired black athletes in terms of both visibility and commercial viability.[56]

But as Wynter also observes, Simpson did not achieve true pop icon status until 1994. On June 17 of that year, Simpson led police on a televised, slow-speed chase in his white Ford Bronco, after which he was arrested for the murder of his ex-wife, Nicole Brown Simpson, and her friend, Ronald Goldman. Although Simpson was acquitted of the murder charges with the help of lawyer Johnny Cochran, who had previously represented Brown in a 1985 sexual assault case,[57] the incident was another in a long line of arrests for violence against women. And like Brown almost two decades earlier, Simpson was convicted in the court of public opinion. Indeed, even in cases of alleged murder, Simpson managed to eclipse Brown, succeeding in killing where Brown failed to kill Bohn-Chin.

How did the Simpson case affect Brown's reputation? In 1999, Brown again went to trial for an act of violence against a woman. After a fraught 911 call by Brown's wife, Monique, he was arrested for beating the window of her Jaguar with a shovel. Although he was acquitted of making "terroristic threats" against her, Brown was convicted of the lesser charge of misdemeanor vandalism with domestic-violence conditions. Monique Brown came to her husband's defense in the media, most notably on *Larry King Live*, where the couple characterized the affair as Brown's understandable response to his wife's premenstrual syndrome.[58] Nevertheless, Brown was fined eighteen hundred dollars, sentenced to three years' probation, ordered to attend domestic-violence counseling for a year, and given the choice of performing forty hours of labor on a work crew or four hundred hours of community service. When he refused the counseling, he was sentenced to serve 180 days in jail.[59]

Following his trial, Simpson, whom a majority of Americans (or at least white Americans) believe ought to have been convicted, went back to playing golf and living the life of a jet-setter, albeit one of reduced means as a consequence of the financial burden of his defense, at least until a civil court found against him in a wrongful death suit. More recently, Simpson was convicted on ten felony counts, including kidnapping, in an attempt to retrieve sports memorabilia by force, and sentenced to fifteen years in prison. Brown, conversely, "took his medicine," represented himself as a political prisoner and a prisoner of conscience, and used his incarceration to make what he defined as a positive impact on society and on his own public image. Simpson may have broken Brown's single-season NFL rushing record, made more money in movies and product endorsements, and may even have been a better murderer, but Brown was a better convict. Brown used the final result of his tendency toward violence, which had injured his reputation and placed his public image on life support, to reverse the public's perception of him. Essentially, his stint in jail made Brown the anti–O. J.

In prison, Brown was interviewed by Jon Saraceno in that most mainstream of media outlets, *USA Today*. Brown commented on his status as a self-styled political prisoner: "If I were domesticated, I would be accepted racially. I'd have approval if I stayed in my place. The worst thing an African-American man can do is be as free as those more powerful than he is."[60] Saraceno concluded that Brown's incarceration proved nothing: "Choosing jail was not a selfless act by a wronged man but the epitome of self-absorption and martyrdom. Fact is, Brown had become politically irrelevant, despite his good works aimed at empowering African-Americans. He now has a platform."[61] No fan of Brown, Saraceno still makes an important point.

SPOKESMAN

Brown parlayed the publicity generated by his incarceration to begin the project of reputational resurrection. He told *Sports Illustrated*'s Don Yaeger, "I'm talking about making major changes in the educational system that would impact an entire race. I'm talking about stopping these young gang members from killing each other."[62] Here, Brown refers directly to his Amer-I-Can Foundation, dedicated to working with gang members through economic empowerment—"green power." By positioning himself not only as a former gang member but as a convict, stoically doing his time, Brown gives himself, and, by extension, Amer-I-Can, street cred.

More recently, reformed ex-con Brown has become something of a spokesman for jailed football players, suggesting in an ESPN interview that Vick use his time in jail to reflect on his actions and learn from his mistakes. Moreover, Brown has become a spokesman for African America, or at least for former African American radical, ex-con athletes reentering the mainstream. Owing perhaps to Ali's slurred speech, Brown is now the go-to ex-athlete turned cultural icon for issues regarding race. On Inauguration Day 2009, who did ESPN seek out for his comments regarding the election and installation of Barack Obama, the first African American president? Brown.

In a 1970 interview conducted while he was promoting . . . *tick . . . tick . . . tick*, Brown tells the *Chicago Defender*, "I don't think about my image and I don't care about it." He continues, "Images are just that—shadows in the minds of people who don't even know you. A man and his image are seldom similar."[63] Despite his protestations to the contrary, Brown was an active, willing participant in the creation of his reputation, which went from golden to brass before recently moving back to sterling, over the course of half a century. In fact, the media's portrayal of Brown, including his self-portrayal, may be seen not only as indicative of his reputational shifts but in large part as their cause. Later in the *Defender* interview, Brown states, "A lot of people in Hollywood get to believing their own images. A cat's in trouble when he does that. If you really know yourself, then what others think is the least important thing in the world."[64] But for Brown, what others think or thought was and remains the most important thing in the world.

NOTES

1. *Jim Brown: All American* (DVD) (HBO, 2004).

2. "Jim Brown: Career Biography and Statistics," Pro Football Hall of Fame Web site, n.d., http://www.profootballhof.com/hof/member.jsp?player_id=33 (February 15, 2009).

3. "Jim Brown," Sports Placement Service, 2009, http://www.sportsplacement.com/sps/#/clients (March 1, 2010).

4. James N. Brown and Myron Cope, *Off My Chest* (New York: Doubleday, 1964), 166.

5. Ibid.

6. Mike Freeman, *Jim Brown: The Fierce Life of an American Hero* (New York: Morrow, 2006), 264.

7. Ibid., 82.

8. Brown and Cope, *Off My Chest*, 116. In the book, Brown and Cope give Stone the pseudonym Marion Farris.

9. Marion E. Jackson, "Sports of the World," *Atlanta Daily World*, December 28, 1956, 7.

10. Freeman, *Jim Brown*, 50.

11. Brown and Cope, *Off My Chest*, 98.

12. Sam Lacy, "Some of the Athletes I Have Known," *Baltimore Afro-American*, June 3, 1961, 13.

13. Ibid.

14. Brown and Cope, *Off My Chest*, 84.

15. Ibid., 140.

16. Ibid., 107.

17. Ibid., 108.

18. Freeman, *Jim Brown*, 59.

19. Ellen Price, telephone interview by author, January 2009. Price is a former Manhasset resident and Brown contemporary.

20. Alex Haley, "*Playboy* Interview: Jim Brown (February 1968)," in *The Playboy Interviews*, ed. Stephen Randall (New York: Ballantine, 1993), 306.

21. Brown and Cope, *Off My Chest*, 107.

22. James Toback, *Jim: The Author's Self-Centered Memoir on the Great Jim Brown* (Garden City, NY: Doubleday, 1971), 17.

23. Calvin C. Hernton, review of *Jim: The Author's Self-Centered Memoir on the Great Jim Brown*, by James Toback, *New York Times Book Review*, May 16, 1971, 44.

24. David Halberstam, *The Fifties* (New York: Villard, 1993), 692.

25. Ibid., 693.

26. Brown and Cope, *Off My Chest*, 39. In 1951, ninety cadets, including most of the members of the football team, were dismissed from West Point for cheating on exams ("The Nation: Trouble at West Point," *Time*, August 13, 1951, http://www.time.com/time/magazine/article/0,9171,889147,00.html [February 15, 2009]).

27. Sid Ziff, "Jim Brown Reveals Cribbing Scandal," *Los Angeles Times*, November 4, 1964, B1.

28. Haley, "*Playboy* Interview: Malcolm X (1963)," in *Playboy Interviews*, ed. Randall, 21.

29. Brown and Cope, *Off My Chest*, 167.

30. Jim Murray, "Jim Murray's Column: Dear Jim," *Los Angeles Times*, September 29, 1964, B1.

31. "Bomb Threat Made against Jim Brown," *Washington Post, Times Herald*, September 23, 1964, C4.

32. Bill Nunn Jr., "Change of Pace," *Pittsburgh Courier*, October 10, 1964, 23.

33. *Ebony* (advertisement), *Baltimore Afro-American*, December 19, 1964, 11.

34. "The Jim Brown Case: Too Sexy to Be Printed!" *New York Amsterdam News*, July 24, 1965, 1.

35. "'Jim Brown Slapped Me on Three Dates,'" *Pittsburgh Courier*, July 24, 1965, 1.

36. "The Spicy Trial of Jim Brown: Grid Star Denies Sex Acts," *Jet*, August 5, 1965, 16.

37. Freeman, *Jim Brown*, 165.

38. A. S. Doc Young, "Good Morning Sports," *Chicago Daily Defender*, July 26, 1966, 24.

39. Vernon Scott, "Actor Jim Brown Runs for Big Gains," *Washington Post, Times Herald*, August 6, 1967, E5.

40. Gloria Steinem, "The Black John Wayne," *New York*, November 11, 1968, 35.

41. Freeman, *Jim Brown*, 205.

42. Steinem, "Black John Wayne," 36.

43. Freeman, *Jim Brown*, 205.

44. Steinem, "Black John Wayne," 39.

45. "Jimmy Brown Is Freed in Assault Case," *New York Times*, June 11, 1968, 22.

46. Toback, *Jim*, 113.

47. Megan Rosenfeld, "Sex, Football, Sex, Politics and Sex: Jim Brown Writes about His Favorite Subject," *San Francisco Chronicle*, September 23, 1989, C10.

48. Steinem, "Black John Wayne," 36.

49. Jim Brown and Steve Delsohn, "Jim Brown on . . . Life and Love in Hollywood" (excerpt from *Out of Bounds*), *Ebony*, December 1, 1989, http://www.encyclopedia.com/doc/fullarticle/1G1-8153059.html (January 17, 2009).

50. Ibid.

51. Ed Guerrero, quoted in Jesse Algeron Rhines, *Black Film/White Money* (New Brunswick: Rutgers University Press, 1996), 43.

52. "Violent Black-Movie Trends Dominate 'Slaughter' Sequel," *Christian Science Monitor*, July 20, 1973, 11.

53. Brown and Delsohn, "Jim Brown."

54. Leon E. Wynter, *American Skin: Pop Culture, Big Business, and the End of White America* (New York: Crown, 2002), 89–90.

55. Jim Murray, "The Most Deserving," *Los Angeles Times*, November 9, 1969, D1.

56. Wynter, *American Skin*, 97.

57. Freeman, *Jim Brown*, 229.

58. *Jim Brown: All American*.

59. Don Yaeger, "Prisoner of Conscience," *Sports Illustrated*, April 15, 2002, 54.

60. Jon Saraceno, "Keeping Score: True Manhood and Perspective Elude Brown," *USA Today*, April 10, 2002, http://www.usatoday.com/sports/comment/saraceno/2002-04-10-saraceno.htm (January 25, 2009).

61. Ibid.

62. Yaeger, "Prisoner of Conscience," 56.

63. ". . . tick . . . tick Star Discusses His Image," *Chicago Defender*, March 3, 1979, 11.

64. Ibid.

AFTERWORD
Sports and the Iron Fist of Myth

—JACK LULE

INTRODUCTION

The stories seem to come from the same dark place. Kirby Puckett goes from Minnesota's cuddly and beloved sports hero to a half-blind, bloated womanizer, despised and dead at forty-five. Jim Brown goes from one of professional football's most respected players to a brooding, dangerous figure who beats women. Mark McGwire and Sammy Sosa go from brawny and beloved home run heroes to disgraced drug users. And O. J. Simpson goes from football, cinema, and advertising star to wife killer, a man who got away with murder.

Even with their distinct, violent edges, these stories are eerily familiar and ominously similar. They tell an oft-told tale, the story of gifted ones who fall from grace. The narratives, as we have seen repeatedly in this volume, call forth Greek tragedy, and it is tempting to read the newspaper accounts and the learned academic analyses of those accounts and nod knowingly over their putative lessons. Hubris and tragic flaws have brought down the heroes.

However, that reading by itself is incomplete. The tragic structure and literary lessons of these stories are only a small piece of their significance and should not distract us from their larger purpose—the invocation of the iron fist of myth. These are not simple, tragic tales. They are myths of admonishment and disapprobation. They sanction and scourge. They punish and cast out. Myth was never made simply to teach or entertain. Myth has one main purpose—the construction, maintenance, and surveillance of social order. It is deadly serious.

THE MEANINGS OF MYTH

Myth today has come to mean many things. For some, myth can mean a false belief or untrue story and often is offered in bland contrast—"myth or reality"? For others, myth refers to ancient tales, the stories of the Greeks or Romans, hoary tales of Zeus, Jupiter, Apollo, and Pluto. Others see myths as the superstitious beliefs of earlier, primitive societies and believe that modern society has "outgrown" myth, that it has replaced those credulous stories and rituals of old with enlightenment, science, and technology.

For many modern scholars, however, myth is never false, never ancient, and never to be outgrown. In this context, myths are understood as stories that express a society's prevailing ideals, ideologies, values, and beliefs. Myths thus are essential social narratives, present in every society, rich and enduring aspects of human existence that draw from archetypal figures and forms to offer exemplary models for social life.[1] Myth, in this view, is indispensable for human understanding of the world.

Philosopher and historian of religion Mircea Eliade studied myths in hundreds of societies, arguing that "certain aspects and functions of mythical thought are constituents of the human being."[2] Moreover, "it seems unlikely that any society could completely dispense with myths, for, of what is essential in mythical behaviour—the exemplary pattern, the repetition, the break with profane duration and integration into primordial time—the first two at least are consubstantial with every human condition."[3]

Carl Jung, too, saw myth as a fundamental part of human life, asking, "Has mankind ever really got away from myths?" He answered his own question: "One could almost say that if all the world's traditions were cut off at a single blow, the whole of mythology and the whole history of religion would start all over again with the next generation."[4]

Joseph Campbell, a popular chronicler of myth, agreed: "No human society has yet been found in which such mythological motifs have not been rehearsed in liturgies; interpreted by seers, poets, theologians, or philosophers; presented in art; magnified in song; and ecstatically experienced in life-empowering visions."[5]

MYTH AND SOCIAL ORDER

Seen in this way, the stories of myth are necessary to human lives and the societies they construct.[6] But how does that work? What is the relationship between myth and society? A simple but classic definition, offered by scholar Bronislaw Malinowski, states that myth is a social charter. That is, myths dramatize and support preferred ways of thinking and acting in society. Myths express beliefs and assumptions, offer rules and norms.

Malinowski made clear the crucial relationship between a society and its myths. An anthropologist, Malinowski approached myth differently from Eliade, Jung, and others I have considered, emphasizing the functions of myth in "primitive" cultures. Many scholars have found fault with Malinowski's politics and perspective, but they still love the breadth of his attempt to make plain the importance of myth for humanity:

> Studied alive, myth, as we shall see, is not symbolic, but a direct expression of its subject matter; it is not an explanation in satisfaction of a scientific interest, but a narrative resurrection of a primeval reality, told in satisfaction of deep religious wants, moral cravings, social submissions, even practical requirements. Myth fulfills in primitive culture an indispensable function: it expresses, enhances, and codifies belief; it safeguards and enforces morality; it vouches for the efficiency of ritual and contains practical rules for the guidance of man. Myth is thus a vital ingredient of human civilization; it is not an idle tale, but a hardworked active force; it is not an intellectual explanation or an artistic imagery, but a pragmatic charter of primitive faith and moral wisdom.[7]

No idle tale, myth is a "hardworked active force" that labors to uphold the social charter and the maintenance of social order. This view has been central to many scholars of myth. Following Malinowski, Walter Burkert stressed that myth justifies and defends social order, writing, "The phenomena of collective importance which are verbalized by applying traditional tales are to be found, first of all, in social life. Institutions or presentations of family, clan, or city are explained and justified by tales—'charter myths,' in Malinowski's term."[8] Kenneth Burke also saw myth involved with the construction and defense of social order. Even within myths that tell the origins of a society, Burke astutely observed the defense of the social charter: "An account of origins is also a way of establishing sanctions. Its narrative stating how things were in the past thereby substantiates the principles of governance to which the faithful should be vowed in the present."[9]

MYTH AND SOCIAL DRAMAS

Burke has also provided us a way to understand just how myth maintains social order. A literary critic and social commentator writing in the middle of the twentieth century, Burke was a wide-ranging thinker who traced connections among stories, dramas, and social life.[10] Burke's model starts from basic premises. First, although *society* is a common, oft-employed term, the word was ambiguous and imprecise. Burke focused not on "society" but on "social order"—how a particular society is organized and kept together in time. In this view, social order is the specific structure of all the things that make up an individual society—rights, authority, power, hierarchy, status, ways of worship, labor, property relations, means of production, means of having fun, and so on. Social order therefore provides a way to talk about a particular society at a particular time.

Though the model emphasizes order, social order is not some kind of fixed, unmoving system, Burke said. Social order is literally acted out each day in "social dramas," the large and small acts and interactions that make up a society. They are written and spoken, official and unofficial, formal and informal—from congressional hearings to parent-teacher conferences to murder trials to ESPN broadcasts. Social dramas give life to social order each day.

Myths lie behind some of the most important social dramas. These myths are not ancient stories tucked away in history, but social dramas acted out every day. For example, myths dramatize the origins of a society, and we can see them today in annual celebrations of the events of 1776, battles over Supreme Court justices, or debates over the original meaning of the Constitution. Myths dramatize values, traditions, and beliefs and can be seen today in news stories of new citizens, television movies of heroic fights against cancer, and numerous other narratives. Myths also dramatize right and wrong, and we can see them today in news accounts of crime and punishment, on detective shows, and on the front pages of sports sections in stories of fallen heroes.

MYTH AND SPORTS

Sport is the last piece of the puzzle we are putting together in our attempt to fully understand the meaning of the dramas surrounding the fallen sports hero. Sports are as essential to understanding social life as politics or culture, and sports have been inextricably entwined with myth. Indeed, sports provide fine raw material for myth. They offer drama and conflict. They offer binary oppositions, which Claude Lévi-Strauss found at the heart of myth, such as winning and losing, success and failure.[11] They recur, often daily, allowing myths to be retold, as myths must be. They often are performed on a public stage. Like myth, sport often is employed to celebrate, inculcate, and instill social values, such as sacrifice, courage, effort, teamwork, and perseverance. For these reasons, myths have been built around sports since the time of the ancient Greeks.

Sports also provide us with heroes. The hero may be humanity's most enduring archetype and the basis for its most pervasive myth. Every society likely has dramatized and personified its core values and ideals in stories of a hero that remind people of values needed to succeed and provide models for emulation. Hercules, Karna, Gilgamesh, Ulysses, Achilles, and Samson are just a few heroes whose exploits are celebrated in myth. The hero, Eliade noted, embraces one of the chief characteristics of myth, "the creation of exemplary models for a whole society." He continued, "In this, moreover, we recognise a very general human tendency; namely, to hold up one life-history as a paradigm and turn a historical personage into an archetype."[12] Myth, after all, in its fullest sense, "supplies models for human behavior and, by that very fact, gives meaning and value to life."[13]

Sportswriters have recognized the process. Tom Boswell, longtime writer for the *Washington Post*, said, "Great athletes have, without knowing it or wanting it, been put in something akin to the position of mythic or religious characters in other cultures in other times. That is to say, they have taken on a symbolic quality. For them, no doubt, this is a mixed blessing—a kind of celebrity squared."[14]

Red Smith of the *New York Times*, often acclaimed as the dean of sportswriters, recognized and defended the process of "godding up" ballplayers: "If we've made heroes out of them, and we have, then we must also lay a whole set of false values at the doorsteps of historians and biographers. Not only has the athlete been blown up larger than life, but so have the politicians and celebrities in all fields, including rock singers and movie stars. . . . I've tried not to exaggerate the glory of athletes. I'd rather, if I could, preserve a sense of proportion, to write about them as excellent ballplayers, first-rate players. But I'm sure I have contributed to false values—as Stanley Woodward said, 'Godding up those ballplayers.'"[15]

MYTH AND THE FALLEN SPORTS HERO

Thus, societies need and construct myths primarily to create and sustain social order, and sports provide fertile ground for such myths—in particular, myths created around the sports hero. We now can return to the grim stories of Kirby Puckett, Jim Brown, Wilt Chamberlain, Mark McGwire, Sammy Sosa, and others and place them in this larger context. All of these men— and they are all men—were superior athletes whose accomplishments were chronicled and celebrated. However, they were set apart from other fine athletes. They attained a larger status. They were mythologized as heroes. On a local, national, and even international level, these men were not lauded simply for their ability to run fast, jump high, or hit a ball far. They came to be heroes and in terms of myth were held up as "exemplary models" whose hard work, sacrifice, dedication, and accomplishments were celebrated in support of social order.

What happens when the hero falls, when the hero proves unworthy of such social status, when the hero fails to live up to his status as an "exemplary model"? Can social order allow such transgressions to go unnoted? We know the answer. But it is good to pause here and consider. Each of these men could have fallen from grace in obscurity. Many wife abusers do not make the news. Violence against women is a too-common occurrence and often does not make headlines. Drug use is rampant in sport and society. We take for granted that the transgressions of each of these sports heroes resulted in high-profile, front-page status and top-of-the-hour storytelling that dominated the news for days and weeks. Their stories could have gone untold. But a powerful force could not allow that to happen. And that force is the iron fist of myth.

THE IRON FIST OF MYTH

Implicit in the understanding of myth as a social charter, a series of stories that dramatize a society's values and norms, and help create and sustain social order is the idea that myth has dark consequences for those who deviate from social norms. As part of its social role, myth vilifies those who diverge too much from the social charter. Myth stigmatizes and ostracizes evildoers. It demeans and degrades. It depicts a kind of public denunciation of those who offend the charter. Not every evildoer receives the social sanction of myth. But the heroes, the anointed ones, the figures once hailed and heralded— their fall cannot go unmentioned and must receive a response.

We can now fully understand the need for this volume and the importance of the analyses. Society constructed large and encompassing social dramas around the rise and fall of Puckett, Brown, Chamberlain, McGwire, Sosa, and others in this volume. These dramas were not tawdry scandals. They were not sensationalistic fare. They were much more than literary cousins to Greek tragedy. These stories were told and attended to as myths brutally enacting the enforcement of social order.

Just as deadly and grim as the public stonings of centuries ago, these stories were made to punish and abuse, castigate and cast out. Myth enforces social order with exacting social dramas that humiliate, degrade, and deprecate. The fallen ones are heaped with scorn, vilified and shunned. Even as I write, the sports heroes of 2009, such as Michael Vick and Alex Rodriguez, endure the savage lesson: Myth will enact and exact public dramas of degradation to those anointed ones who would violate social order.

NOTES

1. Carl G. Jung, *Archetypes and the Collective Unconscious*, trans. R. F. C. Hull (New York: Pantheon, 1959); Mircea Eliade, *Patterns in Comparative Religion*, trans. Rosemary Sheed (New York: Sheed and Ward, 1958); Northrop Frye, "The Archetypes of Literature," *Kenyon Review*, Winter 1951, 92–110; Northrop Frye, *Anatomy of Criticism* (Princeton: Princeton University Press, 1957).

2. Mircea Eliade, *Myth and Reality*, trans. Willard R. Trask (New York: Harper and Row, 1963), 183–84.

3. Mircea Eliade, *Myths, Dreams, and Mysteries*, trans. Philip Mairet (New York: Harper, 1960), 31–32.

4. Carl G. Jung, *Symbols of Transformation*, 2nd ed., trans. R. F. C. Hull (Princeton: Princeton University Press, 1976), 25.

5. Joseph Campbell, "The Historical Development of Mythology," in *Myth and Mythmaking*, ed. Henry Murray (New York: Braziller, 1960), 1–2.

6. Excellent studies of myth and society include Jean-Pierre Vernant, *Myth and Society in Ancient Greece*, trans. Janet Lloyd (Atlantic Highlands, NJ: Humanities, 1980); Martin S. Day, *The Many Meanings of Myth* (Lanham, MD: University Press of America, 1984), 1–32; Ivan Strenski, *Four Theories of Myth in Twentieth-Century History* (Iowa City: University of Iowa Press, 1987); Carl G. Jung, *Man and His Symbols* (New York: Dell, 1964); Mircea Eliade, *The Sacred and the Profane*, trans. Willard R. Trask (New York: Harcourt, Brace, and World, 1959), 205; Joseph Campbell, *Myths to Live By* (New York: Viking, 1972).

7. Bronislaw Malinowski, "Myth in Primitive Psychology," in *Magic, Science and Religion* (Garden City, NY: Doubleday, 1954), 101.

8. Walter Burkert, *Structure and History in Greek Mythology and Ritual* (Berkeley: University of California Press, 1979), 23.

9. Kenneth Burke, *Language as Symbolic Action* (Berkeley: University of California Press, 1966), 390.

10. Kenneth Burke, *The Philosophy of Literary Form* (Baton Rouge: Louisiana State University Press, 1941); Kenneth Burke, *Permanence and Change: An Anatomy of Purpose*, 3rd ed. (Berkeley: University of California Press, 1984).

11. Claude Lévi-Strauss, *The Raw and the Cooked*, trans. John Wrightman and Doreen Wrightman (1964; Chicago: University of Chicago Press, 1983).

12. Eliade, *Myths, Dreams, and Mysteries*, 32.

13. Eliade, *Myth and Reality*, 2.

14. Tom Boswell, *Game Day* (New York: Doubleday, 1990), xvii.

15. Red Smith, *The Red Smith Reader* (New York: Random House, 1982), 16.

Contributors

Lisa Doris Alexander is assistant professor of Africana studies at Wayne State University in Detroit. She received her Ph.D. in American culture studies from Bowling Green State University. Her research deals with issues of race, class, gender, and sexuality in professional sports and popular culture.

Roy F. Fox is professor of English education in the Department of Learning, Teaching, and Curriculum at the University of Missouri. His research focuses on the teaching and learning of writing as well as media literacy—especially how people interact with television, film, and advertising messages. In addition to numerous chapters, articles, and professional recognitions, he is the author of several books, including *Images in Language, Media, and Mind*; *Harvesting Minds: How TV Commercials Control Kids*; and *MediaSpeak: Three American Voices* and is the founder of the Lewis and Clark Center for Integrated Learning and the Mizzou Men for Excellence in Elementary Teaching Program, which seeks to recruit and develop high-caliber male elementary teachers.

Gregory J. Kaliss is visiting assistant professor of American studies at Franklin and Marshall College. He received his Ph.D. in history from the University of North Carolina at Chapel Hill. He has published in the *Journal of Sport History* and is currently revising his dissertation, *Everyone's All-Americans: Race, Men's College Athletics, and the Ideal of Equal Opportunity*, for publication.

Jeffrey Lane, author of *Under the Boards: The Cultural Revolution in Basketball* (University of Nebraska Press), is currently pursuing his Ph.D. in sociology at Princeton. He is the founder and director of Schoolhouse Tutors, a mentoring program for middle and high school students in Manhattan and Brooklyn.

Robert F. Lewis II is a retired corporate executive who earned his doctorate in American studies from the University of New Mexico. He is the author of *Smart Ball: Marketing the Myth and Managing the Reality of Major League Baseball* (University Press of Mississippi).

Thabiti Lewis is associate professor of English and African American literature at Washington State University–Vancouver. He has written about twentieth-century African American literature, images of modern athletes, and race. He has edited two special journal issues, "On Masculinities" (*Ameri-Quests*) and "African American Life and Culture" (the *Willamette Journal*). He is a former columnist and radio talk show host and has contributed freelance to *The Source*, the *St. Louis American*, and *News One*. He is also the author of the forthcoming book, *Ballers of the New School: Race and Sports in America* (Third World Press).

Shelley Lucas is associate professor of kinesiology at Boise State University, where she teaches courses in history, sociology, and philosophy of exercise and sport. Her areas of interest include women's sport history, gender equity in athletics, and media representations of gender, race, and sexuality in sport.

Jack Lule is the Joseph B. McFadden Distinguished Professor of Journalism and the director of the Globalization and Social Change Initiative at Lehigh University. His research interests include globalization and media, international communication, international news reporting, cultural and critical studies of news, online journalism, and teaching with technology. He is the author of *Daily News, Eternal Stories: The Mythological Role of Journalism* (Guilford Press). Called "a landmark book in the sociology of news," the book argues that ancient myths can be found daily in the pages of the news. The author of more than forty scholarly articles and book chapters, he is also a member of the editorial board of *Journalism and Mass Communication Quarterly* and *Critical Studies in Media Communication*. His current book is a study of globalization and the media.

Roberta J. Newman teaches in the Foundation Studies program at New York University, where she teaches a course on baseball. She is the author and coauthor of numerous articles on sports and is the coauthor of a book-length study of the economic ramifications of desegregated Major League Baseball on the African American business community.

David C. Ogden is associate professor in the School of Communication at the University of Nebraska at Omaha, where he has taught since 2001. His research focuses on cultural trends in baseball, specifically the history of the relationship between African Americans and baseball. He has presented his research at the National Baseball Hall of Fame Symposium on Baseball and American Culture, the *NINE* Spring Training Conference on Baseball and Culture, and Indiana State University's Conference on Baseball in Culture and Literature. He has published in *NINE: A Journal of Baseball History and Culture*, the *Journal of Leisure Research*, and the *Journal of Black Studies*.

C. Oren Renick is professor and former chair of the Department of Health Administration at Texas State University in San Marcos and a fellow in the American College of Healthcare Executives, a member of the American Bar Association, and a member of two state bar associations. A frequent contributor to professional journals and presenter at professional conferences, his major scholarly interests are civil rights, civic engagement, continuous quality improvement, managed care, health care law and ethics, and baseball and American culture.

Joel Nathan Rosen is associate professor of sociology at Moravian College in Bethlehem, Pennsylvania, where he coordinates the Africana studies program and serves as founding codirector of the college's Center for the Study of Media in Culture (*CoSMiC*). His research focuses primarily on the relationship between human activity and stratification as informed by cultural idioms such as music and sport. He is the author of *The Erosion of the American Sporting Ethos: Shifting Attitudes toward Competition* (McFarland), is coeditor of and a contributor to *Reconstructing Fame: Sport, Race, and Evolving Reputations* (University Press of Mississippi), and has been published in such varied journals as the *Sociology of Sport Journal*, the *Journal of Mundane Behavior*, *NINE: A Journal of Baseball History and Culture*, the *Journal of Sport History*, and *Media History Monographs*.

Sherrie L. Wilson is associate professor in the School of Communication at the University of Nebraska at Omaha. She teaches classes in media ethics and communication law as well as journalistic writing and editing. She earned her Ph.D. in mass communication from the University of Minnesota and her M.S. in journalism and mass communication from Iowa State University. Before teaching at UNO, she worked for sixteen years as a newspaper editor and reporter.

Index

Aaron, Hank, 20, 22, 23
Ali, Muhammad (Cassius Clay), 48,
    115–16, 131, 132, 178, 185, 188
Ashe, Arthur, 133, 165

Baer, Max, 105, 107
Bankhead, Don, 92
Barkley, Charles, 134
baseball cards, ix–x
Bonds, Barry
    asterisk, 19, 20, 22, 23
    death threats, 17
    home run record, 13, 16, 23
    Latin players, 14
    Pittsburgh Pirates, 11–12
    press and media, 8–9, 11–14, 15–16, 19, 23
    race, 9, 13, 15–16, 18, 19, 20–21, 25–26,
        48, 71
    San Francisco Giants, 12, 24
    steroids, 18, 19–20, 26; BALCO, 17, 18,
        25; grand jury investigation, 19, 22;
        indictment, 24
    Web site, x
Bonds, Bobby, 10, 20, 179
Bostock, Lyman, 34
Bourdieu, Pierre, 122
Braddock, James, 110–11
Breadon, Sam, 86, 87, 90
Brown, Darrell, 34
Brown, Jim
    acting career: Blaxploitation films, 184;
        The Dirty Dozen, 180; *Ice Station
        Zebra*, 180–81; *100 Rifles*, 183; *. . . tick
        . . . tick . . . tick*, 183, 188
    Amer-I-Can Foundation, 187
    autobiographies, 170, 171, 176, 182, 183
    Black Muslim, 171, 177, 178, 181, 183–84
    Paul Brown, 177
    Buffalo Bills, 185

    Wilt Chamberlain, comparison with,
        185
    civil rights, 171
    Cleveland Browns, 176
    Cleveland Indians, 174
    ESPN, 187, 188
    Gaylords (gang), member of, 174–75
    lacrosse, 170, 174
    as a leader, 175
    Spike Lee documentary and, 170, 182
    legal troubles, 171; Brenda Ayres, assault
        of, 178, 180, 181; Eva Bohn-Chin,
        assault of, 181–82, 183, 186; Monique
        Brown, domestic dispute with, 186;
        cribbing scandal, 177; incarceration
        of, 187
    Malcolm X and, 183
    mythmaking and, 172, 173
    NAACP, 171
    NFL, 171, 174, 176, 185
    press coverage, 171; black press, 176,
        178, 179; Cleveland's press, 172; *Larry
        King Live*, 186; *Look* magazine, 177;
        media portrayals of, 188
    race, 170, 172; racial stereotypes, 183;
        sexuality of black men, 172
    Jackie Robinson, comparison with,
        173, 174, 185
    as a role model, 170
    Bill Russell, comparison with, 180,
        185
    Ben Schwarzwalder, 172
    O. J. Simpson, comparison with, 185,
        186–87
    Avartus Stone, comparison with, 172
    Syracuse University, 170, 171
    track, participation in, 170
Brown, Joe, 95
Bryant, Kobe, 122–23, 132

Bülow, Arthur, 106
Busch, Gussie, 96

Campanella, Roy, 92
Campbell, Joseph, xii–xiii
Canseco, Jose, 63
Carew, Rod, 34
Carnera, Primo, 105
Cartwright, Alexander, 97
Cayton, Bill, 47, 48, 51–52
Cerv, Bob, ix
Chamberlain, Wilt
    Forrest "Phog" Allen, 148, 150
    autobiographies, 155, 162
    The "Big Dripper," 160
    Big Seven conference, 150, 152, 154, 155,
        160
    Big Six conference, 146
    black masculinity, 147
    civil rights issues, 163; Jim Crow
        segregation, 149, 152; race (racial
        politics), 147, 148, 150, 155–56, 157,
        162, 163; racial stereotypes, 157, 158,
        160, 166
    Dowdal Davis and, 148–49, 158
    death of, 165
    Harlem Globetrotters, 146, 147, 158, 159,
        161, 162
    high school basketball career, 147
    as a leader, 153–54
    media attention (coverage), 150, 153,
        157, 160–61; Life magazine, 147; Look
        magazine, 162; newspaper coverage
        of, 149, 166; Saturday Night Live skit
        about, 164
    NBA, 147, 161, 162, 165, 166; Rookie of
        the Year, 162
    NCAA, 147, 150, 163
    Oklahoma City University, 156
    as role model for the black community,
        149, 150
    Bill Russell, comparisons with, 150–52,
        162–63
    sex with "twenty thousand women," 164
    University of Kansas at Lawrence, 146,
        147–48; discrimination, 148; history
        with black athletes, 146; leaving, 158–

59; national championship game, 158;
        varsity debut of, 150
Chandler, Happy, 93
Charles, Ezzard, 115
Clemens, Roger, 24
Clemente, Roberto, 95
Conn, Billy, 113–14

D'Amato, Cus, 48, 50, 51–52
Dempsey, Jack, 45, 105, 107
Devine, Bing, 96
Durocher, Leo, 93

Edwards, Harry, 163
Ellison, Ralph, xii

Galbreath, John, 94, 95
Gerbner, George, xi
Giambi, Jason, 18–19
Giuliani, Rudolph, 16
Givens, Robin, 47, 53
Griffith, Calvin, 33–34
Griffith, Clark, 95
Grimsley, Jason, 22

Haak, Howard, 95
Hisle, Larry, 34
Hitler, Adolf, 110, 113
hooks, bell, 135
hoopsaddict.com, 122
Hornung, Paul, 185
Howsam, Bob, 96

Jackson, Jesse, 118, 130, 139
Jackson, Reggie, 34
Jacobs, Jim, 48, 51–52, 53
Johnson, Earvin "Magic," 164
Johnson, Jack, 45, 48–49, 104, 111
Jordan, Michael
    African American culture, 136
    blogs and, 122
    Charlotte Bobcats, 125
    Chicago Bulls, 124
    father James Jordan, 123, 138
    hip-hop and, 133
    marketing of, 126, 127, 128, 131, 134
    minor league baseball, 125

NBA, 124, 125; MVP honors, 124
Nike, 126, 130, 137, 139, 140; Air Jordan,
    125, 126, 139; Jumpman logo, 125;
    Spike Lee's Mars Blackmon, 126, 134;
    sneaker crime wave, 139
political silence (apolitical or political
    apathy), 128, 130, 131–32, 138, 139, 141
product endorsements (promotion),
    124, 129, 135
PUSH, 139
race (blackness), 133, 135, 136, 142;
    racelessness (colorless), 131–32, 134
60 Minutes, 141
Washington Wizards, 125, 127

Kansas City A's, ix
Kiner, Ralph, 94
King, Don, 47, 48, 53–54
King, Martin Luther, Jr., 164
Krause, Jerry, 127

Landis, Kenesaw Mountain, 86, 87–88, 92
Liston, Sonny, 115
Louis, Joe
    amateur career, 103–4
    James Braddock, knockout of, 111
    as celebrity, 108–9
    childhood and early years, 102–3
    Billy Conn, fight with, 113–14
    as enlisted soldier in World War II,
        113–14
    financial problems, 114–15
    funeral of, 118
    name change, 103
    racism, 102, 110, 117–18
    Schmeling: first bout with, 109–10;
        rematch with, 111–12;
        similarities with, 107–8
    Jack Sharkey, knockout of, 111
    turning pro, 105

Marciano, Rocky, 115
Maris, Roger, ix, 62
Martinez, Pedro, 68–69
Mays, Willie, 10, 20, 131, 180, 185
McCain, John, 48
McGraw, John, 88

McGwire, Mark
    Baseball Hall of Fame, 72
    home run race, 13–14, 61–62
    media coverage, 61, 62–64, 65–66, 70–71
    race, 61, 64
    steroid use, 61, 62, 71–72;
        androstenedione, 18, 64; BALCO,
        62; congressional hearings, 65–66;
        Mitchell Report, 63
McPhail, Larry, 90
Mitchell, George, 24, 25, 63
Modell, Art, 180
myth, 191–96

Namath, Joe, 185
Nelly, 141
New York Giants, 88
Nike: Michael Jordan, x; the Temple of
    Nike, xi
Nixon, Richard, 164

O'Malley, Walter, 91, 94
Owens, Jesse, 112

Piazza, Mike, 24–25
Pollin, Abe, 125, 127
Puckett, Kirby
    Baseball Hall of Fame, 30, 31; Hall of
        Fame Induction, 31, 32, 36
    community service, 35, 40
    death of, 30, 38, 40
    domestic problems, 36
    as "everyman," 31, 32
    glaucoma, 31, 35
    legal problems, 37
    Minnesota Twins, 30, 33, 37
    press and media, 37–39
    race, 33–35
    weight problems, 38
    World Series, 31

Reinsdorf, Jerry, 127, 132
Rickey, Branch
    baseball as a "moral equivalent of war,"
        82
    Baseball Hall of Fame, 97
    beer advertising, objections to, 78, 94

Brooklyn Brown Dodgers, 92
Brooklyn Dodgers, 87, 90–94;
    Dodgertown, 89
Caribbean recruiting, 95–96
Continental League, 96
death of, 97
"farm system," 78–79, 84, 86–91, 94
as field manager, 86
free agency, 84, 85
"hard power," 79, 85, 87, 95, 96
media coverage, 77, 84
Methodist Church, 80
minor League teams, 85, 86–89, 90–91
Negro Leagues, 82, 83–84, 92
Ohio Wesleyan University, 80, 81, 91
Pittsburgh Pirates, 94–95
prospect evaluation, 89, 95
reserve system, 76, 79, 96
"smart power," 79
"soft power," 79, 85, 95
St. Louis Browns, 85–86
St. Louis Cardinals, 85, 86, 87, 96; as
    president, 86; training techniques,
    88–89
televising games, 78, 94
World Series, 90, 95
Rickey, Branch "Twig," Jr., 90, 94, 95,
    96
Robeson, Paul, 117
Robinson, Jackie, 76, 81, 83, 84, 92–93, 96,
    173, 174
Robinson, "Sugar Ray," 185
Roxborough, John, 104
Ruth, Babe, 20

Sanchez, Alex, 34
Schmeling, Max
    amateur career, 106
    America, coming to, 106
    heavyweight champion, 107
    Jews and minorities, association with,
        112
    Joe Louis: first bout with, 109–10;
        friendship with, 116–17; rematch
        with, 111–12; similarities with, 107–8
    Luftwaffe, with the, 113

    Nazi Party, member of, 102, 106, 110,
        112, 113
    racism, 102, 117–18
    as teenager, 105
    turning pro, 106
Selig, Bud, 22–23, 24, 63
Sharkey, Jack, 106, 107, 111
Simpson, O. J., 4–5
Sisler, George, 86
Smith, Wendell, 92
Sosa, Sammy
    Baseball Hall of Fame consideration,
        67, 69, 70
    Chicago Cubs, player on, 66
    corked bat, use of, 62, 66, 68
    home run race, 14, 61–62
    media coverage, 61, 62–64, 67–71
    race, 61, 64, 70; as the "Other," 69, 70
    600th home run, 67, 69, 71
    steroid use, 61, 62; BALCO, 62;
        congressional hearings of, 66, 67;
        Mitchell Report, 63
Stengel, Casey, ix
Stewart, Bobby, 50

Thomas, Charles, 91
Thorpe, Jim, 117
Tunney, Gene, 106, 107
Tyson, Mike
    as commercial spokesman, 53
    HBO documentary on, 54–55
    as hero/villain/fool, 49–50, 51, 53–54,
        56, 58–59
    hip-hop music, 45–47, 55–56
    race, 47–50, 52, 56, 57, 58–59
    rape conviction, 54
    tattoo, 57
    James Toback documentary on, 58–59
    WBA/WBC titles, 50, 54, 55

Van Slyke, Andy, 12
Vick, Michael, 179, 187–88

Walcott, Jersey Joe, 114
Washington, Ron, 34
Wright, John, 92